RUGBY'S
GREAT HEROES
AND
ENTERTAINERS

RUGBY'S GREAT HEROES AND ENTERTAINERS

Bill McLaren

Hodder & Stoughton

Copyright © 2003 Bill McLaren

First published in Great Britain in 2003 by Hodder and Stoughton

A division of Hodder Headline

The right of Bill McLaren to be identified as the Author of
the Work has been asserted by him in accordance with the
Copyright, Designs and Patents Act 1988.

6 8 10 9 7 5

A CIP catalogue record for this title is available from the British Library

ISBN 0 340 82728 9

Typeset in 11/15.5 Plantin Light by Servis Filmsetting Ltd, Manchester
Printed and bound in Great Britain by Clays Ltd, St Ives plc

Hodder and Stoughton
A division of Hodder Headline
338 Euston Road
London NW1 3BH

To Bette

CONTENTS

PART THREE

1970s

PART FOUR
1980s

PART FIVE

1990s and the Present

PART SIX

My World XV

PHOTOGRAPHIC ACKNOWLEDGMENTS

The author and publisher would like to thank the following for permission to reproduce photographs:

Colorsport, Empics/Alpha/Sport & General, Getty Images/ Allsport, Getty Images/Hulton Archive, Offside/L'Equipe, Offside/ Mark Leech, Popperfoto.com, Press Association/Tom Hevezi, Simon Wilkinson Photography.

ACKNOWLEDGMENTS

I would like to thank James Hughes for putting my thoughts and memories into order. His visits to Hawick were always a pleasure, and his insight and informed comments much appreciated.

Thanks too to Roddy Bloomfield of Hodder & Stoughton. Fifteen years ago he edited my autobiography, and I was delighted to have the chance to work with him again.

INTRODUCTION

IN PICKING players, matches and subjects for this look at rugby's heroes and entertainers, it has been the spectacular aspect of rugby football that has first and foremost influenced my choice. I have always been one who reacted to adventurous players, the Campeses of this world who love to tilt their lance and run out from defence. As a lifelong lover of the game, I came through a very long spell in the 1950s of defensive, careworn rugby football, when people were frightened to take risks because winning was so important. That was very hard for a commentator!

To give you just one example, there was a Scotland v Wales game in which there were 111 lineouts. That was maybe not typical, but there were a lot of games that turned out rather like that, with the same kind of defensive, careful rugby. I never enjoyed that. First of all, commentary was hard because you had to find so many different ways of trying to entertain your listeners, when in point of fact you were seeing a game of touch kicking and stilted play with very little spectacle at all. Having had to slog through commentary after commentary with that kind of defensive rugby football, it has just been a sheer delight to have come across people like David Campese, and Andy Irvine, and Jason Robinson – mind you, I would have hated to mark Jason Robinson, you would need a double-barrelled shotgun to do that. But I love the fact that he takes people on, he's courageous and trusts his instincts and capabilities.

I've always enjoyed doing commentary on that kind of player, because they've always carried the commentary along with them. Good commentary depends so much on what happens on the field, and if you get a dreich game with 111 lineouts, then you've got a game! Whereas if you've got people like Robinson, Campese, Irvine – Gerald Davies was another who used to delight me because he was another who would take people on, with sidestep, swerve, change of pace, all the arts of deception. Those are the guys who have given me the greatest pleasure.

Of course I've also appreciated driving forward play. I can remember when Dean Richards got a couple of tries against Ireland in 1986 where England simply dominated the Ireland pack, just drove them all over the place in a phenomenal display of forward power and expertise. Big Dean Richards got a couple of tries from pushovers in that match. There have been some magnificent players of that type, and I've had some great times watching grinding forward play, because that's an art too and all part and parcel of the game. With forward power you can sap the puff out of the opposition, and create the situation for the backs to do the fancy stuff later on. Great packs are quite prepared to be patient. They'll grind away and grind away, and then the other lot run out of petrol, and that's when the damage is done.

But I must say that my whole being has been lifted by guys who were brave and trusted their instincts. Gareth Edwards is another great favourite of mine. This is how I described one of the greatest individualist tries I've personally ever seen, scored by Gareth against Scotland at Cardiff in 1972:

> Mervyn Davies takes the tap-down from Peter Brown; it's beautifully laid back for Gareth Edwards. Edwards is over the ten yard line, over halfway ... the kick ahead by Edwards ... can he score? It would be a miracle if he could ... he may well get there ... and he has! Is there anything better than that in international rugby?

I'm sure most of you have seen it on video, but that has to be one of the finest tries of all time because it really encompassed just about everything the human frame needs to provide in any single game:

the stamina, the endurance, the power and strength of his hand-off, the acceleration, the tactical awareness – the wee kick he gave as he got through – he knew just where everybody was!

Incidentally, that's the first time I'd seen Gareth switch the ball from his inside arm to his outside. Even the slanting of the kick, which landed just on the goal line and went just inside the touch-in-goal line, was perfect. That move suggests to me that rugby union really is the greatest of ball games, because Gareth there has just about everything.

A lot of fellows in rugby union of course don't have that kind of feel, or that extra speed. But the great thing about the game is that it provides for the men of six feet six and eighteen stone. Tell me another team game of this kind that can provide for blokes like that. It's the fact that there's a place for everybody, and there are so many skills involved, that makes rugby union the greatest.

PART ONE

1950s

The Background
1935–36 All Blacks
1951–52 South Africans
1953–54 All Blacks
Scotland and Others

Portraits

Wilson Shaw (Scotland 1934–39)
Jean Prat (France 1945–55)
Bob Scott (New Zealand 1946–54)
Jack Kyle (Ireland 1947–58)
Bleddyn Williams (Wales 1947–55)
Hennie Muller (South Africa 1949–53)
Cliff Morgan (Wales 1951–58)
Cliff Morgan in his own words: Cardiff v All Blacks, 1953
Hugh McLeod (Scotland 1954–62)
Tony O'Reilly (Ireland 1955–70)
Peter Jackson (England 1956–63)

THE BACKGROUND

M Y FATHER came from the West of Scotland and he was more a fan of football than rugby. In fact his cousin was Donald Coleman, who played right back for Scotland and became trainer at Aberdeen Football Club. I remember my father taking me up to Edinburgh one day for a cup tie, Heart of Midlothian v Aberdeen. I was about nine or ten, and I was introduced to the Aberdeen team. Of course I was thrilled just to shake hands with players like Willie Mills and Matt Armstrong. In fact I can remember the names of the whole Aberdeen team to this day.

So my father came from a soccer background. But he took to rugby at Hawick, and he was the one who encouraged me to play rugby football and took me to internationals. One of the earliest games I remember seeing was Scotland v Ireland at Murrayfield in 1932, which Ireland won 20–8. My father encouraged me tremendously from the earliest days, and I owe him a lot for the whole-hearted way he fostered my interest in rugby football.

But it wasn't hard to be interested in rugby at Hawick in those days. In fact it was hard not to be interested, because then as now Hawick was a great rugby town. A lot of the Scottish internationals came from there, and I was brought up really in awe of the great ones, people like Willie Welsh, Jock Beattie and Jerry Foster, all super Hawick and Scotland forwards, and all of them were on the pitch at Murrayfield against the Irish back then in 1932.

I particularly remember Jock Beattie – he was such a stalwart in Hawick. He had a joinery business in the town, and he was a big fellow, six foot three and fifteen stone – heavy for those days. But the thing I remember about him was that he had bow legs! How they pulled his leg about those bow legs! I remember during one seven-a-side tournament, a fellow shouted from the side, 'Look oot, Jock, shut your legs – there's a horse and cairt coming!' But he took it all in good part, he was a great leader.

There was a big army encampment in those days about five miles outside Hawick and they used to field a side against the town – they had some good players. I was just beginning to play a bit of proper rugby round about then, and I was thrilled one day to find myself in a Hawick team that was due to play one of those army sides – it was the King's Own Yorkshire Light Infantry, I remember – and I was in the changing room getting ready with the rest of the team, and there was Jock Beattie alongside. He was a veteran by then, of course, his international career was long over, but they persuaded him to come out for this occasion. I was thrilled to bits to be changing alongside the great international who led us out to play that day.

That was early on in my games for Hawick. The first game I played for the town was against Kelso on a snow-covered pitch at our home ground of Mansfield Park – we did daft things in those days! I started out as a centre or stand-off in the semi-junior rugby side, the Hawick PSA. That PSA stood for Pleasant Saturday Afternoons, if you'll believe me, not that it was too pleasant sometimes playing against Kelso or Jedforest – you were liable to get a going-over! Then you would go into the junior side at eighteen years of age. But I was lucky enough to skip that stage and went from semi-junior into the senior side as a seventeen-year-old.

I continued to play centre and stand-off to begin with, but when I was in the army at the end of the war I was picked for a brigade side where they told me, 'Never mind about centre and stand-off. You're a big fellow, you'll play wing forward.' So that was it, wing forward I was, and when I came back I went on to play as a flanker for Hawick. But not long afterwards I took ill with tuberculosis, and that bumped me out of the game permanently, though I did manage to get a final trial for Scotland in 1947, so I was fairly close to international status at one time. Maybe if I hadn't had to go into a sanatorium for two years ... I can moan about my bad luck, but I was lucky in another way: when the TB was first diagnosed the doctor said I'd be four years in bed, but then the 'wonder drug' streptomycin came along and that did the trick in half the time. But all the same, that was my rugby career over. I was in hospital for nineteen months and they didn't let me play rugby again in case it brought back the TB.

I can't deny that in addition to being a teacher, which I've greatly enjoyed, all my life I've had a super job as a commentator, seeing all the great players, the great teams and the great grounds – and all without having to pay to get in! But I would have swapped all that for the honour of walking out at Murrayfield with the thistle on my jersey just once.

That's my one great regret; I would have loved to play for Scotland even just once, because I can think of nothing more uplifting than to stand there as the anthem is being played. But when I complain about it my wife Bette always says, 'What are you moaning about? You've got on fine.' And it's true, but ... Well, never mind, one cap would have done! My old friend Hugh McLeod, the great Scottish and Lions prop forward, who lives in Hawick and comes every now and then for a chat, he has got forty caps. And when I complain he says, 'Hey Bill, you could have yin o' mine. That would do fine for me with thirty-nine and just the one for you!'

Of course, any fellow from Hawick, certainly when I was a boy, just wanted to play for the rugby side. There wasn't a Hawick boy who didn't want to wear that green jersey. It's a little different now because there are people who play football in Hawick, although rugby is still very much the dominant game. But in those days the sole ambition was to play rugby for Hawick, and you were carried along in that ambition by such greats as the players I have mentioned, guys like Willie Welsh, Jock Beattie and Jerry Foster.

So rugby played a big part in my life from an early age. At first I played with a ball made out of paper, which was handy for not breaking windows in the street. I had a powerful fantasy life in those days, kicking off for Scotland, catching the ball for England, passing it down the line, and over for a try by the lamp post – all in my imagination. My ambitions were to wear the green jersey of Hawick and then the blue of Scotland. But there must also have been something in my make up as a boy that suggested that I wanted to be a rugby writer or a rugby commentator, because I also used to write up fictional rugby reports of international matches, using the players of the day, and I would write out on great sheets of paper detailed reports on fictional games. Needless to say, Scotland always did very well in my matches, in fact in one match Scotland beat the Rest of the World 48–5, and the report is there for all to see!

I did a lot of that, and it suggested I was always keen to communicate the game to others. I remember also going into our spare room upstairs at home and sitting there impersonating the rugby commentators of the day. Teddy Wakelam was one, and for hours on end I used to imitate him doing commentary. He had this plummy voice I tried to imitate – without success, I'm glad to say. At that time it never dawned on me of course that this might indicate a desire to cover matches for real, but there you are. It's lucky that as a boy I showed that interest and did that homework, because homework really has been at the very heart of my commentary career. Before every match I would fill up a great sheet of paper to cover every aspect I could think of, down to the names of the physiotherapists.

So as a boy I seemed unconsciously to know what I might be able to do. And I went on with that fantasy commentating right up to the time I was playing for Hawick for the first time as a seventeen-year-old. And when I was in the TB hospital I used to entertain myself and others by commentating on table tennis games between patients. I don't know when I began using those phrases people remember me for, but they sometimes relate to my boyhood days. For instance, when I described Robert Howley, the Wales scrum-half, as 'wiggling his way upfield like a baggy up a Border burn'. A baggy is a small fish we used to 'guddle', to catch in our hands, as boys. When scared, it just wiggles away. People in Hawick were very chuffed about that because 'like a baggy up a burn' is very much a local saying.

The first game I went to was Hawick v Newport, here at our home ground of Mansfield Park, when I was about eight. I remember that my hero of the time, the Hawick and Scotland flanker Willie Welsh, had to go off. I thought he was injured and wouldn't be able to come back on again, and began shedding tears in the stand! But it was only mud in his eye and he soon came back on.

I remember once being out for a walk with my father on a Sunday, and we bumped into Rob Barrie, a Hawick stalwart who got one cap for Scotland, at Twickenham in 1936, though he deserved more. And I was there, at Twickenham, as a twelve-year-old with my father, when Rob Barrie got his one cap! I remember looking up to this giant – he was a flank forward, as I would be one day. But to me he was a giant, and I remember feeling a nervous tingle at just being in his presence.

In fact the first internationals I saw were a couple of years earlier when my father took me to see Scotland v Ireland in 1932 and Scotland v England at Murrayfield in 1933, and I had the excitement of seeing the legendary Iain Smith, the Flying Scot. Then in 1936 my father took me all the way to London, to Twickenham. I'll never forget that first visit to Twickenham. I was amazed at the size of the place because of course I'd never seen a ground with three stands before, huge stands they seemed to me, though nothing to what's there now. That was a very close game with England winning 9–8.

But Scotland had their revenge two years later when they won a wonderful game 21–16, and I had the privilege of seeing that match too. As a matter of fact, that Calcutta Cup match in 1938 was the first ever rugby international to be televised. The Scottish stand-off Wilson Shaw had a superb game, scoring two brilliant individualist tries. No wonder Twickenham has always been special to me.

Something of that special Twickenham feeling endures to this day. I remember how people used to have picnics in the car park. Once I saw a parked car with its engine running – someone seemed to have left it on by mistake. But when the owner was asked to turn it off the answer was, 'I was just warming the claret!'

So there was that kind of a background to my Hawick boyhood, and rugby was the language everybody spoke in the town. Eighty-year-old fellows walking along the High Street would tell you who had scored the previous Saturday, and toddlers who had just learnt to walk would tell you the names of the players; so from the beginning I got a fairly clear indication of how important rugby was. In fact in the town of Hawick rugby was a passion. And soon enough it became a passion for me too, as I got into the game and began to play for the junior sides. And that passion for rugby was felt by a lot of other Border towns – Gala, Melrose, wee Jedburgh, they've all produced more than their share of rugby greats. In fact a Borders rugby game gives you a good idea of the intensity, fervour, rivalry and spirit of the Scottish Borders.

I remember once we had been beaten by Watsonians in the first round at Melrose Sevens, which was something unheard of, Hawick being beaten by a team like Watsonians, whom we all thought of as just city slickers. I was a prop forward in that Sevens, along with a team mate called George Hook, and we were walking along the High Street on the evening after the game when we heard a voice. We didn't even see the guy, just heard this voice coming from a close-mouth: 'Ye want tae hing up your buits, yow per, because ye're bluidy useless.'

So it was against that kind of background that you pulled on the green jersey for Hawick, and when you did you were very aware of the fact that the whole town *expected*. They say England expects, and so did Hawick; there was a lot of pressure on young fellows to carry on the tradition. You were expected not only to play for Hawick but to do well for Hawick, and if you didn't they'd very soon tell you about it.

My father and his workmates would talk to me about all the great Hawick players of the past, and the great internationals. My mother's cousin was Walter Sutherland, who played thirteen times for Scotland as a wing between 1910 and 1914. Jock Wemyss, the great doyen of rugby writers who used to do commentary with me later, once told me he thought Sutherland was the greatest wing he ever saw. Well, Andrew Jock Wemyss had been all over the world, and when I told my mother what he'd said she was thrilled to bits.

1935–36 ALL BLACKS

I MUST have been about twelve when I went one afternoon to the Hawick public library and picked out a book on rugby, I think it was just called *Rugby Football*, and in the centre it had sixteen little pictures showing the action when the England wing Alexander Obolensky went from one end of the field to the other for one of the greatest individualist tries of all time. That was against the All Blacks touring side of 1935–36. The photo sequence showed each step, and I was so impressed by this fair-haired fellow who was playing for England, and was a Russian prince of all things! I can remember to this day how I went over every one of those sixteen pictures which showed the action leading up to that try. I almost had it off by heart: sidestep and sway and so on. And this was the 'auld enemy' England – it wasn't even Scotland! Here was I, very Scottish, but fascinated by this England scorer. I'll never forget Obolensky and his famous 1936 try at Twickenham.

It was an extraordinary try in the respect that he got the ball in the right-hand corner of the field and scored in the left-hand corner. The sequence of photographs brought the whole thing to life, showing him sort of dithering his way across the whole New Zealand side, this flaxen-haired fellow who was very quick, of course. There he was, from one end of the field to the other, and it seemed almost humanly impossible for a player to score a try like that against the All Blacks of all people, who were renowned for sinking opponents, just torpedoing them. The pictures didn't show it of course, but he must also have been gifted with change of pace,

14

because he seemed to sort of stutter, and it showed the kind of try that could be scored by a player who just played it off the top of his head and didn't stick to any particular rule. Since then I have always loved that kind of play, with David Campese and Andy Irvine as its finest exemplars. But it was Obolensky who first caught my imagination, the first Englishman (or rather, the first Anglicised Russian prince) to make a very big impression on me with that marvellous try against the 1935–36 All Blacks. Amazingly, he scored *two* tries in that match.

Jack Manchester of Canterbury was the captain of that New Zealand outfit. It wasn't the most successful All Blacks side of all time. They played twenty-eight, won twenty-four, lost three and drew one, which was almost a failure by New Zealand standards! Manchester's side lost to Wales by 12–13 and to England by 0–13, including that great Obolensky try, and so from that point of view I suppose they would have been regarded at home as something of a flop. Scotland they beat 18–8, and Ireland 17–9. But Swansea also beat them, so it was far from being the greatest team of all time from a statistical point of view.

But before coming across that series of pictures of the Obolensky try I had already seen those All Blacks in action, and I assure you I was mightily impressed. They were the first touring side I ever saw, though I had already been to Murrayfield to see Scotland play Ireland and Wales a couple of years before. But I'll never forget as a boy of eleven years of age, sitting in the enclosure seats at Mansfield Park, and seeing this great fellow, Jack Manchester, walk out, leading the All Blacks side against South of Scotland. He *walked* his team onto the field. When David Sole did the same thing for Scotland in that great Grand Slam match of 1990 against England, a lot of people said it was the first time they had seen a team walk onto the field. But long before him Jack Manchester had done the same thing, and I can remember sitting there as a boy looking at those great big brutes all in black, and Manchester, holding the ball in one hand like an orange pip, wearing a brown-black scrum cap that made him look even more ferocious. My breath was taken away by the sight of those great strong All Black fellows walking onto the pitch.

They beat South of Scotland 11–8, which was quite a good performance from South; the forwards did well. But the lasting memory of that game is the way the Blacks came out. Those big, craggy New Zealand players not only looked huge but also as if they had sharp edges to them. I think a lot of them came from agricultural communities, which tends to make people physically strong and mentally tough. But there was a hardness and a sharpness about their make up that struck me as being somehow different. Certainly they made a great impression, and I have had a huge respect for New Zealand rugby right from that day, the moment Manchester appeared out of the pavilion and walked his team on.

I don't think David Sole got his idea from that, though. I believe David discussed with one or two senior players what kind of a gesture they could make to pose a challenge to England, and he hit on this idea – I think it was his own idea, though the others agreed – that they would walk the team on at Murrayfield in 1990. And it certainly worked well. I've never heard the Murrayfield crowd sing the anthem the way they did that day. Usually it's the Welsh singing of 'Land of my Fathers' that's the thing which just carries you away, makes the hairs stand up on the back of your neck. But that day at Murrayfield the Scottish crowd sang as I've never heard them sing before. I've a feeling that walk-on had much to do with it. It had a tremendous impact, I've no doubt.

It was back on that 1935 tour that Scotland played their first international against the All Blacks. Like the South, they also lost 11–8, but managed to put up quite a good performance. I remember there was a lovely try by Ken Fyfe of Cambridge University, who was a favourite of mine. K.C. Fyfe was a very quick wing, and when he scored a Scottish try that day the whole of Edinburgh went potty. A try against the All Blacks!

And I will always remember too, in that South of Scotland game at Mansfield Park, when the New Zealanders came onto the field, there was this great big blond-haired fellow who everyone thought would be a forward, but in point of fact he was the full-back, a fellow called Gilbert. What an impression he made! A big full-back, well over six feet and weighing fourteen and a half stone, which was very big in those days. A huge man, he seemed to me – we hadn't seen full-backs that size before. He was a tremendous performer, the top scorer on that tour with 116 points.

An interesting aspect of that New Zealand tour and the Scottish match was that this was the first time New Zealand had played three forwards in their front row. They had been more inclined to have a front row of only two. So that was a departure, a front row of three in the scrummage – the first time they had played two props and a hooker.

Also there was a fellow called Tori Reid, twenty-two years old, six foot two and fourteen stone thirteen pounds, which was really big then. He was a Maori, a tremendous forward, and what an impression he made. But why was Tori Reid called Tori? It seems that his Christian name was Sanatorium, I don't for the life of me know why, and the other fellows in the squad cut it down to Tori. He was the only Maori in that New Zealand side, and he thundered about the paddock like a wounded buffalo.

The last game of that tour, the twenty-eighth, was in fact the England international, and that was the match England won 13–0, when Obolensky scored his great try. Obolensky got the pass from Peter Candler, who was one England centre. The other centre was called Peter Cranmer, so there were Cranmer and Candler as the two centres – so I wouldn't have fancied doing commentary with those two playing together! Peter Candler gave the pass for Obolensky's try, and Peter Cranmer actually dropped a goal in that match. It was the only time in the twenty-eight games of that tour that New Zealand had failed to score, and that was a real feather in English caps. Those were the first All Blacks I had ever seen, and I saw them from the enclosure seats at Hawick's Mansfield Park ground with my father and his friends.

1951–52 SOUTH AFRICANS

THE 1951–52 South African touring side was another squad who remain in my mind from more than half a century ago. They were a remarkable outfit, playing thirty-one matches and winning thirty; the only side to beat them was London Counties of all people – and they were packed with internationals. What I particularly remember about the 1951-52 Springboks was a big fellow called A.O. Geffin, Aaron was his first name but he was known as 'Okey', a huge prop forward who was also a tremendous goalkicker. He finished up that tour with eighty-nine points, a big powerful fellow who had this tremendous goal-kicking gift, although he wasn't the fastest runner in the world.

Geffin's kicking technique was simplicity itself: he just stood the ball straight up and down – no nonsense about laying it flat or going round the corner – and he just walked straight on to it and gave it a belt. South Africa beat Scotland 44–0 in that tour, the most dreadful defeat, and Geffin was one of the executioners, kicking seven goals from all over the place. Nowadays the whole procedure is far more scientific of course, kickers go round the corner and hit the ball with the instep to get accuracy and distance. But Geffin just made a hole in the turf, sat the ball straight up, ran on to it, and kicked it with the toe of his boot. And boy, was he accurate. But he didn't look like a goal-kicker, he looked like a prop forward – which is what he was!

It was in that 1951–52 tour that we Scots got our first impression of how South Africans love to scrummage. They saw the scrummage as the first area of ball provision; and also of course an opportunity of sapping the opposition and taking the puff out of them, simply grinding them into the ground. They had huge forwards who made scrummaging a number one priority. That tour really gave us a clear idea of how little we knew about scrummaging in this country, and how we could learn from the South Africans by making scrummaging an attack weapon, and not just something where you put your heads in and got the ball back again. The South Africans used the scrummage to attack, and it was a delight to see how they went about it.

Before the South of Scotland game, which was to be held at Mansfield Park, the Springboks were invited to lunch at the Tower Hotel in Hawick, and I was asked along too because I was on the local newspaper at that time. I found myself sitting beside a fellow called Chum Ochse, who turned out to be the top try-scorer of the tour, a very quick wing who scored fifteen tries. There I was in the company of these huge men in blazers. I was speechless, my mouth open! I was supposed to be taking notes for the *Hawick Express* but I just sat there speechless! Hennie Muller was there, the one they called the *Windhond* (the Greyhound), because he was so quick, a big No 8 forward, one of the greatest of all time. It was his pace for a big man which was so extraordinary; Hennie Muller was definitely one of the all-time greats. In 1949 he was voted the best No 8 in the world.

That was my first commentary game, South Africans v the South of Scotland in 1952 at Mansfield Park, which the Springboks won 13–3. I was on the roof of the pavilion looking straight down the pitch, a dreadful commentary position, because you couldn't see the numbers of the team playing towards you. So identification was extremely difficult. It was OK for the fellows running away from you, but not the other way. I hadn't even seen a training session because they hadn't had one, so I had to do it mainly from numbers – when they were running away from me.

There had been a sprinkling of snow that day, and I remember seeing a number of the South African players out there before the kick-off, and they were throwing snowballs at each other, because they'd never seen the stuff before. Great hulking South African forwards throwing snowballs! It was an amazing sight.

The South Africans lost just the one match, to London Counties, on that tour. The Springboks were leading 9–8 till near the end, but Alan Grimsdell, the No 8 for London Counties, kicked a penalty goal from just inside the South African half, a monstrous goal. That gave the London Counties their win.

I also remember vividly being at the game between that South African team and a combined Glasgow/Edinburgh side in Glasgow, where I saw Chris Koch score three tries. Now that might not seem unusual, except for the fact that Chris Koch was a prop forward and had no right to be scoring a hat trick of tries! But it points to the great strength of that South African side, which was in their forwards. Koch was a wonderfully mobile prop, with a great pair of hands. In the international against Scotland he scored two more tries as well. A prop! When you think of the likes of Hennie Muller, Saltie Du Rand, Basie Van Wyk, and of course A.O. Geffin kicking goals from all over the place, the forwards in that side were really formidable. Koch, a sheep farmer from Boland, once startled his colleagues by practising his scrummaging against a stanchion of the stand at Cardiff and making it quiver with his efforts.

Muller scored a try, three conversions and a penalty goal in the Springboks' 43–11 win over that Combined Glasgow/Edinburgh XV. None of us had seen what we called a 'middle of the back row' forward half as quick as the *Windhond*, nor one capable of slotting goals from all over the paddock. He created a style of No 8 defence that subjected opposing backs to huge pressure and little time on the ball.

Basil Kenyon had been chosen as the captain of the Springboks, but he got an eye injury on that tour and Hennie Muller had to take over as captain. Muller went on to lead the side to a Grand Slam against Scotland, Ireland, Wales and England. A month after the match against the Glasgow/Edinburgh XV I saw him again at Murrayfield as a try-scorer and captain in South Africa's defeat of Scotland. But my abiding memory of that tour was not that win, nor even the sight of Scotland being put to the sword at Murrayfield and beaten 44–0, but Aaron Geffin, that muckle brute of a guy, kicking goals with such accuracy and power.

That 44–0 rout stood as a world record defeat for thirty-five years, with South Africa scoring nine tries, seven of which Geffin converted. It pointed to another area of South African strength that seven of those tries were scored by forwards: Salty Du Rand, Chris Koch (2), Basie Van Wyk, Muller, Ernst Dinkelmann and Willem Delporte.

I had recently been released from the sanatorium where for nineteen months I had been receiving treatment for pulmonary tuberculosis which had been attributed to war service in Italy. I was a 'home patient', one who had experienced a complete cure but was still receiving specialised treatment. I was given permission by my medical supervisor to attend the Scotland v South Africa game provided I 'didn't catch cold'! So I got out of the sanatorium and joined up with Bette, to whom I was engaged – because the first thing I did when I got TB, staring death in the face, was to get engaged to Bette! I met up with her in Edinburgh and we went to Murrayfield. When the score was 19–0 I said to her, 'We're seeing history today,' and by the time the game was over it finished up 44–0, which at the time was the biggest ever international victory. It was terrible to see Scotland get such a hammering; that was one of the most disappointing Scotland sides. For years after that, the South Africans referred to any crushing defeat as a 'Murrayfield'.

All in all the 1951–52 Springboks were a great outfit, and not only in the forwards. They had a wing called Ryk Van Schoor, who got a kick in the head during the Ireland game and was carried off unconscious. But against the doctor's orders he said he was going back on again. 'No you're not,' said the doctor. 'No way.' But he went on all the same. He should never have been allowed to go on, but he insisted and he scored a try, a solo effort. When he was told afterwards about his try he couldn't remember a thing – he had absolutely no memory of it, no idea at all.

The 1951–52 South Africans made a great impression, no doubt at all, with just the one defeat in thirty-one games, especially the speed of Hennie Muller, and the power of Aaron Geffin, who they called 'the Boot'. Geffin was the first one to be called that. Later on they called Don Clarke of New Zealand 'the Boot' as well. Of course, in some ways the two were very similar.

The last game of that touring side was against France, and that was the first official international between the two countries. It was in Colombes Stadium in Paris, and victory went to South Africa by 25–3. France led with a drop goal for a while, before the Springboks swept them away, but the important point is that yet again it was the forwards who scored no fewer than four of the six South African tries: Dinkelmann, Muller, Delport and Van Wyk. And that I think underlines the strength of South African rugby as being in those great, muckle forwards who could produce ball whenever it was needed. It was a delight to see that South African side in action: played thirty-one, won thirty, lost one, and scored 562 points in thirty-one games. Some team!

1953–54 ALL BLACKS

B OB STUART was the captain of the 1953–54 All Blacks, a touring side who lost two games over here and were held to a draw in two more. They lost to Wales 8–13, and then to Cardiff 3–8, and were held to a 6–6 draw by Swansea and 5–5 by Ulster. And in France they lost a couple of games too. But in my opinion the impressive thing about the 1953–54 All Blacks side was that they produced one of the great last lines of defence in the shape of full-back Bob Scott. Scott was a big man, a very adventurous full-back, a fellow who showed everybody in this country that if you have a big man at the back who can shift along at a good pace and is adventurous, it can be absolutely devastating.

Bob Scott certainly wrote his name on that tour, in which New Zealand beat Ireland 14–3, and beat England by 5–0. They defeated Scotland by 3–0 – a Bob Scott penalty goal, I remember, on a filthy day, which just scraped over the bar, and the whole of Murrayfield was blowing to stop it going over. Then they lost to France by 0–3, when the great French flank forward Jean Prat scored a try. Tries were three points in those days.

But the story of the '53–54 All Blacks was mainly Bob Scott, an intruding full-back who was devastating, and he underlined the concept of an attacking full-back rather than someone who was just there to defend. They had some great forwards too, like Peter Jones, a big back-row forward who was a formidable player with ball in hand. And they had grinding scrummagers like Kevin Skinner. I remember that the night before the South of Scotland game here at Hawick Kevin Skinner went out on the town and had quite an evening. Apparently he got in pretty late, but the following day he played the game of his life. It didn't seem to have had any effect on him at all – typical New Zealand prop forward, nothing had an effect, he just kept champing on. Those New Zealanders are a different breed! I was commentating that game and I remember we got a real thumping from them, with Skinner leading the charge. The score – 32–0.

Ron Jarden, the wing, was another of the great personalities of that tour, not only because he was so fast but also because in heavy ground he had that ability to run almost on top of the thick mud rather than through it. He seemed to float over heavy ground. And he had wonderful handling gifts and also good change of pace. Jarden was one of the stars of that tour with seventy-one points, and the top try scorer with ten.

I remember they had great forwards, that lot: Bill Clark, Peter Jones, Kevin Skinner, Nelson Dalzell – who was listed at six foot three and about seventeen stones, which in those days was massive. Ian Clarke was the brother of Don (the Boot) Clarke, and he was a prop forward, but he once dropped a goal for the Barbarians – three points thank you very much – which was ridiculous! If any prop forward in Scotland dropped a goal the coach would tear his head off: you're not supposed to drop goals, you're supposed to scrummage and give the ball to some of the aristocrats behind, not drop bloody goals! And the hooker Ron Hemi, a Maori, he was a very mobile fellow. In fact a feature of that All Black side was the forwards, and the way they kept together in a great black mass moving about the field, very seldom split up into little groups. The midfield may have lacked a bit of ingenuity, but with Bob Scott intruding at pace from the back they were always a danger.

SCOTLAND AND
OTHERS

I SUPPOSE the saddest time in Scottish rugby was that spell between 1951 and 1955 when Scotland suffered seventeen defeats on the trot, seventeen consecutive defeats. That was the period when Scotland lost 44–0 to South Africa at Murrayfield, a time when, in the words of the local Hawick song, 'All was sunk in deep dejection'. That was the situation; we didn't seem able to beat anybody. I suppose if we had a fixture with Bechuanaland we'd have lost that as well. But I'll never forget the game in 1955 which ended that sequence of seventeen defeats in a row. Scotland were playing Wales at Murrayfield, a brilliant Welsh side full of British Lions, and Scotland beat Wales 14–8 to end that terrible run.

Jock Wemyss, who was my summariser in those days, and came in with the little tactical bits, was sitting beside me in the commentary box when Scotland beat that fantastic Welsh team. Jock was the great doyen of rugby commentators and correspondents in those days, with a wonderful memory for detail, and he had only one eye – the other eye had been shot out in the 1914–18 war. When Scotland beat Wales in that game, and finally ended that awful run, and I had finished commentary and had handed over to Jock for his summing up, his first words were: 'Well, I can hardly speak.' And believe it or not, a tear came down from that one eye – it was the first time I had seen that big hulk of a fellow so emotional.

By the way, Jock had played for Scotland and had got several of his caps with one eye. In one match he was playing against France, and there was a French player, called Lubin-Lebrère, who had also lost an eye in the war. So they agreed, believe it or not, to mark each other at the lineouts, and of course on the blind side they tended to feel for each other. The referee, who was from England, chivvied them, but Charlie Usher, the Scottish flanker, said, 'Oh for God's sake, ref, leave them alone, they're both half-blind.'

That 1955 win over Wales at Murrayfield brought to an end the saddest era I can remember. And as I did commentary on quite a number of those matches when we were beaten I tended to get the blame for each one of them! But after that things got better. Hugh McLeod and David Rollo were a couple of very dependable prop forwards who were coming in about then. Hugh was a short, stocky fellow, a great one for fitness, and that was what gave him his edge. He was still running when the rest weren't, and at the end he still had a bit of puff left. He was also a very astute tactician and rugby brain. And David Rollo, a big Fife farmer, was very strong as most agricultural types are.

Scotland began to develop one of their most formidable scrummages at about that time. They had Mike Campbell-Lamerton and Frans ten Bos in the middle row, and they were both very big men by any standards. Campbell-Lamerton was a mighty man, a great mauler, very strong in upper body and a great man for ripping ball away from opponents. He wasn't tactically very astute, but he was very strong.

Scotland has tended to be outweighted by almost everybody, and that has been an ongoing problem with us. The English are nearly always much heavier, and the Welsh too. Even the Irish were bigger and heavier than the Scots in those sad days when we had seventeen defeats in a row. So it was partly because we couldn't dominate up front and the backs were always struggling on poor rations that we got such a run of defeats.

In the period 1950–56 Wales won two Triple Crowns and Grand Slams, one further Championship outright, and twice shared the title. In the opinion of Cliff Morgan, one of the most influential players of that era, this golden age for Wales had less to do with the results than the fact that Wales 'conjured attractive rugby out of highly individual players'. Those players included, in addition to Cliff Morgan, the amazing Bleddyn Williams who, with Jack Matthews, formed a ham-and-eggs partnership at centre, and on the wing Ken Jones, an electric eel of a man with the pace of an accredited Olympic sprinter. Jones reached the 100 metres semi-final in the 1948 Olympic Games in London, but in addition to his terrifying speed he was possessed of a swerve that left the most resolute defenders sitting on their backsides and scratching their heads. Jones played forty-four tests for Wales, forty-three of them consecutively, scoring seventeen tries.

Ken Jones was certainly very special at the time. But in my opinion he was limited as a footballer, and he knew his limitations. He was essentially a finisher, a guy who if you gave him half a yard of space he was gone. His incredible pace was something that most rugby players don't have. But he had to be set up. He wasn't in the same league as his great contemporaries like Cliff Morgan or Bleddyn Williams, he wasn't a footballer to that degree. He was certainly no mug, but essentially he was a sprinter playing rugby. All the same, Jones was a key part of those great Welsh sides of the 1950s.

The early 1950s were the golden age too of the Irish, during a period that came to be known as the Kyle era because it was Jack Kyle's genius that inspired them to their only Grand Slam, in 1948, and a Triple Crown in the following year. Kyle is generally acknowledged to have been one of the finest stand-offs of all time.

The English were no slouches in the 1950s either. They won a Grand Slam in 1957, the Championship in 1958, and a Triple Crown and Championship share in 1960. Their scrum-half Dickie Jeeps was a forthright character, completely fearless and very strong. He combined well with Cliff Morgan during the Lions tour of South Africa in 1955, when his short, sharp pass enabled Cliff to demonstrate the full range of his gifts of deception.

The Lions ran rings round the South Africans on that tour. In addition to the orchestrating genius of Cliff Morgan there was the flashing talent of Tony O'Reilly on the wing, who ran up two tries in four internationals and scored sixteen tries on the tour, and the immaculate midfield partnership of the English pair Jeff Butterfield and Phil Davies, who were superior to the Springboks' three-quarters.

The English also had the great Peter Jackson, of course, who made his debut in 1956. Jackson's try against the Wallabies at Twickenham in 1958 has gone down in history as one of the greatest ever, although the tries he scored against the All Blacks on the 1959 Lions tour were superb scores.

And then there was the English stand-off Richard Sharp. I once saw Sharp scoring a try against Scotland from a set-piece that you weren't supposed to score from in those days. In scrums and lineouts the defensive formations were so set that it was really very hard indeed to make a clean break direct from the set-piece. You needed something else in between like a couple of rucks. But Sharp scored his try from a scrummage just by picking the right line and going at such a lick that he went clean through and no one laid a hand on him. In those days of strong and ordered defences it was a quite remarkable try, one of the great individualist tries that really shouldn't have been scored. But he just picked his angle, and his pace was such that neither flank forwards nor his opposite number got near him – never even touched him. For a big, leggy fellow like Sharp it was an extraordinary score, the pace he generated over a short distance. Usually big guys take a bit of time to get going.

I've already mentioned the notorious 111 lineouts at Scotland v Wales in 1963, In those days you could punt straight into touch from anywhere, and that game was just a war of attrition up and down the touchline. And it was awful to watch. I got a letter from an irate colonel in the north of Scotland, probably in charge of a whole herd of reindeer or something, who wrote, 'Absolute bloody fool, can't possibly have been 111 lineouts, absolutely impossible.' So I wrote back to him and said I respected his view, but not only were there 111 lineouts in that Scotland–Wales game but also, four days later, I covered the Hawick v Melrose game in the Borders League and in that one there were 108 lineouts! I didn't hear from the colonel again. The game was dying then.

Today the kicking game sometimes seems to be creeping back, but now of course, with the laws governing touch-kicking, your punting has got to be very accurate. Otherwise the other side can exploit inaccurate opposition punting. Kick badly to the likes of David Campese, Andy Irvine or Serge Blanco and they will punish you with counter-attack. On the other hand hoist a few Garryowens with accuracy and you really can pressurise even players of the highest quality. After all they just have to wait there, knees knocking, hoofbeats in their ears, gazing skywards and wishing they could call 'yours'!

PORTRAITS

WILSON SHAW (1934–39)
Glasgow High School FP, Scotland
19 caps

Apart from being one of the most kenspeckle Scottish players, Wilson Shaw of Glasgow High School FP had a remarkable record of having scored against England at Twickenham in three consecutive games there: 1934, 1936, and 1938 (twice). It is an unusual statistic, although no great surprise to those who still remember the pinnacle of his achievement in 1938, when he scored two wonderful tries in victory over England by 21–16 at Twickenham, a performance that brought Scotland the Championship and Triple Crown. And I was there!

As a fourteen-year-old I had been to Twickenham in 1936 when Scotland was captained by my boyhood idol Jock Beattie of Hawick, capped twenty-three times as a lock forward. Here I was again with my father and his factory friends, and I have vivid recall of Wilson Shaw leaving England defenders in his wake as he scuttled home for those two tries. No wonder it was called 'Shaw's match', because Shaw was also captain of Scotland that day. And what a captain's inspirational game he played. So much so that he was carried shoulder high from the pitch by his delighted team colleagues. Once he had showered and changed, he entered the tea room and sat down beside an aged English gentleman to whom Shaw made conversation with the comment, 'By golly it really was hot out there today!' To which the aged one replied, 'Yes, but aren't you lucky you weren't playing?'

Shaw was a player of exceptional gifts and thoughtful captaincy who was prepared to run with the ball rather than kick it, and he was blessed with quite staggering pace off the mark that caught opponents unawares and opened up gaps that didn't seem to exist. Yet it took the Scottish selectors quite a while to field Wilson Shaw in his optimum position of stand-off half. His first three caps were as a wing, followed by one as centre and five as stand-off before returning to the wing for three games, to centre for one, to stand-off for another four, and finally two more as centre. So his nineteen caps comprised six as a wing, four as a centre, and nine as stand-off, in which he was partnered at scrum-half by Ross Logan (five times), Tom Dorward (three times), and Willy Brydon (once).

Yet despite such frequent switches, Wilson Shaw was taken to their hearts by the Scottish support because he was such an exciting player, and a gentleman both on and off the field. He captained Scotland in nine internationals, and in the Irish match of 1937 he played on the wing with his brother Ian as his centre. He became president of the Scottish Rugby Union in 1971, and during his term he helped to improve the relationship between the Scottish Rugby Union and the media as well as creating a splendid impression as a fair and understanding figurehead. He also will be remembered for a quite brilliant performance against Jack Manchester's 1935 All Blacks, who won 18–8 at Murrayfield, but could not prevent Wilson Shaw from creating cracking tries by Ken Fyfe (Cambridge University) and Charles Dick (Guy's Hospital). Truly a great Scot whose name is treasured in Scottish Rugby Union annals.

JEAN PRAT (1945–55)
Lourdes, France
51 caps

He has been described as the man who finally put French rugby on the map, and also as the father of French rugby, and there is no doubt that Jean Prat, nicknamed 'Monsieur Rugby' by his friends and supporters in the Lourdes rugby club, was a key figure in the emergence of France as a significant force in the years after the second world war. He amassed a French record of fifty-one caps as a gifted flanker who missed only three international games in more than a decade of service.

Relations between the French Federation and the Home Unions had been severed in 1931 because of alleged professionalism by the former, but in 1945, when France awarded Prat his first cap as a twenty-one-year-old for their New Year's Day game against a British Army side, relations were restored to normal. Prat showed his paces that day, and developed into a gifted flank forward with the speed and running angles to pressurise opposing midfield backs, and with the kind of skills that brought him an impressive haul of 145 test points from nine tries, twenty-six conversions, seventeen penalty goals and five drop goals.

A son of the soil from Lourdes in the Pyrenees, Prat did not seem, at five foot ten and thirteen stone four pounds, to have the physique for survival in the wear and tear of forward play. In fact he looked like a pygmy beside some of the huge French forwards of the time, but he was wonderfully skilled. Strong and quick, he was very comfortable with ball in hand, so much so that he seemed capable of being at home in any of the back division positions.

Prat was famed as a drop goal specialist, and had a big hand in France's first away victories over Wales in 1948 and England in 1951. He could swivel and drop a goal out of the blue, and in that respect he was a little like the great All Black No 8 Zinzan Brooke. They could both drop a goal from forty yards out, much to the rage and frustration of their opponents.

33

Prat's first game as French captain brought an 11–5 win over Scotland in 1953, and he captained France in sixteen internationals before his retirement in 1955. He also played in the same French side as his brother Maurice, a midfield artist, on eighteen occasions.

Jean Prat led France to their first two Five Nations Championships in 1954 and 1955, and he was captain and player-coach of Lourdes when they won the French Championship six times in ten years between 1952 and 1963. He was such an outstanding player, leading by example, that the other members of the team would follow him anywhere.

Prat had a kind of aura about him, and a lot of his skill and application rubbed off on his team mates. Along with Lucien Mias, he became a legendary figure in French rugby, and his brother was also very highly thought of. The Prat brothers made an immense contribution to the evolution of French rugby into a potent force in the postwar years, and Jean Prat's achievement was recognised with an award of a French Rugby Federation gold medal in 1959, followed by the *Légion d'honneur*.

BOB SCOTT (1946–54)
Auckland, New Zealand
17 caps

Some called him the Barefoot Boy, because New Zealand folk would come from miles around to see Robert William Henry Scott kick goals in his bare feet from all over the place – as far as I know he was the first international to perform this feat in public.

The first of Scott's seventeen caps was gained against Australia in Dunedin in September 1946. In the New Zealand tour of Australia in 1947 his brilliant place-kicking brought him seventy-two points in just six games, including fifteen in the second test. All in all he put together seventy-four points in his seventeen tests, including sixteen conversions, twelve penalty goals and two drop goals. His 840 points in first-class rugby union remained a record for quite some time, but it was as an adventurous full-back rather than a points machine that he is best remembered. Scott toured South Africa in an abrasive series in 1949, playing in all four tests.

At five foot ten and twelve stone eleven Bob Scott was quite a big man for those days, but his main talent was his mastery of the various arts of deception, not least of that sizzling sidestep by which he would avoid opponents following up their punted ball. Scott also brought judgement and timing to his intrusion support play, and to his ability to link with and launch his forwards. He had command of a spinning punted ball, and whilst his style and skill were at their peak some fifty years ago, they still stand as a benchmark for aspiring young full-backs in New Zealand.

In 1946 the great South African flank forward Hennie Muller rated Scott 'the greatest footballer I have ever played against'. In 1954, after the Barbarians game against the All Blacks at the end of their tour of the UK, Bob Scott was chaired from the field. According to the *Playfair Rugby Annual* Scott's technique and personality had been the outstanding memory of that tour.

JACK KYLE (1947–58)
Queen's University, Belfast, Ireland, British Lions
46 Ireland caps
6 British Lions tests

There aren't many rugby union players who can claim to have written their names over a particular period of the game, but John Wilson Kyle, better known as Jacky, certainly achieved that. For Irish rugby in the years after the second world war has become generally known as the Jack Kyle era. The reason was simply that Jacky Kyle became the most revered of Irish players as a dominant force when Ireland claimed their only ever Grand Slam in 1948, as well as three international Championships in four years in 1948, 1949 and 1951. With Kyle at the helm, Ireland claimed a level of success that they have not equalled in all the years since, and Kyle also had the most remarkable record against my own countrymen in that he played against Scotland on ten occasions and was never once in a losing side.

I once saw a demonstration of his intelligence and guile at Lansdowne Road, on 25 February 1956, when Ireland were leading Scotland by 11–10. Kyle, noting that an injury to Angus Cameron, Scotland's left wing, had caused the Scots to replace him with a forward, Iain McGregor, showed real patience in waiting for the chance to break. Delaying his run to perfection, he accelerated onto a set-piece scrummage pass from his scrum-half John O'Meara, sprinted with that amazing pace of his up the weakened Scottish flank, and dotted down a try that gave Ireland victory by 14–10.

That was typical of Kyle: observant, tactically astute, sharp in decision-making, and with pace off the mark that made him an extremely hard target to nail down. For more than half a century he remained Ireland's most capped stand-off, with forty-six caps between 1947 and 1958, and it is no coincidence that during his reign the Irish enjoyed by far their most successful run.

Having first played for Ulster as an eighteen-year-old, and also as a teenager in the Victory International just after the war, Kyle announced his entry into International Championship play by excelling against France in 1947. Eleven years later he rang down the curtain on his illustrious career following a 12–6 win over Scotland at Lansdowne Road. Besides playing in forty-six internationals, he captained Ireland in test matches on six occasions.

Kyle was quick, with pattering steps, and frequently managed to accelerate away from enemy tacklers just when they seemed to have him in their sights. Although a comparatively slightly built player of five foot nine and twelve stone six, he once was described as a 'light-weight who packed a heavyweight tackle'. In his forty-six internationals he scored twenty-four points from seven tries and a drop goal. He also toured with the British Lions in Australia and New Zealand in 1950, playing in sixteen of the twenty-three games including all six tests, for six tries. One of these was a remarkable effort of individual brilliance in the first test against New Zealand.

Rugby men in the southern hemisphere rated Jack Kyle as 'a complete footballer', and the great New Zealand full-back Bob Scott called him 'the best player in the Lions team, and in all the years since I have never seen a better first five-eighth'. There was a quality about his play that was truly poetic. Indeed, it is said that a famous Irish poet, when asked to make one wish, answered that it would be to play rugby like Jack Kyle.

Jack Kyle OBE became the first man to win fifty caps against International Rugby Board countries, including his tests for the British Lions. He was a surgeon by profession, and after retiring from rugby spent more than thirty years working as a medical man in Zambia.

BLEDDYN WILLIAMS (1947–55)
Cardiff, Wales, British Lions
22 Wales caps
5 British Lions tests

Bleddyn Llewelyn Williams was not only an outstandingly gifted centre in his own right. As a member of one of the most successful centre partnerships in the history of the game, he also contributed creative ability and a wonderful grasp of basic skills to the rugged physicality and power of Jack Matthews, his renowned partner for

Cardiff, Wales and the Lions. Together they provided an amalgam of all the essentials for a productive midfield pairing. Williams himself had progressed from junior school scrum-half, senior school stand-off at Rydal, and full-back for the Welsh Schools XV, to twenty-two caps as centre for Wales and five test appearances for the British Lions.

Williams was already playing for Cardiff by the time he left school before the war, and in 1943 he scored a hat trick of tries for the Welsh Services XV against the English Services in a 34–7 victory. Because of the war he had to wait until 1947 before gaining his first cap, against England at Cardiff, where inevitably he was in partnership with Matthews, who was also making his first-cap appearance. They proved a very influential combination in Welsh centre play, partnering each other in nine tests, which would have been many more but for injuries. Williams scored eight test tries and a record 185 tries for Cardiff, which included another record, still standing after half a century, of forty-one Cardiff tries in one season (1947–48). He was chaired from the field after Cardiff beat the All Blacks 8–3 in 1953–54, and he captained Wales to their 13–8 win over those All Blacks in December 1953 (see pp. 42–44).

He was vice-captain of the 1950 Lions in New Zealand, but played as captain in three of the tests after Karl Mullen was injured. Williams showed great tactical and leadership skills in that series, as well as being rated the outstanding midfield player of that tour. At five foot ten and thirteen stone, Bleddyn Williams was in every sense a solid citizen, not easily torpedoed, and he had a sizzling side-step and gifts of passing improvisation that enabled his wings to prosper. He had been a key performer when Cardiff, Wales and the Barbarians beat the 1947–48 Wallabies, but despite his superb individual skills, which marked him out as a superstar, he was always one who put team before personal interest.

HENNIE MULLER (1949–53)

Transvaal, South Africa

13 caps

They called him the *Windhond* of the Veld, and sure enough Hendrik Scholtz Vosloo Muller, known as Hennie, seemed possessed of the speed of a greyhound. His impressive pace is underlined by the interesting statistic that, as a fourteen-year-old schoolboy, he ran the 100 metres in 10.5 seconds.

Injuries prevented Muller from gaining more than his thirteen caps, in which he scored three tries, two conversions and a penalty goal. Only one of his international matches ended in defeat. He also captained South Africa to eight test wins in nine games.

Hennie Muller's speed, combined with his adhesive but soft hands, made him a formidable citizen as a roving loose forward with a hard edge to his endeavours. At five foot eleven and thirteen stone ten, he hounded and harassed opposing backs in the days when loose forwards at lineouts could position themselves virtually in the midfield opposite the opposing centres. His blond hair, and his way of standing with hands on hips, marked him out as a dangerous force liable to fill opponents with apprehension. Bob Scott said of him that he was 'as fast as a track sprinter and as alert and hungry as a hawk'.

The home countries had received some warning about the influence of Hennie Muller, for on the South African tour of New Zealand in 1949 he had created havoc among the New Zealand backs. Indeed, South Africa's Mr Rugby, Danie Craven, reckoned that Muller was the fastest loose forward he had ever seen. It was Craven who gave him the nickname of *Windhond*.

In October 1951, when I made the two-hour journey by car to Glasgow with a group of friends to see the Glasgow/Edinburgh v South Africa game, my abiding memory is of a devastating display by Hennie Muller, not least in his remarkable work rate and his edge of pace. There were knowledgeable South African adherents who reckoned that Muller could have played for South Africa on the wing. The Springboks beat Glasgow/Edinburgh 43–11, and part of Muller's contribution comprised a try, three conversions, and one penalty goal. Not bad for a forward!

However, amazing though it may seem, Muller was outscored on that occasion by another forward – a prop! Chris Koch, a wonderfully mobile player, went over the line to score on no fewer than three occasions in the course of that game. Nevertheless, it is Hennie Muller who stays in my memory.

I remember also on that occasion that the Glasgow/Edinburgh back division contained three players with the surname of Cameron. My own first commentary game was at about that time, when I covered the Springboks v South of Scotland at my home ground of Hawick's Mansfield Park, so I could sympathise with whoever was doing the job at Glasgow and feel deeply relieved that I had not been called upon to provide commentary on that game!

During that 1951–52 tour the South African captain Basil Kenyon suffered eye damage and Hennie Muller took on the leadership in nineteen of the tour's twenty-two games, including the Grand Slam of the internationals: Scotland 44–0, Ireland 17–5, Wales 6–3, England 8–3, and France 25–3.

Hennie Muller's sad death in 1977 at the age of fifty-three was mourned by rugby supporters all over the world.

CLIFF MORGAN (1951–58)
Cardiff, Wales, British Lions
29 Wales caps
4 British Lions tests

At one time, whenever Scotland were due to play Wales, much of the Scottish team talk centred around ways and means of limiting the threat posed by Clifford Isaac Morgan of Cardiff and Wales. For not only was that gifted product of the Welsh stand-off factory a crafty tactician who seldom missed a trick, but he also had all the gifts of deception that enabled him to operate brilliantly in cluttered confines, and he was sharp into his running, which carried with it a deceptive body lean and sway that often spoofed opponents. That acceleratory pace was a key element in his armoury and was demonstrated to spectacular effect when, in the first 1955 South Africa v Lions test match at Ellis Park, Johannesburg, he scored a quite amazing try in days when loose forwards could bring pace and pressure to bear on opposing runners.

That try, direct from the set-piece, was scored against a South African loose forward trio of Basie Van Wyk, Stephen Fry and Dan Retief. Some trio! Cliff made a huge impression on the South African game during that tour, where he revelled in the firm grounds that helped him to display the wide range of his talents and, not least, to conduct with flair and versatility an orchestra that included such greats as Tony O'Reilly and Jeff Butterfield.

His twenty-nine caps as stand-off was a Welsh record for some thirty-eight years, and he was an influential figure in the Welsh sides that won a Grand Slam in 1952, won outright Five Nations Champions in 1952 and 1956, and shared the Championships in 1954 and 1955. In 1956 he was captain. He was very astute, so much so that in one international he inspected the pitch and also the wind conditions with such care that he actually ensured that Wales would have wind advantage in both halves. This he did by punting to one touchline in the first half, and to the other one in the second.

Later he became head of BBC Outside Broadcasts as well as a brilliant commentator with a wonderful turn of phrase, and an enthusiasm and love of the game which he transmitted to his listeners and viewers. He was a delight to work alongside, and had a lovely way of putting broadcast colleagues at ease, with a little tap on his forehead accompanied by a reassuring, 'Now don't forget, McLaren, it's up here for thinking and down there for dancing, innit?'

He presented the programme 'Rugby Special', with Alan Mouncer as producer and me as commentator. We were the three who came in at the start. As well as the presentation Cliffy did the inter-round summaries. One of his many great performances as commentator was when he described with enormous passion that famous Gareth Edwards try for the Barbarians against the All Blacks in 1973. It was just brilliant.

Cliff Morgan was a truly great player. I have often felt that if he played today he would probably score fifty or sixty tries in a season. We have to keep in mind that Cliff was stand-off for Wales at a time when defences were really claustrophobic, and opposing players were allowed to lie right up on the attackers, and the amount of room in which a back could move was limited to the nth degree. And yet Cliffy scored some great tries. He was wonderfully quick, with tremendous pace off the mark; and also as cunning as a bag of weasels. He could assess tactical situations, and today I think he would be even greater than he was in his own day.

Cliff Morgan in his own words

Cardiff v All Blacks, 1953

It was a staggering game, with a big build-up and a terrific front-row battle. In particular I remember Stan Bowes, our tough naval prop, playing opposite Snow White, an equally rugged New Zealander. They struggled and hit and fought in that front row all through that game, and yet until the day that Stan died in the early 'nineties, Snow White would come across to see Stan, or he'd pay for Stan to go and see him in New Zealand, and they kept that friendship going for thirty-seven years. There is a special relationship, a kind of intimacy between opposing front-row forwards which I have always admired. I noticed it first when I played with Cliff Davies, and later Billy Williams and Courtney Meredith and other great props.

The All Blacks' full-back was Bob Scott, one of the first to come into the three-quarter line to make an extra man and create a gap through which tries could be scored. Bob was a phenomenon. He kicked equally well with each foot, and part of his normal training was to kick goals from the halfway line with his bare feet. He forced us to think up another signal. If he came into the line, somebody would shout, 'Scott's in!' and we'd have an extra man there to tackle him. But he also made us think more adventurously. I'll never forget Bleddyn [Williams] saying, 'We've got to try things, and if we fail we fail, but we've got to be different.'

So once when the ball came out from Rex [Willis], I tried a little chip over the top of the New Zealand pack, chased after it myself, and as they all came out of the scrum to nail me, I caught it, and passed it immediately to Bleddyn who shot it out to Gwyn Rowlands on the wing. He was boxed in on the touchline but kicked inside to where our flanker, Sid Judd, who was majestic, won the race for the ball to score a try. At that point, only six minutes into the game, you knew there was something on that day. And it's true, the game was decided already. Gwyn converted the try and kicked a penalty; Ron Jarden kicked a penalty for them; and we won 8–3.

That still left us with seventy-four minutes' defending to do. But the 45,000 spectators were unbelievable; I've never known them so solidly behind us, even playing for Wales. I felt that every yard you ran you'd been pushed forward by the crowd, and every time you kicked to touch, the ball went twenty yards further because the crowd were willing it to do so. People said in those days that Cardiff couldn't tackle, that we never had a tackler. Well, we did tackle, we did fall on the ball and keep possession. And then in the last moment of the game, Geoff Beckingham took the scrum against the All Blacks' put-in, Rex just lobbed the ball out to me and I whacked it up into the north stand, out of the way, because I knew it was the final whistle. We were the only club side, as Wales was the only home country, to beat New Zealand on that tour.

Every year since then, the Cardiff side who brought off this victory have held a reunion in Cardiff on the Friday evening before the date of that match. Sadly we are down to nine now, but the survivors get there from wherever they are, paying their own way and buying their own meal. Once I remember flying from Geneva to London Airport, catching the train at Reading and arriving for a seven o'clock dinner party at half past nine. We have no speeches, just conversation, and only one toast – to absent friends. This is at nine o'clock, which is nine in the morning in New Zealand where our old opponents – and most of them are still alive – have a similar anniversary breakfast. After the toast we make a quick phone call: Bleddyn, our captain, speaking to theirs, Bob Stuart. It keeps the true spirit of the game alive, and that's the most remarkable thing as far as I'm concerned. We've always wanted to whack New Zealand, but also to be with them afterwards to share the bumps, the bruises and the memories.

(From Cliff Morgan: *The Autobiography Beyond the Fields of Play*, Hodder & Stoughton, 1996.

HUGH McLEOD (1954–62)
Hawick, Scotland, British Lions
40 Scotland caps
6 British Lions tests

Hugh McLeod, who comes from Hawick like myself, was one of the best tight-head props Scotland has ever produced and a man for whom I have always had the highest respect and admiration. Although only five foot nine tall, and weighing a mere fourteen stone, he was a mighty scrummager and a very down-to-earth personality who wasn't afraid to speak his mind. In fact he was one of the great personalities of the game, always very blunt and forthright. One day in 1962 he was asked to lead the Scottish pack against a powerful Welsh side at Cardiff, but he told the selectors that he didn't want to, he would rather concentrate on his own game. But they insisted, and so, much against his better judgment, he agreed.

On the Friday afternoon the Scottish side had their training session, but it seems that some of the forwards had been chatting away and interrupting him, so he gathered them around him, Frans ten Bos, Mike Campbell-Lamerton and the rest. 'Come here, my wee disciples,' he said, and I can still hear him in his broad Scots. 'I've been asked to lead this pack, and to be honest with you I don't want to do it. I'd rather concentrate on my own job. But I've been persuaded by the chairman of the selectors and the rest of them. So if any of you fellows want to lead the pack tomorrow, just let me know and I'll put in a word for you at the right place. But meanwhile, the next man that opens his trap, I'll put my boot right up his arse.' And I remember one of the Anglo-Scots, I think it was Campbell-Lamerton, saying: 'You know, I didn't understand half of that, but it sounded fearfully impressive.' And the Scottish pack went out the next day against that great Welsh side of 1962, and they wiped Wales off the field. It was a filthy day, and the Welsh were beaten up front, absolutely put to the sword, and the great stalwarts of the day were Campbell-Lamerton and his lock partner, Frans ten Bos.

I remember another time when Hugh McLeod spoke his mind with considerable effect. Hugh and I were in Paris for the 1963 match against France, and we were leaving the restaurant when we ran into Frans ten Bos who had just come out of the team hotel. The three of us had a coffee together, and I could see that Hugh had something on his mind – in fact he was sizzling. Then he said, 'Frans, I want to tell you something. I've seen you playing quite a lot and, to be honest I think you're a big lump of potted meat. If I was half your size I'd pick up the first Frenchman who looked at me tomorrow, and I'd throw him over the bloody stand.'

Ten Bos looked amazed. But when we went out of the restaurant, McLeod stamping on in front, leaving me and ten Bos following, Frans tapped my shoulder and said, 'I'd follow that little bugger anywhere.' And on the morrow he played the game of his life, he was like a raging lion. He knocked people over, he clattered into them – I'd never seen him play like that. And I'm sure it was what Hugh said that made him do that, no one had ever spoken to him like that before. Scotland won that game 11–6, never an easy thing to do in Paris.

Hugh McLeod was a regular in the Hawick side when he was seventeen; he was playing for Scotland not much later, and he toured with the Lions in South Africa (1955) and Australia/New Zealand (1959). Above all, he was a fine rugby brain, always on the look-out to adapt moves and ploys he had picked up in other countries, and this led to Hawick's dominance at the time.

TONY O'REILLY (1955–70)
Old Belvedere, Leicester, Ireland, British Lions
29 Ireland caps
10 British Lions tests

Having played in a final Irish trial when only eighteen, Tony O'Reilly was capped first against France in Dublin in 1955 after just five games with his club Old Belvedere, playing as a centre. According to a contemporary account of that game, his 'red hair made him easy to identify on the field, while his physique made him a difficult opponent to stop ... but he promised more than he attained in the Irish jersey'.

O'Reilly scored eleven tries in twenty-nine major internationals (five for Ireland and six for the Lions), hardly a small achievement, but it was with the Lions in South Africa in 1955, when he was just nineteen, that he achieved his most impressive scoring feat. In that tour he amassed a haul of sixteen tries, which was a record for a tourist in South Africa. In fact O'Reilly boggled the minds of the Springboks on that tour, making an impact as great as Jonah Lomu in 1995.

When the Lions toured Australia and New Zealand in 1959, O'Reilly and England's Peter Jackson took the country by storm with marvellous wing play that spawned thirty-three tries between the two of them, seventeen by O'Reilly, which was a record for a tourist in New Zealand.

O'Reilly played twenty-two of his twenty-nine Irish caps consecutively, and he also figured in ten tests for the British Lions. At six feet two, and close to fifteen stone, he was an impressive sight and a hard man to put on the floor when at full pace. His test career lasted until 1970, during which he became something of a cult figure with young followers.

O'Reilly became president of Heinz but never stepped back from poking fun at himself, which he did with rare abandon when he and Ireland's scrum-half Andy Mulligan formed a double act of huge entertainment value at meetings of the Ireland squad and indeed of the British Lions. One of his heroes, the Irish flanker Ronnie Kavanagh, was a fitness freak who urged O'Reilly to harden himself by combat-type training in the mountains. But O'Reilly was having none of it. 'Kav,' he said, 'it's not guerilla warfare, it's rugby we're playing. We're not going to be asked to ford a stream at Lansdowne Road.'

Once he played for Barbarians at the Melrose Sevens tournament in the Scottish Border country, and turned out in a pair of rugby boots with no ankle guards on them. It was the first time, said one Border supporter, that he had seen a player taking part in Sevens wearing dancing pumps.

When Tony O'Reilly was recalled to the Ireland side as a thirty-three-year-old for the game against England in 1970, after being out of the international scene for seven years, he was by then becoming something of a giant in business. So folk weren't exactly taken aback when he arrived for the Friday afternoon Irish training session in a gleaming Rolls-Royce, from which there also emerged the chauffeur, who handed the great man his rugby boots, which were badly in need of a brush and polish. That story reached the Saturday morning papers so that during the actual game against England, when O'Reilly, as he himself described it, 'made the grave mistake of going down on the ball at the feet of the England forwards', a voice from the crowd bellowed out, 'Yes, and kick his bloody chauffeur as well!'

PETER JACKSON (1956–63)
Coventry, England, British Lions
20 England caps
5 British Lions tests

My friend Hugh McLeod, who toured with the Lions in South Africa in 1955, and in Australia/New Zealand in 1959, rates Peter Barrie Jackson of Coventry and England as the greatest wing with whom he ever played. And few who saw him would disagree with that assessment, for the Coventry wing had all the essential gifts with which to tease, torment and outwit opponents, who found him as elusive as a will-o'-the-wisp.

Jackson was slim of build and pale of complexion. At five foot eleven and twelve stone eight, he looked in danger of being blown away in the hurly-burly and physicality of the rugby union game, but he was much too sharp in thought and action for that, and much too wily too. With his strong belief in what he could do with ball in hand, Jackson gave a long line of illustrious opponents a very hard time, revelling in taking them on whatever their size. In his repertoire he could call on flaring speed, subtle change of pace, a bewildering body swerve, and safe handling skills, and he had a forest animal's instinct that enabled him to compete successfully in cluttered environments. He also could call on a subtle kind of hitch kick to his running which frequently duped opponents, as did his lightning jink and flaring acceleration.

Such was his grasp of the variety of attacking methods that he proved an unpredictable target for opposing defenders, with his ability to play off the top of his head, and his array of feint passes, as well as his clever use of the chip kick ahead which he could put into operation with skilled placement. At times he spoofed opponents by going through the motions of the chip kick only for them to discover too late that he had not kicked at all but was still in possession.

For all his apparently frail physique, Jackson was seldom dispossessed, and proved an instinctive support runner and clever link man, once being described as having the skills to run in tries beyond the capabilities of others. Jackson also had strong views on tactics, as when he disagreed with the practice at one time of wings throwing into the lineouts. In his view wings should be free of such obligation so that they could concentrate on their roles in attack, as indeed they have done ever since the throwing-in role was taken over by hookers.

First capped against Wales at Twickenham in 1956, Jackson's last international appearance was against Scotland in 1963, when he featured in an England side who won the International Championship. His haul of just twenty caps for his country seems hardly to do justice to his remarkable gifts, nor does his collection of only seven international tries. Once described as a cross between Nijinsky and Stanley Matthews, and by the famous New Zealand broadcaster Keith Quinn as 'the speedy ghost', Jackson did indeed create the impression that he was floating rather than running, a wraith who ghosted his way past and round defenders.

Jackson's near-supernatural powers of deception spawned two

famous tries that took the breath away. That for England against Australia in injury time at Twickenham in 1958 was an amazing effort in limited touchline space, leaving seven would-be tacklers staring into space and taking England to victory by 9–6. The other was in the fourth Lions test against New Zealand in 1959 when Jackson, launched by Ken Scotland's feed, showed all his wonderful control of pace, lift-off, sidestep, and sway. The All Blacks were left bemused by that astonishing jinking run, performed at top speed, which brought him a jewel of a try. The Lions won the fourth test by 9–6, their first victory over the All Blacks since 1930.

It was on that British Lions tour in 1959 that Jackson demonstrated the full range of his huge talent and, along with Tony O'Reilly, took New Zealand by storm. Jackson scored sixteen tries in eighteen games on that tour, O'Reilly seventeen tries in twenty-three games, and those notoriously hard to please New Zealanders heaped praise on them for their extraordinary feats.

1960s

France
South Africa
1963–64 All Blacks
1966–67 All Blacks
1968 France's First Grand Slam
Scotland

———————— Portraits ————————

Don Clarke   (New Zealand 1956–64)
Colin Meads   (New Zealand 1957–71)
Colin Meads in his own words: The art of second-phase rugby
Wilson Whineray   (New Zealand 1957–65)
Ken Gray   (New Zealand 1963–69)
Frik Du Preez   (South Africa 1961–71)
Benoit Dauga   (France 1964–72)
Brian Lochore   (New Zealand 1964–71)
Pierre Villepreux   (France 1967–72)
Gordon Brown   (Scotland 1969–76)
Gordon Brown in his own words: Scotland v Springboks, 1969

FRANCE

I REMEMBER France in the late 1950s and 1960s, when they had some tremendous performers and were already playing that running game for which they have become famous. They were so adventurous, they had such flair, such a desire to run and handle, while we tended more to kick the ball into the corners in those days. Perhaps that kind of open play was second nature to the French because so much of their rugby was played in the south-west in fine weather conditions, so it became their natural style. And they produced some wonderful rugby with it, there's no doubt of that. They were Five Nations Champions in 1959, 1960 (shared with England), 1961, 1962, 1967, 1968 (when they won the Grand Slam) and 1970 (shared with Wales).

A potent rugby force. On the other hand, get them on a wet day and it could be a very different story. I remember once I went to stay at the same hotel as the French team in Paris before a match so that I could identify them for commentary purposes. That was in the late 1950s – 1957 I believe. The day before, the French officials had given me a very hard time at the training ground where I had gone to see the players for identification purposes. They must have thought I was spying on them, because after a while a very large gentleman with a nose that indicated a career as a professional boxer issued from the club house and approached me menacingly, repeating '*Non! Non!*' I tried to explain to him my mission, and the importance for a commentator of knowing who the players were. But it was an unsatisfactory conversation, and I retired to my hotel room, the memory of his glowering presence still with me.

The next morning I heard the rain pattering on my window when I woke but, thinking nothing of it, I went downstairs to the restaurant and had breakfast. There was no one else about, the place was silent as the grave. Then at about eleven o'clock the French team began to come down – they must have had breakfast in bed. They wandered off to the hotel lobby, and stood around staring through the front door with long faces, looking at the rain, and then began muttering and moaning, *'Pluie! Pluie!' 'O malheureux!' 'C'est terrible!'* and so on. All fifteen of them were standing there at the front door of the hotel, and it almost seemed as if they really would have preferred not to play.

They were dry-weather boys, of course, and were appalled to see the wet stuff! It was cold as well, a coolish rain. The Scots on the other hand were really chuffed, of course, and just got stuck into them when the game got going. I remember how Hamish Kemp went about the place like a devouring flame, flattening everything in sight. In the end Scotland beat the French 6–0, with Ken Scotland landing a penalty goal and a drop goal. The pitch was a swamp but, even so, the French should really have defeated Scotland because they had some very skilful players. If the truth be told, they had beaten themselves. In spite of their fine players, their whole confidence just evaporated as soon as they saw that rain. It looked very much as though they had defeated themselves, just because it was wet.

The French used to be very prone to psychological upset, but I don't think that's the case any more. They're more phlegmatic today, and able to take things as they come along. And they're mentally better equipped, I think. They still play most of their rugby in better weather than we do, and I've no doubt that when Scotland play France, we would be happier to get some rain and some heavier going, but we don't see any clear advantage over the French in rain any more. The French today are better disciplined, better organised, better coached. They have learnt to accept the fact that you have to play in wet weather sometimes.

What worries me, though, is that when the French see rain they may depart from their traditional style. That would be a shame, because there's nothing more uplifting – especially if you're a Frenchman – than to see France in full flow. It's a delight! It's sad when rain reduces them to ordinary levels. I think there was a suspicion of the old attitude as recently as 2003, when Ireland pipped them at Lansdowne Road in rather soggy conditions. Once again, they looked the better side ball in hand, but never managed a try even when they got over the Irish line.

In the 1960s they had a lock forward, Benoit Dauga, who was a terrific player. He was one man who didn't lose his head or get upset easily. Dauga was a big fellow, six foot six, with a big hook of a nose, and he had a glowering look about him, he exuded menace. Before taking up rugby he had been a basketball player, and he was wonderfully gifted, with delicate touches here and there. His deflection off the top of the lineout was superb, and he was a terrifically good forward with ball in hand as well. A great all-rounder was Dauga, and he would have stood out in any country, wherever he played. But it was that sinister look about him that impressed. He would have made a great villain in a film, but he was a favourite of mine, I must say, because I like seeing big skilled men in action.

Walter Spanghero was another. I think Walter was more gifted than his brother Claude, who also played for France. Walter Spanghero was like Dauga in that he was quick about the park and had great hands. French forwards tend to handle well, even front-row forwards. It's part of their culture.

The French backs at that time were also very much worth watching. I would shortlist Jo Maso at centre as one of my all-time greats. He had adhesive hands and just floated across the ground like a high-speed ghost. And he enjoyed taking risks. In fact he was a highly unorthodox citizen who had developed this trick of passing the ball behind his back at speed – it became known as the Maso flip. I loved his sense of adventure, and so did the French spectators, but the selectors took a different view and frequently dropped him. The opposition was grateful!

At their best the French are a delight with sleight of hand and adventurism key elements in their attack style. But they have produced a number of genuine hard men, some of whom have been guilty of foul play that most would draw the line at. That was a shame for the French are skilled participants capable of handling wizardry that takes the breath away. But have a look at a French team photograph and the forwards tend to have a villainous look to them, like so many Long John Silvers! Tough guys, without question. Once a Scottish referee was sent to France to officiate at a French club match and on his return he expressed the view: It's not a referee these boys need. It's a missionary.'

Lucien Mias was their inspirational captain, although he only captained France in six internationals. He was another lock forward, and a great player, a magnificent leader, and a considerable rugby brain. Mias led France to win a totally unexpected test series against the Springboks in 1958, and set the tone for their brand of graceful but uncompromising rugby. Lineout peeling was introduced at about that time by the French under Mias.

In fact lineout peeling was Lucien Mias's brainchild, and it was a real innovation, though of course everybody copied it afterwards. Mias was a big lock forward with long hair – he looked like an out of work artist. But he hit on this idea of launching forwards off the lineout and peeling round the front or, even more dangerously, round the back. It was a devastating ploy, and so hard to stop. If they peeled out of the back of a lineout the poor opposing stand-off found himself staring at a horde of great brutes running at him when he was expecting a little twinkle-toed opponent like himself.

Peeling round the lineout is a ploy we don't use much these days, although in 2001, in the Ireland v England test at Lansdowne Road, Keith Wood used that move to devastating effect against England. In fact he scored a try that deprived England of their long anticipated Grand Slam, much to the glee of the Celtic nations. Peeling hadn't been used for quite a time. But in the late 1950s, when they first introduced the move, those French were brilliant at it, and took everybody completely by surprise.

I think the French called that move *percussion*. They threw the ball to the back of the lineout where it was flicked down by a forward, often Christian Carrère, and then they launched a forward at the opposing stand-off. The guy they usually launched was Amédée Domenech, who was one of the fastest prop forwards I have ever seen. In fact he once played against England as a wing. According to my friend Hugh McLeod, the Scottish prop, Domenech was no great scrummager but he was fast all right.

In that French *percussion* move, when Domenech took the flick-down and went out the back of the lineout, he would run straight for the opposing stand-off, who was already saying his prayers because he was going to have to stop this charge. Once Domenech had committed their stand-off, then the French quickly replenished the ball and that was when they let it go down the line – because they knew the opposing defence line was minus at least one body, and sometimes two if Domenech had flattened the stand-off and went on to the next guy.

They did that move so well, and Domenech had such good hands for a prop forward, besides being quick, though he was built like a barrel. The French didn't catch and feed it from the lineout, they took it off the top so it was quicker and more explosive. And because the ball was thrown to the tail, Domenech was running out into open space, heading straight for the stand-off or the inside centre.

I liked Domenech. He saved a youngster once. He was on his way to an international, and on the bank of a river he saw a kid in difficulties, drowning, and he jumped in and rescued her. Then he went on his way, soaking wet, and then played the match as if nothing had happened.

So Domenech was the first man off the lineout peel. With the likes of Dauga backing up, and the lock forward Chevalier, that move was tough to stop. The French didn't like rucking, they preferred to maul it – that way they stayed on their feet – and the next guy who took it would be a great big lock forward, and he went a bit further, and then he peeled in turn, and it was like a roly-poly movement.

When they hit it right it was not only devastating but it was also wonderful to watch. And of course the French forwards handled magnificently, Christian Carrère and Dauga, and people like that. So one or even two defenders could be taken out, and if they then shipped it down the line there was room on the outside, and the outside man would go over for the try. I was amazed when I saw *percussion* first at a training session, that launching of forwards from the set-piece. I was always very interested in moves and tactics, and when I began to work out what they were doing I could see they were years in front of everyone else. Back home I found myself talking to Hugh McLeod, and although I obviously couldn't give him details, I warned him to be on guard. But when it came to the day Hugh was as surprised by the move as everyone else. Afterwards he said to me, 'What a shock I got!' We'd never seen that before. That *percussion* took the rugby world by storm.

McLeod didn't leave it at that – he brought lineout peeling back to Hawick rugby, and Hawick were elevated to championship status in Scottish rugby for quite a period purely as a result of McLeod bringing back from his international experience that French move. Hawick were doing lineout peeling long before anyone else in Scotland, and it caught Scottish club rugby by surprise.

Hugh McLeod also brought back from his Lions tour in New Zealand the value of creating ruck ball – secondary phase ball – rather than scrummage and lineout ball, which the New Zealanders had perfected. After every match in New Zealand with the Lions, whereas the other guys would be drinking and singing and so on, Hugh would be sitting with the local New Zealand coach and pulling out from him all the little bits and pieces of tactical know-how, which he then brought back to Hawick. That's basically why Hawick had such a record of championship wins through the 1950s and 1960s; it's not too much to say they dominated Scottish rugby. And that was very largely due to McLeod and his interest in the tactical aspects of French and southern hemisphere rugby. I don't think he ever got the credit he deserved for that. It took the other Scottish clubs at least a couple of seasons to realise what we were doing.

But it was the French who invented the peel move, and that was only one of the ways in which they stamped their mark on rugby in the 1960s. It was in 1959 that the Tricolores won the title outright for the first time. But after that they were Champions for four years in a row, and in 1968 they won their first Grand Slam.

SOUTH AFRICA

SOUTH AFRICA had a tradition of relying on its mighty and skilful forwards in the 1950s, even though this approach was challenged and tested almost to destruction by the British Lions tour of 1955 with brilliant performances by the likes of Cliff Morgan and Tony O'Reilly. But the Springbok tours of the 1960s brought some exciting players to these shores, including the flanker Jan Ellis, regarded as one of the best ever to play for South Africa. Ellis combined well in an outstanding back row threesome consisting of himself, Piet Greyling and Tommy Bedford. On the wing was Jannie Engelbrecht, who scored eight tries in his thirty-three tests between 1960 and 1969. At centre John Gainsford, of Western Province, was South Africa's most capped midfielder, playing thirty-three times for his country between 1960 and 1967. He was a typical South Africa centre: physical, imposing and with a lot of pace. He was a peerless crash tackler who intimidated opponents with the ferocity of his engagement. And then there was Frik Du Preez, the magnificent second-row forward who dominated the scene from his first international tour in 1961.

Captain of that tour was Avril Malan, and he was one of the great leaders. He had a certain aura about him, and of course he was a big man as well. He and Du Preez were partners in some ways. I remember I felt very sorry for Malan once. It was the Springboks' match against the Barbarians, of all people, and it was at Cardiff. Malan had taken the ball at the lineout and was charging flat out up the touchline, ball in hand, when Haydn Mainwaring, a great muckle lump of a full-back, hit him with a shoulder charge. That would be illegal today, and Mainwaring would have been cautioned, at the very least. Poor Malan was defenceless, just running up the touchline as hard as he could, and Mainwaring hit him sideways on. Malan was blasted into the enclosure seats as if he had been fired from a gun. All the Wales crowd thought it was wonderful, but I felt sorry for Malan. You are really defenceless when you're flat out and a guy comes in sideways on and you don't see him until too late. It really shook Malan. It almost put him in hospital.

In general, that Springbok side was a pleasure to watch. They also had a kind of camaraderie about them that was impressive. Like many South African teams, as a squad they were very together. I think perhaps they felt that the world was agin them. And I suppose in some ways they were right. But what came out of it was a sort of camaraderie that was keener and tighter than you would find anywhere else. They banded together and looked to help each other more, that was my impression, partly because of the criticism they'd had. They seemed to get on pretty well with each other, to have a common bond, with no worries about not getting on. Certainly when I was with them they were very much a team, and over the years they produced some tremendous rugby.

1963–64 ALL BLACKS

THE 1963–64 All Blacks, captained by Wilson Whineray, played thirty-four games and won thirty-two, which was a pretty impressive performance even by the standards of the New Zealanders who don't believe in losing.

That 1964 achievement owed a lot to a certain Don Clarke, who played in twenty-five of the thirty-four games, and scored a total of 136 points, including five drop goals. Clarke was different from most full-backs I had seen before in that he looked more like a lock forward – he was over six feet and fifteen stone – but played as a full-back. All in all he was a pretty formidable fellow. A lot of people thought he could be embarrassed by diagonal kicking to the corners, because he wasn't the quickest player in the world. But he made up for that by having a great positional sense, and he was very seldom caught out.

Clarke was also formidable coming into the line. He had a booming punt that could transfer play miles back upfield, and as a goal-kicker he was amazing. In their first test in New Zealand, in 1959, the Lions had scored four tries, but Don Clarke kicked six penalties, and the final score was 18–17 to New Zealand. The Lions were by far the better side to watch, but Clarke was the match-winner. He kicked goals from everywhere.

I believe I once saw him kick a goal from halfway with his bare feet. That was his little party piece, his music hall act, kicking a goal from halfway with his bare feet. Perhaps he got the idea from his predecessor, Bob Scott. But he was an amazing fellow, and if he had been a bit quicker he would really have been something else. Even so, as an intruding full-back Clarke was a formidable proposition because of his size, and of course there was a great worry for the opposition, who had to be careful about offending anywhere inside their half because he could kick from halfway – with his bare feet if necessary!

That was a tremendous pack of forwards too, with Wilson Whineray, Denis Young, and Ken Gray. And then they had Waka Nathan, Brian Lochore and Kel Tremain – what a threesome that was – as their three loose forwards. And there was the incomparable Colin Meads, and alongside him a big fellow called Allan Stewart, or sometimes it was Stan Meads, Colin's brother – the two Meads brothers played together for New Zealand in 14 tests. Waka Nathan was called the Black Panther, for the predatory relish with which he pounced on opposing backs. He never lost in fourteen internationals for the All Blacks.

Whineray, the captain, wasn't regarded as the most hurtful of scrummagers – although he was very adequate as a scrummager – but he certainly got about the park, he was very mobile. He scored a try against the Barbarians in their last match when by sheer instinct he was in the right position, and then had to run about thirty yards to score. That was Whineray, not the most devastating scrummager in the world, but a highly mobile prop forward with a real sense of direction. And of course he was a wonderful captain, and had a great feel for the job. Whineray's leadership was one of the key factors in that tour.

The wings on that tour, Malcolm Dick and Ralph Caulton, scored thirty-three out of a total of 111 tries – that's how many tries they scored on the tour! Don Clarke, as I mentioned, scored 136 points including five drop goals. And they had a fellow called Mark Herewini who was a lovely little player, neat and tidy, sharp, twinkling footsteps, great handling skills. He also scored well, seventy-four points, and he dropped five goals on top of that. So those All Blacks were very well aware at that time, when defences were fairly tight, of the value of the drop goal. If you're finding it very hard to breach the opponents' defences for tries, the drop goal will do! Five for Clarke and five for Herewini certainly underlined that. Perhaps we don't use it enough – it's an easy three points. For a long time it was practically ignored as a scoring device, but it seems to be coming back in now – and it can turn a match round.

1966–67 ALL BLACKS

ALTHOUGH THE Australians of 1984 and 1988 were the most adventurous and exciting touring sides I have ever seen, I think the most efficient and impressive from a success point of view, in statistical as well as playing terms, were the 1967 All Blacks. They came over here and played fifteen games, winning fourteen and drawing just the one. It was East Wales who held them to a draw, 3–3, in a match for which I was on commentary duty.

Those All Blacks were a wonderful side for underlining the simple basics of rugby football: first of all you've got to win ball. Secondly, when you win ball, you run straight. Thirdly, when you get tackled you create ruck, and therefore provide ball of second- and third-phase quality that is by far the best ball to run. So they produced this concept of having one big centre who would take the first pass from the stand-off, and the centre would run at the opponent and deliberately create a ruck situation; because it was from the ruck that the All Blacks wanted the ball to flow along the back division.

Those All Blacks were the most devastating rucking forwards, because they were quite ruthless. If there was a guy in the road where they were rucking the ball they just rucked him out with it. In fact there were occasions where an opposing forward was shot backwards! The Blacks, in driving into the ruck, would take short prancing steps that were meant essentially to shovel back the ball, but if there was an opponent there they would shovel him back as well, or trample over the top of him.

The New Zealanders I think were the first to underline the value of ruck ball or maul ball as a second, third or fourth phase of possession. The initial phase was scrum or lineout, but they emphasised this concept of the second- or third-phase situation where you actually won ruck or maul ball, and were able to run against a defence that was not set, and had been broken up because of the drive. They had this big fellow Ian MacRae of Hawke's Bay, a large, powerful centre (as he would have to be), and his main job was to take the pass from the stand-off, deliberately drive into the tackle, create the ruck, lay the ball, and then the forwards would champ over the top. They did it brilliantly, because their rucking was ferocious – and it was frightening. There's no doubt that guys who went down with the ball against the New Zealanders were often praying as they did so, because the Blacks just champed and stamped in there and didn't give a monkey's what they rucked back so long as they got the ball.

Ian MacRae was their contact man who created the situation from which the All Blacks were able to ruck, using it as an intimidatory exercise as well as a ball-winning one. He was big enough and strong enough to be able to do that. So he was inevitably the target when they came off the set-piece in the lineout, nine times out of ten they would guide themselves towards MacRae, because he was the one who could create that situation where they could trample over everybody and heel the ball. MacRae was the one who made the dent and sucked in the opposition, and then they shifted the ball down the line. The wings benefited so much from that. That's why they scored so many tries, because the opposing defence was cracked first by the likes of MacRae, who not only took one out but another had to go in. So MacRae had a considerable input in those All Black sides, a physical man, a key man in that style.

It was frightening stuff all right. Today it's been developed to such an extent that we now have, in my view, too much dangerous footwork where players are actually liable to be badly hurt, with some fellows deliberately putting their boots in where they shouldn't be. But the Blacks were the first to underline the value of ruck ball as a start of the next phase, rather than the initial phase when the defences were all set. Rucking was really aimed at breaking up the opposing defence line by sucking people into the ruck and running against guys who were not in set positions. And it was devastating. There's no doubt that many if not most of New Zealand's tries in that era stemmed from the ball being rucked, and then crisp handling along the line with maybe someone coming in.

So these were the simple basics that the 1967 New Zealanders stuck to, and the result was: played fifteen, won fourteen, drawn one. They beat England 23–11, Wales 13–6, France 21–15, and Scotland 14–3. They didn't play Ireland because there was a foot-and-mouth scare at the time, but I think there's no doubt they would have beaten Ireland too. They also had a pretty useful back division: Fergie McCormick, the stocky little full-back, scored a hundred points on that tour, while Dick, Steel, MacRae, Kirton and Laidlaw were no slouches either.

But the thing about that side was the quality of the forward play. The test pack had Ken Gray, Bruce McLeod, Alister Hopkinson, Sam Strahan, Colin Meads, Kel Tremain (one of the all-time greats), Brian Lochore who was captain, and Graham Williams as flank forward. Ken Gray was one of the greatest props I have ever seen, and yet he looked like a lock forward, he was such a big fellow. In fact he was so big that he played an important part as a ball-provider in New Zealand's lineout play – very unusual for a prop forward. Hopkinson was another tough guy. Sam Strahan was a youngster, but he had the great Colin Meads alongside him as his mentor. And that loose forward trio – harum-scarum Williams flying about all over the place, not to mention Tremain and Lochore. That was a magnificent pack. All in all, the 1967 All Blacks were among the most formidable touring sides I have ever seen. And it was a great side through sticking to fundamentals: win the ball, run straight, create the ruck, and use it in second and third phase for handling against broken defences (see pp. 78–79).

They had a wonderful game at Twickenham against the Barbarians, which really the Baa-Baas should have won but for a late try by Tony Steel, the wing. That game gave a good example of how the New Zealanders evolve moves and use them. I saw them practising in pouring rain during that tour, and about fifteen to twenty times they went through a move in which Brian Lochore, the captain and No 8 forward, stood off and took a pass from the breakdown, and he then created the back division move. They practised it time and time again, the rain lashing down (I was sitting in the car, no way was I going out in that stuff!). But not a soul complained as they slogged away with scant regard for the weather, trying to achieve classic transference in such conditions. They just kept on running through their drills.

Then came the Barbarians match, with the All Blacks defending their unbeaten record in the very last game of their tour. The scores were level in injury time – and what did the New Zealanders do? They produced that move with Lochore standing off, making an extra man, and Tony Steel ran and scored the crucial try for an 11–6 win. That really brought home something to me about those New Zealanders, how not only do they practise the moves, but they make sure that when the time comes they remember and use them. That was so significant. The Barbarians deserved to win that match, but late on in the game, when the Blacks looked as if they were out the window, they ran that move. It worked perfectly. I can still see Lochore standing off as a kind of fly-half, and running on, and then the ball went down the line, and Steel was over in the corner.

The All Blacks were then, and still are, great ones for getting the basics right. They don't make many mistakes, and they work really hard at eliminating error. And everything they do is at top speed, crash-bang-wallop! It's bred in the bone: 'We're New Zealanders and we're supposed to win!'

1968 FRANCE'S FIRST GRAND SLAM

1968 SAW the first Grand Slam in French history, and it's a strange fact that France played no fewer than thirty-one players in the four games, including six new caps. There was an aura of sadness about that French Slam because Guy Boniface, a lovely centre, and Jean-Michel Capendeguy, who had been chosen as a wing in the game against Scotland, had both been killed in separate road accidents. The French wore black armbands in the first match of that Slam, which was against Scotland.

In that game, which France won 8–6, the French selectors had picked J. H. Mir as scrum-half, and told him so, but suddenly changed their minds at the eleventh hour to recall the Camberabero brothers, Guy and Lilian, as half-backs. Mir did get a cap later, against Ireland, but it was unusual, to say the least, to be chosen for a match and then find you weren't playing in it. Mir should have taken those selectors to court!

France gained their narrow victory over Scotland when Stuart Wilson failed to touch down Camberabero's miskicked attempt at a drop goal, and Bernard Duprat, the French wing, came tearing up and fell on the ball for a try, which was a bit of a dead loss from the Scottish point of view. Wilson also had the chance of a last-minute penalty goal that would have won the game for Scotland, but unfortunately he didn't hit it quite right. So it just wasn't poor Wilson's day.

France then beat Ireland 16–6 when Ireland was without Mike

Gibson, who was of course one of their greatest players. In that match the Irish lock forward Mick Molloy suffered a cracked fibula, but having gone off the pitch he suddenly came back on again, and played with a broken bone! Not only that, but the Irish hooker Ken Kennedy also got hurt, damaging a knee, so Ireland were in an awful state. That brought out a call for injury substitutions, which hadn't been allowed before, and it was the pressure arising from that game which introduced the rule about injury replacements. Now of course there can be tactical replacements too, and you get guys going on and off like yo-yos. It can be a commentator's nightmare, keeping tabs on everyone when you get six different new players on the field.

Another fact I recall about that Ireland v France game was a drop goal by Jean Gachassin, a tiny little wing they called Le Papillon (the Butterfly) – he was also known as Peter Pan – who dropped a goal out of nowhere. I really don't know if he meant to or not, it came as such a surprise!

Then France played England, and beat them 14–9. Believe it or not, France actually made nine changes for that game, dropping Benoit Dauga, who for me was the greatest French forward of them all. There were three drop goals in that game – by Guy Camberabero, Mike Weston and Claude Lacaze.

The game that clinched the Grand Slam for France was against Wales at Cardiff, and they played out of their skins to win 14–9, with Guy Camberabero dropping a goal from thirty-five yards. He also kicked a penalty and a conversion, and his brother Lilian scored a try as well. So the Camberabero brothers were the heroes of the hour. They were such wee fellows, you really wondered how they survived in the rougher areas of rugby football, but by golly they could play!

But for me the great feature of that match was the performance of Walter Spanghero. He was a tremendous forward who was really a back row, a No 8 or flanker, but they played him at lock as well.

He had a running battle with Dauga – they just didn't get on, apparently – which was ludicrous because they were the two best French forwards I've ever seen. In the second half the French had a try from Christian Carrère, who was another of the great flank forwards, a really stylish player.

So that was France's first Grand Slam since they entered the Championship in 1909. They've won a good few since then, but that 1968 side was one of the best. There were backs like Gachassin and Claude Lacaze. And there was a lovely blend with Jo Maso, one of the most creative backs I've ever seen, and Claude Dourthe, who was a crash-bang merchant, an unsmiling type like Dauga. Maso did the scariest things, like throwing the ball over his shoulder or behind his back without looking. And the whole thing was fuelled by a terrific set of forwards who grafted and worked tirelessly.

I think a lot of people were pleased when France broke through at last, because they did so in style. Though it was significant that in the four Championship matches they scored only seven tries, which isn't a great haul, until you remember that Ireland and Wales scored only four, England only three, and Scotland I'm sad to say scored only one try in the whole series, and that by Jim Telfer (Melrose) in the 6–3 victory over France.

SCOTLAND

AFTER THE disappointments of the 1950s, Scotland began to make progress on the international front in the 1960s, and this was due not least to the development of the scrummage.

Ian McLauchlan was a forerunner of skilled front row play. He came under the tutelage of Bill Dickinson when he was at Jordanhill College, the physical education college in Glasgow. They had a very good XV at that time, winning the Scottish club championship, and I think Bill Dickinson had been a hooker himself. He made a really intensive study of the art of scrummaging, and brought new ideas to it.

McLauchlan was only about five foot nine and thirteen stone ten, but because of his development under Dickinson he became one of the all-time great scrummagers. And yet when you looked at him you just saw a small, plump fellow. You wouldn't have given him house room, but boy! he created plenty of discomfort for men three or four stones heavier than he was. There's a famous picture from the Lions tour in South Africa in 1974 where McLauchlan has lifted a twenty-stone South African prop forward so that his legs are literally dangling in mid-air! They would probably penalise that now, for 'destabilising' the scrum. Well, I think they're probably right, better to be safe than sorry. But at the time McLauchlan was doing it it was legal. A little shift of the shoulder here, a pull there, if you know what you're doing it doesn't take an awful lot to make your opponent very uncomfortable.

That excellence in scrummaging was really done with gym work, working on the right muscles and so on, under Bill Dickinson's guidance. Bill Dickinson became coach for Scotland after Jordanhill. He certainly had a ruthless touch to him, and looked as if he would have trampled over anybody. His Jordanhill College were a tough outfit; he had them trained up to be really hard. And he had the same effect on the Scottish pack. His team talk before they took to the field was a real call to arms, and after it they went out there slavering at the jaws to get stuck in. The pack in those days was a very hard eight, and Scotland had a very successful spell when Dickinson was there.

I think he niggled some of the hierarchy because he wasn't 'sporting'. Winning was the object for him and Scottish forward play under Dickinson was a fearsome thing! We were pretty ruthless, and the crowd seemed to love it. There's a savage in everybody, and Dickinson was the man to bring it out. Scotland certainly had a productive pack in those days, and it was all down to Bill Dickinson. He was the first Scottish coach, appointed despite very strong opposition from the old guard. He presided over a pack that was feared, not because of their size but because of their technical expertise, all brought about by Dickinson.

We were lucky in the lineout too in those days, particularly towards the end of the decade, with Gordon Brown and his brother Peter, and Alastair McHarg. Gordon Brown was the donkey, the workhorse, the blood-sweat-and-tears guy, and McHarg, a good scrummager but one who liked to be out in the open which upset some of the purists. Lock forwards weren't meant to do that in those days! The two Browns and McHarg were exceptional as a threesome for the lineout. Peter Brown was a very good No 8 forward, and captain of Scotland in ten internationals. They played him mostly as a lock forward, but Peter was a flamboyant character who liked to be out and about and I always felt that as a lock he was straining to get away from the middle of the scrummage, whereas at No 8 he could express himself more.

There was a curious look to Peter Brown, as though he wasn't quite joined together in the right way. He had great splay feet, but he was very skilled for such a big man. Whenever Peter Brown played Scotland's lineout was productive, because he was a very crafty lineout operator as well as being a very big man into the bargain. He had a good positional sense and educated hands, and I also recall his peculiar goal-kicking method, when he would turn his back on the ball before the run-up. He had a talent for the unusual, and no one who saw it will forget the way he once rose like a rocketing pheasant in a Scottish trial at Murrayfield, and headed the ball into touch like a footballer.

All in all the Scottish packs of the 1960s and 1970s were very well-rehearsed outfits, and they frightened people a bit! And Bill Dickinson was behind it.

PORTRAITS

DON CLARKE (1956–64)
Waikato, New Zealand
31 caps

At six foot two and seventeen stone seven he had all the appearance of a lock forward, but Donald Barry Clarke was a full-back of enormous skill. Hailing from the Waikato province of New Zealand, Clarke played thirty-one tests for his country, in the course of which he scored 207 points, comprising two tries, thirty-three conversions, five drop goals, thirty-eight penalty goals, and two goals from the mark.

A first-class cricketer who might well have represented his country as a fast bowler, Don Clarke made a huge impression on the All Blacks' tour of the United Kingdom in 1963–64, when he played in all five tests and scored 136 of New Zealand's 341 points in the twenty-five games in which he played. The legendary Colin Meads, his colleague on that and other tours, regarded him as the finest full-back of his generation.

I recall with some amusement the reaction of the Scottish Borders crowd when their South of Scotland heroes held those 1964 All Blacks to 8–0 at our home ground of Mansfield Park. The South full-back was a stocky, tough, uncompromising individual called Jim Gray from out of the local club of Hawick. Inspired by the challenge from a New Zealand great, Gray played a stormer. So much so that the delighted Borderers reckoned Gray was a better full-back than Clarke!

Clarke was a formidable adversary, for he had a mighty hoof, safe hands, a thumping tackle, impressive power on the run – and of course he could kick goals from all over the pitch. New Zealanders still recall how, in the first test in Dunedin in 1959, the British Lions scored four tries (then worth three points) but were defeated by the full-back's magnificent kicking. For Clarke thumped over six penalty goals to give New Zealand victory by 18–17.

Don Clarke was one of five brothers who turned out for Waikato, all five playing together in a single game in 1961. One of the Clarke brothers, Ian, also toured the United Kingdom with the 1964 All Blacks as a prop, and indeed captained them on another occasion. Ian Clarke created one of the highlights of the 1964 New Zealand tour in the UK when he was chosen to play for the Barbarians against his New Zealand colleagues. He dropped a goal from a mark – notching up the only Barbarian score in a defeat by 36–3. It was a fine effort, but in the kicking department his brother Don ruled supreme. Not for nothing was he known throughout New Zealand as 'the Boot'.

COLIN MEADS (1957–71)
King Country, New Zealand
55 caps

Colin Earl Meads was a mighty man who often struck fear into others. I recall Earle Mitchell of Edinburgh University, a Scottish lock forward, being deputed to mark the legendary New Zealander at the lineout in the Murrayfield test of 1967. Afterwards, on being asked by his friends how he had fared, Erle said, 'I just looked him straight in the eye and told him that I would not tolerate any non-sense from him during the game. But,' he added, 'I whispered it.'

As hard as teak, and a formidable figure at six foot four and sixteen

stone six, Colin 'Pinetree' Meads was renowned as a totally uncompromising performer, utterly committed to the New Zealand cause.
He played a record fifty-five tests for the All Blacks, scoring seven
test tries and, believe it or not, one conversion; and on top of that,
just to demonstrate his versatility as well as his command of the basic
forward skills, he once slotted a drop goal for the King Country.

Meads was just twenty when he was first capped against Australia
in Sydney in 1957, and he proved a first-choice lock for New
Zealand in fourteen seasons from 1957 to 1971. Incidentally, he
shared eleven of those fifty-five tests in the New Zealand boilerhouse with his brother Stan. They were together in all four of the
tests in the 1966 whitewash of the British Lions. Meads also played
as flanker and No 8 – his first test was as a flanker – but it was as a
lock that he achieved huge fame and supporter idolatry. It is not too
much to say that he dominated world rugby throughout the 1960s.

Colin Meads was no slouch when it came to scoring his seven test
tries, and he wedded an iron hard physique, built up on the King
Country farm which he worked with his brother Stan, to a thorough
grasp of the basic skills. This marked him out as a formidable
runner with ball in hand, as well as a totally committed labourer in
the darker regions of the forward game.

It is said that in one international test scrummage the New
Zealand loose-head prop forward, who happened to be Meads's
captain, Wilson Whineray, was getting some trouble from the
opposing tight-head, trouble of a not particularly legal kind.
Whereupon he asked of Colin Meads, whose head jutted out
beneath him, 'Have you got a spare arm, Pinetree?' 'Sure have,
skipper,' came the answer. A large fist drove up through the middle
of the scrummage, and the All Blacks' loose-head prop had no
further trouble from his rival. If there should be any doubt about
the extent of his toughness and courage, Meads once broke two ribs
during the 1971 British Lions tour of New Zealand, but finished the
game and captained his country again five weeks later.

Meads always was supremely fit. It is said that, as part of his fitness programme, he would run up and down a mini-mountain near home with a North Island Cheviot sheep tucked under each arm. He played nineteen seasons for King Country, and it is sad that his magnificent test record was tarnished by his ordering off by Irish referee Kevin Kelleher in the 1967 Scottish game at Murrayfield. All the same, Colin Meads has been, in the eyes of many of the game's supporters, the greatest All Black of them all. In fact, in 1999 he was named Player of the Century at the New Zealand Rugby Football Union Awards dinner, and surely there are not many who would argue with his selection.

Colin Meads in his own words

The art of second-phase rugby

If you don't go into a game *believing* you can win, prepared to overcome your opposition so that you *will* win, what is the point? Rather a loss, while striving to win, than a draw while striving not to lose. The difference between those two outlooks is plain. Scotland's whole approach [in 1963–64] was defensive. They thought only of stopping us, so much so that when we made mistakes, and we made plenty, the Scots were not tuned to turn them against us and into points ... This complex of theirs which told them they could not win led to great skill in one area of the game of rugby which, for the sake of the game, simply has got to be cleaned up: killing the ball by lying on it, failing to release it as the law dictates you should. There must be the strongest effort to bring uniformity to referees' interpretations of the offence which I see as the most frustrating illegality in the game.

This denial of possession to a team geared to attack, leads to the sort of rucking which British crowds – and British referees – find so reprehensible in All Black forward play. It also leads to game stoppages, and this is very serious in a spectator sport which already has too many grey patches. Of all countries in the world Britain has most to answer for in this, yet of all countries in the world Britain most vehemently demands 'open, running rugger'.

In this same context we in Whineray's team were regarded with scorn by some critics because, they said, we scored our tries from second phase. Where, they asked, were the classical tries from set-piece passing and individual skill in beating a man? They accused us of the crime of standing flat to the advantage line at the oposition put-in. At the very beginning of the tour Wilson Whineray was asked by a pressman whether the All Blacks would play 'open, attacking rugby'. Whineray said that if opposition teams were pre-pared to, so were we.

What happened? From the first match, against Oxford University, when we might have expected some sign of the intent of British teams to meet us half-way, the Oxford backs stood as flat as last year's beer not only on our ball but on their own! And that was to be the pattern of 'attacking football' virtually throughout the tour. It was the very thing disciplined and efficient second-phase rugby was designed to over-come. Ours was winning rugby, but more than that, it was try-scoring rugby. We scored 64 tries through our centres and wings. The British are strongly inclined to demand attacking rugby miracles from touring teams while setting out themselves to negate any such possibility.

(From Alex Veysey, *Colin Meads – All Black*, William Collins (New Zealand) Ltd, 1974)

WILSON WHINERAY (1957–65)
Canterbury, Waikato, Auckland, New Zealand
32 caps

At Auckland grammar school he was a scrum-half, and then he played as a back row in provincial rugby for Wanamatu; but it was as a prop that Wilson Whineray finished up for Auckland and New Zealand. He is generally considered to have been the most successful captain that New Zealand ever had, a leader with the ability to inspire his colleagues to play to the top of their talent.

Whineray got thirty-two caps between 1957 and 1965 as a loose-head prop forward, and became captain as a twenty-three-year-old against Australia in 1958. So he captained New Zealand in thirty of his thirty-two tests, a remarkable record that endured till 1997. He was the youngest New Zealand captain for thirty years, holding the post against the Lions in 1959, South Africa in 1960, France in 1961, Australia 1961 and 1962, England in 1963, and South Africa in 1965. And he captained the All Blacks in the famous 1963–64 tour of the UK.

Whineray will probably always be remembered for the try he scored against the Barbarians at the end of that 1963–64 tour, when the All Blacks beat a classy Barbarians side 36–3, and the final try was scored by Whineray himself, doing what a lot of people reckoned he did best – supporting the ball-carrier. He had to run about thirty to forty yards, but he was at full lick and he really was quite quick.

There were some people who pointed the finger at Whineray as a genuine test prop forward, claiming that he could be sorted out by a determined scrummager. But he played all those tests as prop for New Zealand, and you don't play tests for New Zealand unless you know what you're doing. He might not have been a destructive scrummager, but he was more than adequate in holding his own. The fact was that he was very highly regarded by his fellow players as a captain. They would have followed him anywhere, not just because he had a nice way with him but he was gritty as well, and tactically very sound.

That Barbarians try in 1964 beautifully rounded off a highly successful tour, with Whineray chomping in as he did best, with the ball in his hands. Most people saw him as that kind of forward, rather than a prop who grinds his opponent into the dust. His trademark move of running onto the ball from lineouts was so closely identified with him that it is now known as the 'Willie-away'.

Whineray was a great one for reading a game, and also very fair. I don't think I ever saw him do anything reprehensible, and that was an important aspect as well. After that try for the Barbarians he was carried off the field shoulder-high and the crowd all sang 'For he's a jolly good fellow'. It was a beautiful ending to the tour, that this guy who had been so impressive as a captain and as a personality should go out on that lovely sweep of quality rugby that those All Blacks produced, and then to be chaired off the field. Knighted in 1998, Sir Wilson J. Whineray OBE, of Auckland and New Zealand, is quite a gentleman.

KEN GRAY (1959–69)
Wellington, New Zealand
24 caps

At six foot two and seventeen stone he looked more like a lock forward than a prop, and indeed he did play for the All Blacks as a lock, and also for Wellington against the 1959 Lions. But Kenneth Francis Gray, a physically hard farming type, came in time to be rated as the world's greatest prop forward, and he was likened in his value to the All Blacks side alongside none other than Colin Meads.

Meads of course was renowned and feared everywhere he went, but Gray had a touch of that about him as well. To look at you might have thought him a bit elongated for a prop at well over six feet – most props are about 5ft 10in – but his height gave the All Blacks terrific options at the lineout because he was a splendid jumper. And so he gave them an additional lineout service that a lot of countries didn't have. He would soar up to a prodigious height, and of course in those days there was no lifting, you had to do your own jumping. Gray had that quality. But it was mostly as a kind of hard, flinty, agricultural type that he made his mark. And he was always supremely fit of course; perhaps he was like Meads and went about carrying North Country Cheviot sheep up and down mountains. Meads and Gray certainly had in common the fact that they both scared the living daylights out of people.

Certainly they were cornerstones in the great All Black packs of the 1960s, and Gray had the admirable record of having played in twenty-four All Black test matches of which only two were lost. What a fearsome sight he was when he got his motor running! No doubt there were signs there that he had a shortish fuse, and that he had an uncomplicated way of settling arguments, but what a player he was! He could scrummage equally well as loose-head or tight-head, and he had huge value as a lineout purveyor, providing New Zealand with auxiliary service, usually at number two in the line.

Gray could also get himself about the paddock at a fair rate of knots, and in addition he had safe hands so that he never looked out of place in a handling attack. As a twenty-four-year-old on the New Zealand tour of the UK and France in 1963–64 Gray made a huge impression as an all-purpose prop. He played in all five test matches, and with the tour captain Wilson Whineray and hooker Denis Young formed a solid front row which had an aggregate forty-five stones – fairly beefy in those days.

When the All Blacks were back on the 1967 tour, Gray played in nine of the fifteen games, and in the tests against Wales, France and Scotland. In between those two tours, Gray had underlined his leadership qualities as captain of Wellington in wins over the South Africans in 1965 and the Lions in 1966.

There is no doubt that Gray impressed rugby folk in the United Kingdom and France as one of the greatest forwards ever to wear the silver fern. He also was a man of strong principle who so dis-

Alex Obolensky, a Russian prince in England colours, challenged by Scotland's Kenneth Fyfe in England's 9–8 victory at Twickenham, 1936.

Jack Manchester runs out at the head of his 1935 All Blacks for the game against Somerset and Gloucester. At Hawick, I saw him *walk* his team out to menacing effect!

Hennie Muller, the *windhond* (greyhound) from South Africa, leads out the Springboks for their match against London Counties at Twickenham on 15 December 1951. It proved to be the tourists' only defeat (11–9).

Bob Scott, the inimitable Auckland and New Zealand full-back, toured with the All Blacks in the UK, 1953–54. His penalty goal at Murrayfield won the match against Scotland 3–0.

South African players celebrate their 25–3 victory over France in Paris, 16 February 1952. Prop forward Chris Koch provides the vehicle for Hannes Brewis; lock Ernst Dinkelmann is on the left, centre Tjol Lategan on the right.

Jean Prat (No 6), one of the most gifted forwards ever to represent France, converts Guy Basquet's try in their 11–3 defeat of England at Twickenham, 24 February 1951.

Peter Jackson, Coventry and England wing, clears to touch against Australia at Twickenham, February 1958. Jackson's superb individualist try won the match for England by 9–6.

Tony O'Reilly of Old Belvedere, Ireland and the British Lions, takes the field against Wales at Lansdowne Road, March 1956. He was then nineteen years old but had already toured with the Lions in South Africa.

Sometimes they caught him – often they didn't. Welsh fly-half Cliff Morgan with the British Lions against South Africa in Johannesburg, 1955. Voted the player of the tour, he went on to forge a career as a radio and TV broadcaster and producer – a rare talent, a super friend.

Jack Kyle, for many years Ireland's most capped stand-off (forty-six), who orchestrated their only Grand Slam (1948), sees off an England attack during the international at Lansdowne Road, 9 February 1957.

Don 'the Boot' Clarke, New Zealand's prolific goal-kicker and full-back, lines up one of his punishingly accurate penalties in the All Blacks' 1964 tour of the UK. In a thirty-one-test career, Clarke claimed 207 points.

Hugh McLeod, Scotland and the Lions' groundbreaking prop, peels off a lineout during the 1961 international against England at Twickenham.

'Pinetree' Meads foils Jean-Michel Cabanier's attempt to topple him as he heads for the French line in Paris, 25 November 1967.

The 1968 France team, the first to win a Grand Slam, pose for their group photograph before taking on Wales at Cardiff – a 14–9 victory that clinched the Slam for them.

One of the great attacking French full-backs, Pierre Villepreux kicks a penalty against England at Twickenham, 1971.

Jean-Pierre Rives, the legendary French flanker who led his country to their 1981 Grand Slam, initiates yet another onslaught on the line in their victory over Wales in Paris.

Benoit Dauga, the fearsome French lock known as the 'Control Tower', displays his considerable ball-handling ability during an international against England, February 1971. On the left, the Spanghero brothers, Claude and Walter.

Willie John McBride, captain of the 1974 Lions in South Africa, is chaired from the field by three Scots – Andy Irvine, Gordon Brown and Ian McLauchlan – after winning the third test 26–9 to ensure an unprecedented series victory.

Ireland's Mike Gibson, the greatest complete all-round rugby player I have ever seen, leaves his Welsh opponents grasping at air in the Wales–Ireland international of January 1977.

agreed with South African politics that he did not tour there with the All Blacks in 1970, despite pressure on him to do so.

The rugby world was saddened when Gray died of a heart attack in 1992, aged 54.

FRIK DU PREEZ (1961–71)
Northern Transvaal, South Africa
38 caps

Frederik Christophel Hendrick Du Preez was undoubtedly one of the finest back-five forwards ever to be spawned by the South African game. For here was a big man – six foot two and fifteen stone six – who could run like a stag and leap like a salmon, and who had adhesive hands and could move ball out of tackles. He was so versatile: seven of his test caps were as flanker and thirty-one as lock. In all he played eighty-seven games in South African colours, and went on six overseas tours.

The great Lions coach Carwyn James rated Du Preez very high as being 'the only lock in modern times who had every one of the skills necessary to the completely equipped forward'.

A former Schools stand-off, Du Preez was impressively quick for such a big man, and was hard to knock over especially when flat out, with the ball tucked securely in one arm or placed firmly on a hip. The 1968 Lions in South Africa had reason to remember Du Preez, for in the first test he thundered round the front of the lineout like an express train, and champed through three opponents for a sensational try. He had already made his mark on the Springboks tour of the UK in 1960–61 when he claimed his first cap in the England game at Twickenham, in which he slotted the conversion of Doug Hopwood's try for South African victory by 5–0.

A corporal in the South African Air Force at the time of the tour to the UK, Du Preez played in sixteen of the thirty-two games, including tests against England and Scotland, and claimed fifty-eight points from three tries, fourteen conversions and seven penalty goals. In all, Du Preez played in successful series against Australia, the Lions, France and New Zealand, and enjoyed ten wins before his first test defeat, by France, in 1964.

Once Du Preez was penalised for being lifted at the lineout (then an offence) but in fact there had been no lift. The referee just didn't believe a player could achieve such height of jump without being lifted; but Frik could! He had a huge leap from a standing start, and the ref was sure he had been given illegal support. And he was a fine ball-handler too. He was like a wild boar, an amazing guy.

Du Preez was a one-off, there was nobody like him. A dour man who seldom smiled, he was a dedicated rugby player. I was disappointed that, when in 2001 *The Times* asked me to pick my World XV, and I chose Du Preez as lock alongside Colin Meads, out of all the forty – replacements and all – who turned up for a celebration dinner in London, the one missing person was Du Preez.

BENOIT DAUGA (1964–72)
Mont de Marsan, France
63 caps

'Mean and menacing' was how some described Benoit Dauga of the Mont de Marsan club, and certainly he didn't smile a lot. But he was tremendously skilful too, as was once vividly brought home to me at a French training session I was watching, for identification purposes, the day before France took on Scotland in Paris. Dauga climaxed a brilliant handling sequence by pivoting on his left foot before sending a drop goal rifling between the uprights for all the world like a gifted stand-off. I almost felt like applauding!

Dauga's stockings were always rolled down to his ankles, and he presented a fearsome appearance, carrying a permanent glower on his features which gave him the air of a genuine hard man. But he was also a wonderfully rounded player, with impressive stamina and commitment, who could operate equally effectively anywhere along the lineout and in any one of the back five forward positions. He was frequently described as France's 'control tower' because of his lineout expertise, which owed much to his ball-handling skills, honed as a result of his experience as a basketball player.

Dauga was six foot six in height and weighed seventeen stone five. He was discovered almost by accident, when the French selectors attended a combined services match where they wanted to run the rule over two other locks. But they came away raving about the tall, slim Dauga who stole the show. His abilities made him a key member of some outstanding French forward packs of the 1960s and 1970s.

Dauga carried an aura of brooding menace, and certainly could never be described as a shy, retiring violet; but he was also a forward of exceptional gifts who was prepared to stand up for himself and for France whatever transpired. He was of farming stock, so was naturally hard and strong. First capped against Scotland in 1964, he shared the French boilerhouse on fifteen occasions with Walter Spanghero, with whom he was not always on good terms. In fact he had a running rivalry with Spanghero, whom he replaced in gaining his fiftieth cap against Wales at Cardiff. It was a pity they did not get on because they were two great forwards and in unison had so much to offer.

Dauga captained France in nine major internationals, of which four were won, three lost, and two drawn. He was a key member of France's Grand Slam side of 1968, and he toured with France in South Africa in 1967 and in New Zealand and Australia in 1968, and as captain in 1971. New Zealanders and South Africans were much impressed by Dauga. Among the South Africans who heaped praise on him was the great Danie Craven, who described him as the greatest forward ever to visit South Africa. The legendary French flanker Jean Prat described Dauga as 'the greatest forward France ever has produced', an assessment that found an echo in the opinion of the great New Zealander Fred Allen, who marvelled at the Dauga gifts during the French tour of New Zealand.

A restaurateur by profession, Dauga shared with Michel Crauste the French record of a forward – sixty-three caps. Dauga's caps were gained as lock and No 8, and he scored eleven test tries. The rugby world was saddened when he suffered serious neck damage and paralysis in a national championship club game. Hospitalised for months, he exhibited exceptional determination and good sense in fighting back to recovery when the whole of French rugby applauded a genuine great.

BRIAN LOCHORE (1964–71)
Wairarapa, New Zealand
25 caps

It was during their 1967 tour of the British Isles that I watched the All Blacks at practice in driving rain, and with the ball as slippery as an orange pip, prior to their last game of the tour, against the Barbarians (see p. 68). The move involved their No 8 and captain Brian Lochore in a standing-off role, and they just kept going through the play time and again in those filthy conditions.

Came the day, and the All Blacks were struggling to defend their unbeaten record with the Baa-Baas leading 6–3 and only two minutes left. Then Ian MacRae, the New Zealand centre, scored a try to make it 6–6, with Lochore playing a key role. In injury time, with the scores level, Stuart Wilson, the Scottish full-back and Barbarians' captain, just failed to find touch, and who but Lochore should gather in the ball, take it upfield, and then from the ruck make an overlap using that stand-off play they had been practising. The result: a try by the wing Tony Steel for an 11–6 New Zealand win to preserve that unbeaten record.

It seemed in every way appropriate that Lochore should make such a timely contribution, for he had been an inspirational figure throughout the tour in which the All Blacks had played fifteen games, won fourteen and drawn one. I was thrilled to bits when I was sent to cover in commentary the New Zealand game against East Wales at Cardiff Arms Park. It was a spectacular affair, the Welsh lads running in the ball from all over the pitch, inspired by the presence of Gerald Davies, Barry John, Gareth Edwards and John Dawes. The game ended as a 3–3 draw, but many felt that the Welshmen were unlucky not to be the only ones to lower the colours of those gifted 1966–67 New Zealand visitors.

Lochore had the unenviable task in 1966 of succeeding as New Zealand captain the highly successful Wilson Whineray. But the six foot three, fifteen and a half stone farmer from Wairarapa did so as to the manner born, and proved a popular leader who encouraged his colleagues to produce a high-quality combination in an attractive playing style. As a result they achieved an international Grand Slam, with wins over England, Wales, France and Scotland. The Irish match was cencelled, but it wasn't easy to see how the All Blacks would have been defeated by a not very strong Irish side, had that match taken place. The composition of the New Zealand pack in that last match against the Barbarians gives an idea of the strength of that outfit: Jazz Muller, Bruce McLeod, Ken Gray, Colin Meads, Sam Strahan, Kel Tremain, Brian Lochore and Waka Nathan. Some pack!

In 1987 Brian Lochore was coach of the All Blacks side that won the first World Cup. It was during that event that Ian Robertson the BBC commentator saw Lochore and Colin Meads waiting for traffic to pass before they crossed the road. 'Let's go across and ask if those old men would like us to help them across the road,' he suggested. I took one look at those sons of the soil and declined Robertson's suggestion. Those two great hulking brutes, you must be joking! And I wouldn't do it today either, especially as he's now *Sir* Brian Lochore.

PIERRE VILLEPREUX (1967–72)
Toulouse, France
34 caps

It was during the second test, New Zealand v France in Wellington in 1968, that Pierre Villepreux, the French full-back and a physical education specialist, startled the crowd by lining up a penalty goal attempt from fully seventy yards. Some in the crowd laughed; others declared that Villepreux would require divine intervention to claim the three points. But by using his instep, and with perfect timing, the slimline Villepreux – five foot eleven and twelve stone twelve – made the perfect strike that had height to spare as the ball soared between the uprights. An amazing goal!

Villepreux was, and probably still is, a favourite son of Toulouse, where as player and coach he created and shared in huge success for his particular style of full-back play, and enhanced the reputation of his famous club. He was an adventurer who revelled in the wide spread of handling attack, and delighted in tilting his lance, sometimes in the most audacious and startling fashion. It was risky, but that was Villepreux. He made the full-back berth a vivid source of counter-attack, for he was quick into his running, and no slouch thereafter with his long loping stride and superb balance.

He gained his first cap against Italy in 1967, and created such a reputation for swift intrusive play, and counter-running, that opponents had one key aim – to keep the ball away from Villepreux. They made it a rule always to find touch; otherwise Villepreux would explode out of defence and cause alarm bells to ring in opposing ranks.

It was hardly surprising that Villepreux was the first Frenchman to be invited to play for the Barbarians, for the free spirit that was Villepreux found natural expression in the ranks of that famous nomadic club. He proved a successful coach, not only of Toulouse and the French squad as assistant to Jean-Claude Skrela, but also of Italy and Tahiti. All of those he coached were encouraged to hone their individual and unit skill, and to seek a widespread handling style that proved a delight to play and a joy to watch.

Villepreux reached a national final with the Brive club in 1965, and with Toulouse in 1969. He also had a close rivalry for the French full-back berth with Claude Lacaze (Lourdes and Angoulême, thirty-three caps). However, Villepreux was at one time rated as the finest full-back in the world game, and assuredly he lit up the action whenever he played. Not only that, but in his thirty-four cap appearances he claimed 163 points from a full house; two tries, twenty-nine conversions, thirty-two penalty goals and one drop goal.

GORDON BROWN (1969–76)
West of Scotland, Scotland, British Lions
30 Scotland caps
8 British Lions tests

I have a vivid recall of a Scottish club championship game in the 1960s when West of Scotland were visitors to Hawick, who in that season had a highly productive lineout. But no one seemed to have warned a young West of Scotland lock forward, Gordon Lamont Brown, about this, for he proceeded to dominate the lineout whether at two, four or six. It was a performance which underlined the Scottish selectors' wisdom in pinning their faith in the six foot five and sixteen stone ten Brown, who had the build of a bison, and who gained thirty Scottish caps, thirteen of them in the same pack as his brother Peter (who was capped twenty-seven times).

Gordon was first capped in Scotland's 6–3 defeat of the 1969 touring Springboks, and his second cap was against France. But for the Welsh game that was to follow, the selectors opted for Peter at lock and Gordon on the bench. However, by a remarkable turn of events Peter was injured during the Welsh match, and lo and behold his replacement was none other than his brother Gordon. He played a great game and proved to be a rumbustious, uncompromising lock forward who shared Scotland's engine room twenty-one times with Alastair McHarg of London Scottish, six times with Peter Stagg of Sale, once with Iain Barnes of Hawick, and twice with Alan Tomes of Hawick.

A product of Marr College in Troon, Gordon Brown was known affectionately as 'Broon frae Troon' and was an immensely popular player, not least on tours by the British Lions. He made an impact on three such tours: 1971 in Australia and New Zealand, with four-teen out of twenty-six games, including two of the four tests; 1974 in South Africa, with twelve out of twenty-two games, and three of the four tests; and 1977 in Australia and New Zealand, with four-teen out of twenty-six games, with three out of the four tests. So on the three Lions tours he played in forty of the seventy-four games, including eight of the twelve test matches. In New Zealand in 1971 Gordon Brown, the junior lock in the party, was regarded initially as a back-up player, but he applied himself with such wholehearted enthusiasm as to be promoted to Willie John McBride's boilerhouse partner in two of the four tests.

With the Lions in South Africa in 1974 Gordon Brown truly laid claim to being one of the outstanding lock forwards in the game, for he scrummaged with such vigour and technical knowledge that he undermined an area of expected Springbok superiority, and he rev-elled in the hurly-burly of lineout engagement. For Brown played his part in the Lions' refusal to be intimidated by the Springboks, and did not hesitate to use a bit of knuckle where that was indicated in accord with the Lions' call to arms, their famous (or notorious) '99' call (see pp. 132–33).

It spoke volumes for his positional sense and his handling skill that Gordon Brown scored a record for a touring forward of eight tries in twelve games with the Lions in South Africa. Two of those tries had crucial impacts on two of the test matches.

The whole of the rugby world mourned the death of Gordon Brown in 2000.

Gordon Brown in his own words

Scotland v Springboks, 1969

Bang! bang! on the door. 'Let's go, lads,' and we were away down the corridor to the top of the tunnel. By this time I had an unbelievable lump in my throat and tears in my eyes. If anyone had asked me something I would have been unable to reply. We were given the come-on by the steward at the bottom of the tunnel. We started to trot. I could see the crowd away on the far side of the terracing, their Lion Rampant flags dancing and waving in the wind. I could hear the band playing 'Scotland the Brave'. The farther down the tunnel I trotted the more I thought I would never get out of that wee hole at the bottom. I seemed to be getting bigger and bigger with every stride. In all the dreams I had had about this moment, I had underestimated fifty-fold.

When the band finally left the pitch I took up position to field the kick-off. When the whistle blew and the ball flew towards me I could hardly see it because of the tears in my eyes, such was the emotion of the moment. I caught the ball and the whole Springbok pack caught me! The emotion evaporated and the game was a reality.

In no time at all I was back in the dressing room hardly believing that the game was already over. It had all gone so quickly and I was feeling on top of the world because we had won by 6 points to 3. We scored the only try of the match by Ian Smith, our full-back, following a devastating break at centre by John Frame.

The champagne flowed at the North British Hotel that night and I was desperately trying to take in as much of the atmosphere, the feelings, and the events as was possible because I knew that day was unique. During the match I ran faster, jumped higher, and scrummaged harder than ever before, such was the adrenaline being pumped through my body. Yet at eleven o'clock that night I felt as fresh as a daisy. Reality reasserted itself on Sunday morning when I attempted to rise from my bed – I could not move an inch! Every bone, muscle and ligament in my body was at screaming pitch as though they had been through a mangle. I very slowly struggled to a bath and after soaking in it for two hours I started to feel some little relief. It took me two weeks to recover fully from that match.

Despite his obvious disappointment at not being chosen [my elder brother] Peter had been, nevertheless, genuinely delighted at my selection. He gave me valuable hints on my build-up to the game. I retained my place for the following game against France, at Murrayfield, but our defeat then had the press calling for some changes.

I was working at the bank, patiently awaiting news of Scotland's team to go to Wales, when I was told there was someone on the phone who had to do with rugby. I rushed to the phone and the conversation went like this.

Me: 'Hello?'

'Great news – I'm back in the Scottish team!' my brother yelled excitedly down the phone.

'Fantastic!' I shouted. 'Who's out?'

'You are,' he replied.

(From Gordon Brown, *Broon from Troon*, Stanley Paul, 1983)

1970s

Wales Supreme
The Barbarians
Sevens: the Abbreviated Game

Portraits

Willie John McBride   (Ireland 1962–75)
Mike Gibson   (Ireland 1964–79)
Gerald Davies   (Wales 1966–78)
Barry John   (Wales 1966–72)
Gareth Edwards   (Wales 1967–78)
Phil Bennett   (Wales 1969–78)
Mervyn Davies   (Wales 1969–76)
David Duckham   (England 1969–76)
Ian McLauchlan   (Scotland 1969–79)
JPR Williams   (Wales 1969–81)
JPR Williams in his own words: The 1971 Wales Grand Slam
Fergus Slattery   (Ireland 1970–84)
Fran Cotton   (England 1971–81)
Fran Cotton in his own words: The Lions in South Africa, 1974
Andy Irvine   (Scotland 1972–82)
Graham Price   (Wales 1975–83)

PART THREE

WALES SUPREME

IT WAS in 1969 that Barry John and Gareth Edwards combined for their first full season together, bringing a Triple Crown to Wales, and thereafter the men from west of Offa's Dyke became almost impossible to beat. That decade from 1969 to 1979 will always be remembered as the golden era of Welsh rugby, when the Welsh side were absolutely unstoppable and Wales won the Triple Crown six times. Only an outstanding French side prevented them from adding to the three Grand Slams achieved in this decade. Thanks largely to the exciting rugby being played by the Welsh sides, by the 1970s the Five Nations tournament had become a must-watch series in northern hemisphere rugby, with matches becoming all-ticket sell-outs, gaining huge popularity and a large television audience.

Throughout the 1970s it seemed that Wales was regularly producing the best players in the world, certainly to judge from the evidence of the 1971 and 1974 Lions tours. Grand Slams in 1971, 1976 and 1978 stood out as peaks in a mountain range of Triple Crowns. The world was privileged to watch a procession of outrageously talented players of the likes of Barry John, Gareth Edwards, JPR Williams, Mervyn Davies, Phil Bennett, the Pontypool front row of Price, Faulkner and Windsor – the list just goes on. That generation of Welshmen were at the heart of the victorious British Lions tours of 1971 to New Zealand and 1974 to South Africa, perhaps the finest group of players ever to pull on a Lions jersey.

It was my good luck to be doing commentary during that golden era of Welsh rugby, between 1969 and 1979, when they played forty-three games, won thirty-three, lost seven and drew three. They were all-conquering: six Championships, five Triple Crowns, three Grand Slams. It was a halcyon time for Wales when they won two great Grand Slams in 1976 and 1978, scoring 102 points in four games in the first, and sixty-seven points in the second. There were some huge victories, such as in 1976 when they beat Scotland 28–6 and Ireland 34–9. In those two Grand Slams they scored nineteen tries and conceded just seven, and that in itself gives you an impression of what a formidable side they were.

Those wonderful Wales sides of the 1970s had everything that's great about the game: skill, grace, power, finesse. They were a truly wonderful combination of stars, often irresistible, a side twenty years ahead of their time. Their magic still stirs the soul today. Every time I sat down to commentate on a Welsh game I looked forward to another command performance, with magical interplay involving both backs and forwards. And of course the likes of Gareth, Gerald and Mervyn were mainstays in the Lions sides of 1971 and 1974 when we taught the All Blacks and the Springboks a thing or two.

Those Welsh were a great sight. They had JPR Williams at fullback, virtually the complete player in that position. Maybe he was not the fastest in the world, but he made up for that with power and strength and rugby know-how. Take for instance that great Barbarians' opening try against New Zealand in 1973. Gareth Edwards scored it, but it needed JPR Williams's instant and perfect pass while being tackled head-on around the neck. This demonstrated sublime amateur-era skills and imposing professional-era physicality. Combining them at the highest level requires utmost courage and confidence. He always had both, and hardly ever had a bad game.

And then there was Gerald Davies, the greatest right wing I've ever seen. He will always be in my World XV. There were powerful men in midfield too with Ray Gravell and Steve Fenwick, and on the other wing JJ Williams, a flying machine, a Commonwealth Games sprinter – wonderfully gifted three-quarters and full-back positions there. And how about the likes of Phil Bennett, a player who could change a game with a single piece of magic. Barry John at stand-off before him, of course, and Gareth Edwards at scrum-half.

And when you look at their forwards, Faulkner, Windsor and Price; Geoff Wheel, Cobner, Derek Quinnell, Squire – there's power there, and there's strength and skill there too. A great scrum-maging outfit, and a good lineout: Wheel a tremendously strong forward, one of the great mauling forwards; and a gifted loose forward trio, maybe not the fastest flankers of all time, but Cobner, Quinnell and Squire were powerful, they combined well, they were great tacklers, and they just kept on running.

So when you look at that kind of XV it's no wonder Wales did so well. They were just a great side and it was a delight to see them in action. And it was also a delight to do commentary on them because they played a kind of total rugby in which at times backs played like forwards, and forwards like backs, with backs prepared to ruck and maul if they had to, and forwards who were capable of running and handling so well. They were such a rounded outfit that they could cope with virtually any situation, with tremendous pace on the wings and power at full-back. JPR Williams was such a great intruding full-back because he came in at such clever positions – his decisions about where and when to intrude were almost always spot-on.

THE BARBARIANS

A RUGBY club without a home base, where membership, which is by invitation only, includes an amazing assortment of the world's greatest players, and where everyone is committed to play open rugby – that's the Barbarians.

It was at an oyster supper in Bradford more than a hundred years ago that the idea was conceived of a travelling rugby side who would go and play here and there, and try to boost rugby in certain areas. WP Carpmael, a Blackheath forward who happened to be on tour with a London side, was the founder, and it just developed from that oyster supper. The first game was in Yorkshire, and it was a huge success because they didn't go out merely to win but still more to enjoy themselves. Thus they became established as a free-flowing rugby-playing outfit, and they have stuck to it ever since.

Initially a ramshackle bunch who played in black-and-white shirts under the flag of the skull and crossbones, they are now the most famous club in the world, drawing members from the northern and the southern hemispheres. The breakthrough came in 1948, when they were asked to field a side against the Wallabies, the idea being that the gate money would allow the tourists to go back to Australia by way of Canada. The match, which the Baa-Baas won 9–6, was a great success, and it's interesting that the Wallabies have now become famous for playing just such an open style of rugby typical of the way their 1948 Barbarian opponents at Cardiff Arms Park played. Ever since then, touring sides have traditionally played the Barbarians at the end of their tours in a kind of unofficial test, in a game where flowing rugby has been the rule.

The Barbarians are special because they remind us about what's available in rugby union when people play with a bit of risk. Rugby union has gone through periods when it has become so carefully planned, when everything has been so covered, that it has been in danger of getting stereotyped. But the Barbarians matches, with very few exceptions, have reminded us of what a delight rugby union can be when it is played with a sense of adventure and an element of risk. That's important, because the game can get bogged down, with not nearly enough of that type of Barbarians play, when they take risks, throw the ball about, and run from their own line.

That has been the Barbarians' style right from the very start. Their aim has been to entertain both themselves and the people watching. And they have done it so well, apart from one or two rare exceptions. There was one game, against the 1961 Springboks, when the Barbarians shut up shop, shut the door, and took no risks whatever. They were confronting an undefeated side in the tourists' last match, and they won 6–0, but it was in a style so against the Barbarians' spirit that there was quite a bit of criticism of that game. That was also the occasion of Barbarian full-back Haydn Mainwaring's bone-crunching shoulder-charge on the Springbok skipper Avril Malan, when Malan was sprinting down the touchline for a certain try. The sound of that collision could be heard all round Cardiff Arms Park, and Malan spent the night in hospital (see pp. 60–61).

In the early 1960s the game of rugby union was in danger of losing its credibility with the public, such was the domination of lineouts and touch-kicking. This reached its lowest level in 1963. But a year later Wilson Whineray's All Blacks changed rugby thinking, and gave forwards the freedom to run with the ball. The Barbarians played their part in that turnaround with a thrilling match against the Blacks that helped rescue the sport.

It was against the All Blacks, of course, that the Barbarians scored one of the greatest tries of all time, in 1973. I've seen tries that were as good as that, but to have produced that special one against the

Blacks of all people, players who shut the door on everybody, was quite extraordinary. The build-up was brilliant, and the final execution with Gareth Edwards's dive – incredible! I was supposed to do the commentary for that famous game when Gareth scored that sensational try. It would have been a lovely game to do, but I was unwell, and Cliff Morgan did it brilliantly with such tremendous passion.

So as a general rule the Barbarians were a delight to do commentary on because they just swept the commentary along with that style of rugby. It was a potent reminder to all of us of what the game had to offer if we were prepared to embrace it and take the risk.

An unofficial committee is in charge of selecting Barbarian sides. They tended to ring up and say, 'Do you think we should have so-and-so? OK? Let's put him in then.' It was all somewhat haphazard and unofficial, but they seemed to muddle through in their selection, and of course right from the very start they laid down that no one was to be invited to play for the Barbarians who wasn't prepared to play that style of rugby football. In the midst of a time of tight defences and careful rugby they shone like a star in the firmament. And it's amazing that with very few exceptions they have held to that style from the beginning to the present day.

It's fun to see their training sessions – it's all so shambolic. Somebody is deputed to take it the day before the match, and there's a lot of 'Hi, how are you? Long time no see!' and that kind of thing. 'Will you take the goal kicks?' 'Well, I don't know ... OK, I'll do it.' It's amazing how the side can gel at all, but I think that in the heart of every rugby player there's a desire to be flamboyant, which is often suppressed because coaching is usually directed towards eliminating error. If you play flamboyant rugby there has to be an element of risk – somebody will drop the ball, the pass will go forward, or whatever. But the Barbarians have traditionally never bothered too much about that. They have just wanted to enjoy themselves because they are of the view that if they enjoy themselves so will the spectators.

Micky Steele-Bodger is in charge these days, a great guy who gets things done, who is wholeheartedly in love with the club, and guarding its traditions. He has done admirable work for the Barbarians. I just hope they can survive in the professional era. It's a worry that the Barbarians' spirit and style are not quite in accord with the modern game as it's played today, where winning is often all that matters. The Barbarians play to enjoy themselves and to entertain, but now everyone else is often playing to win and they don't give a damn whether they entertain or not. It's a test for the Baa-Baas, and nowadays too there are so many commitments on top players that it's not as easy for Barbarians to get the quality. In the old days to play for the Barbarians was, in the player's mind, virtually akin to having a cap – a huge invitation that gave immense pride to the players concerned, and I hope that isn't being eroded as well.

I hope there will always be Barbarians, playing in that style that is very much their own, because it's so essential as a means of reminding us of the kind of rugby football that can be produced by players who, while not being stupid, nonetheless chance their arm a bit and are prepared to take a bit of a risk in order to entertain. But that's hardly the way the professional boys play it. So there's a wee clash there, but I hope the Barbarians will always be the Barbarians and always play in that style, because it's a delight to see. Okay, it may seem a bit artificial now because the rest of rugby football is very much percentage stuff where you don't take many risks, but I think the Barbarians have a very important part to play yet. It worries me sometimes that people talk about them being out of date or out of fashion, because rugby must always have in mind the sheer joy of uninhibited running rugby football.

SEVENS: THE
ABBREVIATED GAME

THE SEVENS game was born in the Borders of Scotland. The first Sevens tournament was in 1883, and it was founded at Melrose, the brainchild of Ned Haig, a butcher's apprentice and half-back at the Melrose rugby club. The club was in financial trouble, so Ned had the notion of raising money with an abbreviated version of the game. His original idea was to have a regular tournament as a way of pulling in the crowds, but playing several games in one afternoon with fifteen players on each side would never work, so the teams were reduced to seven men. The idea just spread like wildfire. All the other Borders clubs took it up, because apart from being a very attractive style of rugby, it was also a great money-making idea which drew big crowds. To this day Melrose makes enough out of its Sevens tournament to keep it going for the rest of the season. And now the game has spread everywhere, it's not just in the Borders but all over the world.

Every Borders club has a tournament, with five in the spring at the end of the season, and three in the autumn at the beginning. No one is allowed to tamper with the tournament. The secretary of the Scottish Rugby Union once rang Bob Brown, who was the Melrose secretary, and told him that the Melrose Sevens would have to be postponed because Scotland were going to have an international on that day. Bob's reply was, 'You have a look at the Greenyards [the Melrose club ground] on the second Saturday of April, and you tell me if there's no mair Sevens being held. There'll be a Sevens held, and you can do what you like with your bloody international!' The Melrose Sevens went ahead.

Bob Brown was secretary of the Melrose club for years and years, and for him the Melrose Sevens were sacrosanct. He's in the Weir cemetery now, up on the hill behind Melrose. You can just about see the ground from there, and I often think of Bob, who was such a lovely person with a wonderful sense of humour. He would defend the Melrose Sevens to the death.

And perhaps he was right, because Melrose is very special, not only because the game was born there, but also because it is renowned for having the best draw for the Sevens. They pick sixteen teams so it's a straightforward draw with each team playing the same number, and they have always reached out for quality class guest sides, not just from England but from all over the world – Randwick from Sydney, Australia, for instance, David Campese's outfit. So the Melrose tournaments have had a special aura, not least because of the great players who have come along to Melrose, this wee town in the Borders, to play in the Sevens.

I'm very fond of the Sevens game myself, especially the Melrose tournament, but it can be a beast of a job to do commentary on because you've got sixteen teams, and most of them you're seeing for the very first time when they run onto the pitch. It's not too easy to do commentary in those circumstances, I can tell you. But it's a thrill to see all those great players coming down to Melrose.

When Randwick came to play, the Greenyards ground was like a swamp, and I can remember Melrose fellows saying, 'Let's see how good Campese is in this rain.' But of course as soon as he got the ball Campo just took off, half-skidded, did a little hitch kick, left two opponents sitting on their backsides, and dived over for a try in the corner. That's how good he was!

Now of course it's the Hong Kong Sevens that have caught the limelight – but you'd better not tell that to anyone at Melrose. When I went out to Hong Kong for the first time, in 1976, I was amazed because I never thought the Chinese would take to it in such a big way. But their organisation was brilliant, and their fervour extraordinary – a lot of Chinese folk whom I wouldn't have thought of as natural rugby fans, all screaming their heads off. Now the Hong Kong tournament is a global event, and all the great sides from the southern hemisphere compete there as well as the minnows.

The Fijians were the real eye-opener in the earlier Hong Kong Sevens, winning in 1977, 1978, 1980 and 1984. Those fellows have a natural love of throwing the ball around. They don't really fancy rucking and mauling and scrummaging, but give them a bit of open territory and a rugby ball and it's a different thing altogether. The Hong Kong Sevens are just made for them. They turn out a team of really big fellows of six foot five, but they're so athletic, so unorthodox. They'll throw the ball miles across the pitch and take it with one hand, flip it behind their backs without looking, it's amazing. Ally that to sheer physical power and pace and they're devastating. That's their forte – throwing the ball about. In Sevens there are huge areas to exploit but it's not so easy in fifteen-a-side.

I suppose Waisale Serevi is the most kenspeckle player at the Hong Kong Sevens, with his ability to check and turn and twist and his ball-handling gifts – he's full of wiles. And it's not just the Fijians; if you see some of the others playing Sevens like Sri Lanka or Japan, it's a delight, it's firecracker stuff.

The New Zealanders tend to put together the most efficient package these days. They have the physicality for a start, right out to the wing. The New Zealand sides had people like Christian Cullen and Jonah Lomu, but they were often people you'd never heard of, people who had been chosen because they were Sevens specialists. Today the New Zealanders have a pretty strong dominance in the abbreviated game. They've been in nine of the last twelve finals.

In 1993 a World Cup of Sevens was held, appropriately in Scotland, again in 1997, this time in Hong Kong, then in 2001 at

Mar del Plata in Argentina where Australia was beaten in the final by New Zealand.

In 1998 Sevens rugby was also included into the Commonwealth Games for the first time, New Zealand taking gold then and again in 2002 in Manchester. Since then Sevens rugby has taken another big leap forward with the creation of a World Sevens series – a truly international series of tournaments involving sixteen nations, played in countries as varied as Argentina, Chile, England, Malaysia, China and Australia. New Zealand was crowned the inaugural IRB World Sevens series champions, and since then has dominated the abbreviated game by winning a third straight Sevens title in 2001–2002.

Hong Kong Sevens final: recalled from my match worksheet notes

Fiji v New Zealand, 1995

The whole of Hong Kong wanted to see a New Zealand v Fiji final, because they were the giants of seven-a-side rugby. The Fijians were great big fellows, long striders and quite ruthless in their own way. They were huge, except for Waisale Serevi, the renowned Sevens stand-off, who was calling the shots and doing all the scoring for them. A tremendous little player he was.

And the New Zealanders – they had a side with only three players folk would recognise: Christian Cullen was one – he was only nineteen then – and Eric Rush, one of the greatest seven-a-side forwards of all time; and Jonah Lomu was there, that was his second year in the Sevens. He scored a try in each tie, that was the kind of irresistible force he was. The other players were people we had no idea about – Bradley Wood, Peter Fleming, Adrian Cashmore, Joe Towiwi, Joe Windiri – and Andrew Blowers who is now playing in England. And there they were, producing just magical seven-a-side rugby that brought them a victory over the Fijians, who were themselves magnificent seven-a-side specialists.

The Fijians just revelled in Sevens, being out in the open spaces and throwing the ball around in spectacular fashion. Sevens was just made for them, led by Serevi, who was only five foot four and eleven stone eleven, but cheeky and with all the gifts, leaving opponents wondering where he'd gone – he was just tremendous. In the Hong Kong Sevens of 1991 he had scored fifty-one points in four games, so he was a star turn. But all the Fijians were a delight to see, great big men handling the ball as if they were stand-offs. And of course they were intense rivals to the New Zealanders, for whom winning was all that mattered. So New Zealand v Fiji was the top of the tree as far as Sevens was concerned.

That game the ball was never still; very few lineouts, hardly any scrummaging, most of it running and handling – those Fijians were a delight to do commentary on once I'd got to know them and was able to get my tongue around their names! But the New Zealanders deserved to win because they were the best side in the tournament. The big difference in the final was that New Zealand won more ball. They knew that if they stopped the Fijians getting ball they could stop them scoring, and that was the story of the final. They worked it well, playing fluent Sevens football, and the skill levels were quite extraordinary, the way that both sides found space so beautifully.

If you want to show people how to play Sevens in the most effective way, then just show them a video of the New Zealanders and Fijians playing in that 1995 final, which was a classic. New Zealand won because they got their priorities right, you don't score if you don't have the ball. But the Fijians did it off the top of their heads, and they were so exciting to watch because you never knew what they would do next. You couldn't get a more exciting or revealing seven-a-side final than that match featuring the Fijians and All Blacks at Hong Kong, 1995. It was top of the tree!

PORTRAITS

WILLIE JOHN McBRIDE (1962–75)
Ballymena, Ulster, Ireland, British Lions
63 Ireland caps
17 British Lions tests

He would never claim to be the most skilful of lock forwards, and he was never liable to break the sound barrier, but there have been few players in the history of the game who could motivate their colleagues into deeds of derring-do with greater effect than the Ballymena, Ulster, Ireland and Lions lock forward Willie John McBride. He held a record of test appearances by a lock forward of eighty, of which sixty-three were for Ireland and seventeen for the Lions, for whom he made five tours, a record he shared with his fellow Ulsterman Mike Gibson.

Willie John was a tough guy who, as captain, inspired the Lions to that unbeaten tour of South Africa in 1974. He had a famous catch-phrase on that tour: 'We take no prisoners.' And that uncompromising approach, plus his massive commitment and fire, made him an inspiring leader. Once I was present when a young Irish new cap on the eve of the game asked Willie John what it would be like. Puffing on his pipe Willie John looked the lad straight in the eye, put his hand on the boy's shoulder, and then told him: 'Jaisus, Oi tell ya, it'll be a long, hard road.' As one who had toured South Africa as a Lion in 1962 and in 1968, he knew full well the sheer intimidation that existed there as part of the game.

Willie John doesn't pull his punches, and in the New Zealand

Lions test in Auckland in 1971 he and the equally legendary Colin Meads had a rare old set-to with punches flying but, at the end, they left the field together, and each had a huge respect for the other. McBride already had demonstrated his powers of inspiration on that 1971 tour when he took over as pack leader from the injured Ray McLoughlin, and he set a strong example to the Lions forwards who reacted with fire and fury to the Ulsterman's lead.

He did the same in South Africa in 1974 when the Lions set records galore – the first major series the Springboks had lost since the turn of the century, and a record Lions haul of 729 points and 107 tries in their twenty-two games, seventy-nine Lions points in four tests. The Lions' 28–9 win in the second test was the biggest defeat ever suffered by South Africa. There also were records by Alan Old (thirty-seven points against South West Districts) Andy Irvine (156 points) and the four tries by JJ Williams in the test series.

All that underlined Willie John's finest hour as having followed his captaincy of Ireland in 1974 to their first Five Nations Championship in twenty-three years. Then, in 1975, in his thirteenth season of international rugby, he scored his only test try for Ireland with a typical charge against France. Needless to say, it brought the house down.

MIKE GIBSON (1964–79)

Cambridge University, Northern Ireland FC, Ulster,
Ireland, British Lions
69 Ireland caps
12 British Lions tests

Of all the gifted artists one has been privileged to see in action, Cameron Michael Henderson Gibson of Ireland has to be one of the most complete fellows ever to strut his stuff on the international stage, and one also who made a huge contribution to the success of the 1971 and 1974 Lions in New Zealand and South Africa respectively. For me Gibson had all the qualities of a great rugby player: the skill, the tactical appreciation, the marvellous acceleration, the instinct for what is on.

Only a class player could have performed with such distinction in various positions at test level – sixty-nine Irish caps of which forty were at centre, twenty-five at stand-off and four as a wing. He also represented the British Lions eight times as centre and four times as stand-off. Amongst three-quarters, Mike Gibson is the greatest complete all-round rugby player I have ever seen. The sort of chap you could play in any single position along the line and he would fit in without the slightest bit of bother.

Mike Gibson had the distinction of being the first international replacement, when he took over from the injured Barry John (collarbone) in the opening Lions international at Ellis Park, South Africa, in 1968. Before then, teams just had to soldier on as best they could. He also equalled the record of having been on five Lions tours. Perhaps the true measure of his greatness was when that giant of New Zealand rugby, Colin Meads, paid special tribute to the Ireland maestro as a key figure on Lions tours down under.

In addition to his physical attributes, Gibson possessed a rugby brain and a calmness under pressure which set him in a class of his own. Meads was not alone in regarding him as the linchpin of that superlative Lions back line in 1971, when the Lions were stomping through New Zealand, virtually invincible. Gibson's own comment on that midfield axis of Barry John, John Dawes and Gibson is revealing, when he said, 'The three midfield men were all of one mind and, when Barry had the ball, I tried to think in terms of something seemingly impossible or unorthodox and then got into that position.' But Gibson was the man the New Zealanders picked out as the number one of them all.

Gibson had all the skills and an edge of pace that often caught opponents by surprise, as well as an intuitive feel for what was on and what wasn't. First capped in the 18–5 Twickenham defeat of England in 1964 he possessed a sizzling sidestep, a wonderful control of pace, and could take and give a pass in a blink. And although he presented a somewhat slimline figure (five foot eleven, twelve stone ten) he was as tough as old rope and a thumping tackler, courageous to a fault. He also was a keen student of tactics, with unorthodox touches to his style which made him all the more difficult to mark, and he was always supremely fit and very alert to the possibility of tactical advantage.

It was testimony to his remarkable fitness and application that, at the age of thirty-six, he yet should be in Ireland's two shock test wins over Australia in 1979. At one time Gibson held the world record of eighty-one test appearances – sixty-nine for Ireland, twelve for the British Lions – and he remains Ireland's most capped player and is regarded by many as Ireland's greatest. He was awarded an MBE for his services to the game and was inducted into the International Rugby Hall of Fame in 1997.

When Ireland sent a Sevens squad to the World Sevens at Murrayfield in 1979 they played Gibson at scrum-half. Needless to say he played there as to the manner born and was hugely instrumental in an underrated Ireland side reaching the final. That was the day when Ireland had just thrown a team together, and they nevertheless got to the final and gave the English team a real battle. And they hadn't done any training at all. It was Willie Duggan who said on that occasion, 'If we ever take this game seriously we'll make a real apple crumble of it!'

GERALD DAVIES (1966–78)
Cardiff, London Welsh, Wales, British Lions
46 Wales caps
4 British Lions tests

With pattering footsteps, wonderful control of body movement and deceptive pace change, Thomas Gerald Reames Davies proved one of the most gifted and elusive wings ever to decorate the Welsh game, and one who earned the total respect of New Zealanders, notably during the British Lions 1971 tour down under.

I first marvelled at the Davies magic when covering the Scottish Borders seven-a-side circuit in the earlier 1960s, as well as the Middlesex sevens at Twickenham, when Gerald Davies proved a short-game natural in the successful Welsh college Sevens of that era. Even in those early days Gerald Davies hinted at being destined for great deeds because he had all the equipment required by an international wing, albeit when I first saw him in action it was as a centre three-quarter. All his gifts were already on display.

Gerald had a delightful way of expressing himself as well. Once when he contributed to a try against Scotland by Terry Cobner I suggested that the try should have been disallowed as Gerald had played the ball instead of releasing it after a tackle. 'Oh,' he said in somewhat pained response, all innocence, 'that wasn't quite my impression!'

He was the kind of wing you hoped you'd never have to mark because he could work miracles of elusiveness even in close or cluttered confines, and there was in his armoury a cheeky little chip ahead that caused all kinds of panic buttons to be pressed whenever he took off. I remember one such effort that brought the house down at Cardiff in 1972 as it led to a Davies try in the 35–12 defeat of Scotland.

But perhaps his most memorable game was at Murrayfield in 1971 with Wales heading for a Grand Slam but down to Scotland by 14–18. With time almost up Delme Thomas won a lineout deflection inside Scotland's 25. JPR Williams intruded into the line, and Gerald Davies scooted home and tried to get as close to the posts as possible to make the goal-kick easier. It still was a tester of a goal-kick from out on the right touchline, but John Taylor piloted it home for a quite dramatic Welsh win by 19–18.

That try came from a move they had practised and practised, but practice makes perfect, and when the pressure was on everything came together. This was regarded by many as one of the greatest games ever played, and it was the admirable Welsh commentator Alun Williams who said afterwards: 'When I think of 1918 I will think not of the Great War but of this great game of rugby.' I was on commentary duty that day and my Scottish disappointment was tinged with admiration for a superb Welsh score by a great Welsh side.

Nevertheless I could have shot him with a double-barrelled shotgun, both barrels! But that was a great side, no doubt about it. Carwyn James the coach had a strong influence, of course, with his power to make the Welsh players believe in themselves, and he was also a great tactician. But the fact was that all at once from 1969 to 1979 the Welsh had seven or eight world class players who all came together at the same time and just gelled brilliantly. It was a coincidence, really. But it could happen again. That was a halcyon era and a delight to commentate on, no doubt about it. That Welsh side just carried the commentary along because of the sheer open quality of their play – it was total rugby, players interchanged roles so memorably. It was a lovely time for Welsh people.

In all Gerald Davies scored twenty tries for Wales in forty-six internationals, a record he shared with the inimitable Gareth Edwards until Ieuan Evans raised the mark to thirty-three tries in his seventy-two internationals. I would put Gerald in my World XV without a moment's doubt.

BARRY JOHN (1966–72)
Cardiff, Wales, British Lions
25 Wales caps
5 British Lions tests

There wasn't an awful lot of Barry John, and at five foot nine and eleven stone eleven, he would never rate as one of the greatest bone-crushing tacklers in the rugby union game; but he was a crafty operator who could shepherd opposing ball-carriers into the lanes he wanted them to run, and he was gifted in so many other areas as to have earned the nickname 'the King', following his wondrous exploits with the Lions in Australia and New Zealand in 1971. Many people claim – and not a few New Zealanders among them – that John permanently changed the All Blacks' approach to the game after that tour. It has been said of him that he dominated British rugby at a time when British rugby dominated the world.

Barry John didn't seem so much to run as to float over even the most treacherous surfaces, and he had a deceptive sway of the hips, and a way of offering the ball, that very frequently deceived opposing defenders. He also had punt control that could land the ball on a sixpence, and a command of pace and direction of pass that helped colleagues to reach their potential.

Phil Bennett, his successor as stand-off in that golden decade of Welsh rugby, the 1970s, said of him: 'King John was a one-off genius. He had an arrogance which put him in a class apart from his contemporaries, but it was arrogance in the right manner, a self-belief that gave him the confidence to try things that other players simply would not imagine.'

He proved a crucial element and a brilliant orchestrator in one of the most effective half-back partnerships of all time with Gareth Edwards, and they were at the heart of some of the most memorable achievements by Cardiff, Wales and the British Lions.

When they came together as a ham-and-eggs partnership,

113

Edwards was concerned to provide a safe service to his partner, who however put him at ease with the assurance, 'Don't worry, Gareth, you just pass it, and I'll catch it.' He almost always did so with a quiet confidence that was not boastful but which proved a source of inspiration to colleagues.

Nor was he any form of drilled robot. Rather, he seemed to make it up as he went along, with a quiet faith in his abilities, and he could torture opponents by exploiting their weaknesses, as in the case of the New Zealand full-back Fergie McCormick. In the first test in 1971 John put McCormick to the sword with a series of huge garry-owens and agonisingly out of reach touches that destroyed the All Black's confidence to the extent that he was never selected to play in another test. Barry John was that kind of player.

He partnered Edwards in twenty-three major internationals over a six-year period, during which Wales won a Grand Slam in 1971, Championships in 1969 and 1971, and a Championship share in 1970, as well as Triple Crowns in 1969 and 1971. Capped first against Australia at Cardiff in December 1966, he gained twenty-five Welsh caps and scored ninety points, which was a Welsh Championship record.

He also played five tests for the British Lions, and he scored thirty points in the four tests against New Zealand in 1971. In all games on that tour he registered 188 points, which was double the previous mark for a Lions tour. His other Lions test was in South Africa in 1968, when he suffered collarbone damage that denied him the opportunity of demonstrating his wonderful skills to South African rugby folk. Few in the game would argue with the choice of Barry John as stand-off in arguably the most gifted Lions back division of all time: JPR Williams, TGR Davies, J Dawes, CMH Gibson, DJ Duckham, B John, and GO Edwards. What an outfit!

My decision not to select Barry John as stand-off in a World XV of all-time greats stirred up a hornets' nest, especially among Welsh supporters. One wrote: 'Imagine an outside-half with priceless tem-

Prop Ian McLauchlan, Scotland's 'Mighty Mouse', takes on Natal during the sensational Lions tour of 1974, when he regularly out-scrummaged far bigger players. He could also shift, and handle with the best.

Gerald Davies, the most gifted wing I've ever seen, who could come off either foot in a blink, held a Welsh record for tries. Here he is on the way to yet another try against England in 1971.

Mervyn Davies, for me the greatest loose forward of them all, out-jumps Christian Carrère to win valuable lineout ball against the French in Wales's 1971 Grand Slam victory in Paris.

Barry John of Wales demonstrates his ability to punt to touch with his left foot too! Mervyn Davies is in close support.

Gareth Edwards, the dominant figure in Wales' halcyon days in the 1970s, stretches for a try against Scotland in 1978. This was the last of Edwards' twenty international tries. Wales won 22–14.

David Duckham, Coventry and England wing, sizzles off his left foot in seeking to evade Bryan Williams (Auckland) in the England–New Zealand game at Twickenham on 6 January 1973.

JPR Williams, the majestic Wales full-back, and a doctor who made a practice of opening up opposing defences with his clinical intrusions, takes on the Scots at Cardiff, 1976.

Fergus Slattery, the Ireland and Lions flanker – and one of my all-time greats – is playing for the Barbarians here, and creating his usual mayhem.

Scotland's Andy Irvine evades a Welsh tackler in the 1977 international at Murrayfield. For me, Irvine was one of the game's greatest entertainers.

Captain Courageous! Bill Beaumont, England's inspirational captain, leads from the front in a dour match during the Argentine tour of 1981.

Colin Deans, Hawick and Scotland, was not only the fastest hooker of his time, but also worked hard to achieve accuracy in lineout throwing and very seldom missed his target.

John Rutherford, Scotland's influential fly-half of the 1980s, scatters the Irish with a booming punt during the 1984 international. Behind him is scrum-half Roy Laidlaw – the other half of a ham-and-eggs partnership.

Phillippe Sella of France, the most capped player of all time with 111, breaks through Welsh lines in the 1986 international at Cardiff.

Ollie Campbell, Ireland's extraordinary points machine, thumped over six penalties and a drop goal – all of Ireland's points – in this 21–12 victory over Scotland in 1982. It was the most amazing display of goal-kicking in adverse conditions that I have ever seen.

Serge Blanco, perhaps the most swashbuckling French rugby player of all time, and one of the great attacking full-backs, captains France in the unforgettable World Cup quarter-final against England in Paris, 1991.

perament, able to sidestep off a knife edge, run the finest angles, drop or kick goals with either foot, find touch on a sixpence, score or create great tries. Imagine Barry John!'

GARETH EDWARDS (1967–78)
Cardiff, Wales, British Lions
53 Wales caps
12 British Lions tests

It was on the Friday prior to a Scotland v Wales game at Murrayfield that Gareth Edwards, who was due to share the BBC television commentary of the game, was enjoying his second great passion, trout-fishing, just below the bridge in Kelso in the Scottish Border country. Two Welsh supporters, bedecked in red and white almost from head to foot, leaned over the bridge and enquired of Gareth: 'Hya Gar, what you doin' down there?' Whereupon Gareth looked up with a broad smile and replied: 'I'm signing bloody autographs, in't I?'

Gareth loved his angling. Gareth's father told him he lost form towards the end of the season because his legs got rusty from standing knee-deep in the water with his rod and line. And Gareth once said to me that he would rather play and outlast a sixteen-pound salmon than score a try for Wales. I'm not sure that he really meant that but I know that the thrill of the bite and subsequent challenge to outwit his prey gave him immense pleasure. In that, as on the rugby field, he was every inch the competitor who used every device in the search for success.

Gareth Edwards was the most formidable scrum-half I ever have seen, with the muscular frame of the physical education specialist that he was, with impressive upper body strength, a powerful frame, a hand-off like a trip hammer, punt control, and a relish for tilting his lance at all comers. He also had a low centre of gravity so that he was a hard man to torpedo, especially when he was going at full lick.

Gareth formed a gifted partnership with Barry John, not least in twenty-three tests for Wales and five for the British Lions, and he later developed a potent liaison with the gifted Phil Bennett. That was in my opinion at the heart of that tremendous Lions test success against the Springboks in 1974.

The Edwards career has been littered with records of all shapes and sizes. He was just nineteen when capped first against France in 1967. He played a record fifty-three Welsh internationals in a row, shared with Gerald Davies the Welsh record of twenty international tries until that mark was exceeded by Ieuan Evans (thirty-three tries in seventy-two internationals) and Gareth Thomas (twenty-nine tries in sixty-six internationals). He was the youngest Welsh captain at twenty years and seven months, and he led his country in thirteen major internationals. He was a dominant figure in the Welsh halcyon era that spawned three Grand Slams, seven Championships and five Triple Crowns.

Gareth Edwards of course will long be remembered for that amazing try he scored for the Barbarians against the touring All Blacks in 1973 when he launched a move deep in his own half and was on his feet and at top speed in just seconds to miraculously be in position miles upfield to take the scoring pass from Derek Quinnell. It has been rated the greatest try of them all. Yet there are many Scots who would point to the try he scored against Scotland at Cardiff in 1972 as the most spectacular of all, when from a lineout in the Welsh 22 he erupted, punted ahead and won the race for the touch at the corner, then ran back downfield, mud-bespattered from head to foot to the thunderous applause of Welsh and Scots alike.

And to think that he could have played soccer for Swansea Town, who were keen to have him on their books, and he also had been the

All England Schools 200 metres hurdles champion. Gareth Owen Edwards – a talent and a half! He also developed a taste for Hawick Balls, a mint sweet manufactured in my home town, and I used to take him a tin of them whenever I was on commentary duty in Cardiff. Indeed, I made the point to him that he never would have come near to twenty tries for Wales if he hadn't boosted his strength with those delicious Hawick sweetmeats! Gerald Davies liked them too. Maybe if I hadn't introduced them to Hawick balls they might not have scored those tries against Scotland!

PHIL BENNETT (1969–78)
Llanelli, Wales, British Lions
29 Wales caps
8 British Lions caps

'This has to be the try of the Championship!' Those were my words in a BBC commentary of the Scotland v Wales game at Murrayfield in 1977 when Phil Bennett, with another of his famous flashing sidesteps, cut inside Scotland's covering defence to scuttle home from forty yards for a quite brilliant try that launched Wales towards victory by 18–9. That sidestep had the Bennett copyright. Who can forget that sequence of flashing sidesteps that bamboozled the 1973 touring All Blacks and set alight that sizzling move for the Gareth Edwards try for the Barbarians, described by some as the greatest try of them all?

Bennett, a modest fellow who let his play do the talking, was a superbly equipped stand-off, versatile enough to be played by Wales as a wing and centre as well. When Barry John's residence as Welsh pivot came to an end in 1972, it said a great deal for Bennett's application and determination that he was able to succeed such a talent as Barry John's, and to make just as big an impact.

Bennett had safe hands and a variety of punt, and once slotted two drop goals in the 26–9 defeat of the Springboks in the third Lions test in 1974. Bennett also had wonderful control of pace so that he could change gear with no apparent effort, and his gift for sniffing out space was a major factor in his instinctive support play.

An OBE with twenty-nine caps and eight Lions tests, he was capped first as a replacement against France in 1969, and went on to captain Wales in the 1977 Championship and the 1978 Grand Slam. He amassed 166 points in his twenty-nine cap internationals, from four tries, eighteen conversions, thirty-six penalty goals and two drop goals.

It was in South Africa with the Lions in 1974 that Phil Bennett reached genuine world class status, when he played in eleven of the twenty-two games, all four tests, and was second top scorer to Andy Irvine with 103, of which twenty-six were scored in the victorious test series. He is still remembered in South Africa, not only for his points-scoring but also for his searing breaks, not least his marvellous fifty-yard scoring run in the 28–9 second test defeat of the Springboks.

In 1975, the Welsh selectors saw fit to drop him initially, and in the 1975–76 season he was not even named as a replacement. However, he inevitably regained his place, and in 1977 became only the second Welshman to skipper a Lions tour, having captained Wales throughout the season. That rain-drenched tour in Australia and New Zealand was disappointing, and Bennett's confidence dipped, affecting his game to some extent. But all the same he finished top scorer with 125 points, playing fifteen of twenty-six games and all four tests. He retired from international rugby in 1978.

MERVYN DAVIES (1969–76)

London Welsh, Swansea, Wales, British Lions
38 Wales caps
8 British Lions tests

From his first cap against Scotland in 1969 to his last against France
in 1976, Thomas Mervyn Davies OBE, known affectionately as
Merv the Swerve, played in thirty-eight consecutive internationals,
having emerged as a slimline twenty-two-year-old from the London
Welsh sides of the 1960s to establish himself in the hearts of many
rugby adherents as the greatest loose forward of them all. An
obvious class act, I had little hesitation in picking him as my No 8
in the World XV I was invited in 2001 to select for *The Times*.

Certainly he gave magnificent service to Welsh international
sides, notably in five Championship-winning outfits and also as
captain of Wales in the 1975 Championship and in the 1976 Grand
Slam. He also was a key figure in the most successful Lions tours of
New Zealand in 1971 and South Africa in 1974, when he played in
twenty-five of forty-eight games and in all the tests. That great New
Zealand legend Colin Meads nominated Davies and Ireland's Mike
Gibson as the most influential figures in the Lions' historic success
in New Zealand in 1971.

Davies was a magnificent all-purpose loose forward with admirable
discipline and total commitment, who excelled in providing high-class
ball from the tail of the lineout, and whose tidying and service work at
the scrummage base was enormously productive. For Wales and the
Lions he created a splendid alliance with scrum-half Gareth Edwards,
who has himself spoken of the huge contribution Davies made to the
success enjoyed by all the scrum-halves fortunate enough to work with
him.

Although not exactly a racehorse, Davies nonetheless could cover
ground rapidly with his long striding style, and that, allied to his
extraordinary powers of anticipation, frequently got him first to the

breakdown and therefore a sure provider of quality possession. He also didn't hold back in his tackling, which could be ferocious.

Davies played a major role, in company with the likes of JPR, Gerald Davies, Barry John and Gareth Edwards, in what was rated by Welsh supporters as the second Welsh halcyon era of the seventies (the first being the 1950s). In 1975, after his achievements with the Lions in South Africa, he became captain of Wales, leading them to success in two seasons. The whole rugby world was saddened when Davies's playing career came to an end after he suffered a brain haemorrhage during a cup tie in 1976 and had to undergo major surgery. But for that he would almost certainly have captained the Lions in New Zealand in 1977. Of the nine tests in which he did captain Wales, only one was lost.

DAVID DUCKHAM (1969–76)
Coventry, West Midlands, England, British Lions
36 England caps
3 British Lions tests

Among players whose attractive style makes them a commentator's delight I would rate very highly David John Duckham of Coventry, Warwickshire, West Midlands, England and the Lions. There have been few more thrilling sights in the rugby union game, and specially for supporters of England, than that of David Duckham in full flight, blond hair riffling in the wind, and with one arm poised to administer a pulverising hand-off – a weapon which he set alongside a flashing sidestep, persuasive feint pass, and change of pace and direction to render him a highly formidable target for opposing defenders. Duckham was a great sight when in full flow, and taking into account his impressive physical statistics of six foot one and fourteen stone seven, he was a very difficult man to put down. I never saw him lose control of his body movement – a wee wiggle of the hips put him on the right angle and he was gone. For a big man he was very much in control of what he was doing.

Initially in tandem at centre for England ten times with the bulky John Spencer of Headingley, Duckham was switched to wing position on the Lions tour of New Zealand in 1971 and settled to the new task with unfettered enthusiasm and skill. In fact he proved a huge success in arguably the most potent Lions back division ever fielded, comprising JPR Williams, John Bevan, John Dawes, Mike Gibson, David Duckham, Barry John and Gareth Edwards. Duckham took New Zealand by storm, playing in sixteen games, including three of the four tests, and scoring eleven tries, six of them, amazingly, in the one game, the 39–6 defeat of West Coast Buller.

That wasn't the only time he achieved a singular scoring feat. He once romped home for five tries in the Coventry v Fylde game in 1969, and he amassed five more for the Barbarians against Leicester, also in 1969. Capped first against Ireland in Dublin in 1969 he scored a debut try in England's 15–17 defeat; and when he gained his thirty-sixth and last cap against Scotland, at Murrayfield in 1976, he had become the most capped England back of all time and with a tally of ten international tries. His standing in New Zealand became even higher when he captained West Midlands to a 16–8 defeat of the touring 1972 All Blacks. He also captained Coventry, Warwickshire and the Barbarians. And yet throughout his career he had notoriously poor possession – it's calculated that in his thirty-six internationals he received an average of fewer than three passes per match. Needless to say, he would go looking for the ball if it didn't come to him.

In all he was capped thirteen times as centre and twenty-three as wing, and never were his splendid all-round qualities more significantly demonstrated than by his superb display in the Barbarians' 23–11 defeat of the touring All Blacks in 1973, when David John Duckham once again had New Zealanders gasping in admiration with his flair for attack from the deep and with that hip sway at pace. In that match Duckham played in a back division that included JPR Williams, Mike Gibson, Phil Bennett and Gareth Edwards, all-time greats every one, and yet to some spectators it was Duckham who was the sharpest and most thrilling runner of them all on that day. No wonder that the Welsh crowd chose to call him *Dai* Duckham!

It was another aspect of his play that the ball or the movement seldom died at David Duckham, for he was a gifted link player as well as a lethal finisher. David Duckham always will hold a place in the hearts of all England rugby union adherents as the archetypal England cavalier who had all the ingredients for greatness. He was, as they say, a wing who could truly fly.

IAN McLAUCHLAN (1969–79)
Jordanhill, Scotland, British Lions
43 Scotland caps
8 British Lions tests

When John (Ian) McLauchlan challenged for a cap in 1969, Scottish supporters looked with disbelief at this tubby little fellow who, at five foot nine and thirteen stone and ten pounds, seemed too small to take on the rigours of scrummaging, driving, and support play at the highest level. He proved them all wrong by establishing himself as one of the most successful loose-head prop forwards ever fielded by Scotland, with a strength and technical knowledge that enabled him to hold his own, and more than hold his own, with opposing prop forwards far bigger than himself.

As we have seen, he owed much of this ability to take on bigger men successfully to his mentor Bill Dickinson, who coached McLauchlan when he was a physical education student at Jordanhill

College in Glasgow, and later guided McLauchlan's fortunes as the first official coach to Scotland's national squad. Dickinson was a scrummaging expert, who knew how to ease pressure and how to exert pressure, so that McLauchlan, a tough fellow from out of Tarbolton in Ayrshire on Scotland's west coast, was able to give far bigger opponents a really hard time. This he could do because he had built up his own strength with weight training and thus could bury opposing tight-heads, or send them skywards, in days when a certain amount of licence was permitted front-row denizens.

McLauchlan however was not just a scrummager, but a prop with pace and good hands, and with sound positional sense that frequently got him into support and pressure roles, as when he scored a charge-down try in the first Lions test against New Zealand in 1971. Nicknamed 'Mighty Mouse' for his extraordinary feats on that Lions tour, McLauchlan, whose forty-three Scottish caps covered the decade 1969–79, captained Scotland in a record nineteen tests, of which ten were won, and put steel into the Scottish forward effort during his reign by his own approach and uncompromising attitude. 'Do that again, son, and I'll fill you in!' was one bit of advice proffered to an international opponent who had gone over the score.

On the two most successful Lions tours, to Australia and New Zealand in 1971 and South Africa in 1974, McLauchlan astonished the locals by his scrummage efficiency and by his mobility about the pitch, as well as his ability to step up his game whenever the opposition challenge presented itself. He relished battle and undoubtedly proved one of the most successful combatants of his time.

On that 1974 Lions tour of South Africa McLauchlan's scrummaging superiority over larger opponents – and some of those Springboks were giants – enabled him on occasion to hoist them clean off the ground. McLauchlan was also an awkward shape, which made scrummaging opposite him a difficult proposition, and because of his strength he was able to place huge pressure on his opposite number in the scrummage or force him to scrummage at awkward heights.

JPR WILLIAMS (1969–81)

London Welsh, Bridgend, Wales, British Lions
55 Wales caps
8 British Lions tests

I was watching the Welsh squad at their Friday training session before their home match against Scotland. It was a foul day, with the wind howling and the rain beating down. The forecast for the match day was just as bad. As they completed their preparations and left the field I suggested to JPR Williams the full-back that it would be a severe test of his skill and concentration if the conditions were as bad on the morrow.

'Well, Bill,' he said, 'if someone drops the ball you'll know it isn't me!'

At the time I thought that was very cocky, considering how evil the conditions were likely to be. Yet in the actual game JPR didn't mishandle a single ball, even when the Scots got after him with a series of clever punts. That was JPR, confident and highly competitive, and one of the most physical backs I've ever come across. He seemed to revel in the unsavoury chores of tackle, fall, jump and catch, frequently with enemy hoofbeats pounding in his ears.

He was never quite as sharp in acceleration as, say, an Andy Irvine or a Christian Cullen, yet JPR was no slouch and presented a formidable physical threat at fourteen and a half stone, as well as a sure grasp of the basic skills, and an acute sense of what was on. That physical presence never was more marked than in the relish with which he sailed into tackles and by the zest in which he took on the role of prop forward in the London Welsh Sevens. On one famous occasion in 1976 he shoulder-charged a flat-out Jean-François Gourdon, the French full-back and wing, with a form of engagement that shook the rafters, sent Gourdon flying into touch, and gave that big son of France the impression that the sky had fallen in. Of course nowadays that would be regarded as dangerous play and open to penalty. But it saved the Grand Slam for Wales and put Monsieur Gourdon into the third row of the National Stadium.

JPR had an uncanny positional sense by which, for example, he registered six international tries, five against England, including two in the 21–9 Welsh win at Twickenham in 1976. A year earlier the Japanese had been fed up with the sight of him as he thundered home for three tries in the 87–6 Welsh win in Tokyo. And when Wales needed someone to fill in as a flanker against Australia in 1978 JPR stepped forward and got himself stuck into the role as if he had been a flanker all his rugby life.

That was one occasion in his fifty-five Welsh caps when he was not at full-back. JPR was one of the finest full-backs to reap advantage from the Australian dispensation that so encouraged full-backs into attack mode. Although no flying machine JPR yet exploited that area of rugby law quite brilliantly because he set a zest for counter-attack alongside clever assessment of when and where to make his intrusion. He never hesitated to come into the line at full blast, and once went over for a try against England with two men on his back.

JPR remains the most capped Welsh full-back and always will be remembered as a splendid all-purpose operator with immense courage and application. He could drop goals too, as for the Lions in the final test against New Zealand in 1971. The score 14–14. The series won!

JPR Williams in his own words

The 1971 Wales Grand Slam

The home matches were against England and Ireland, and these were won fairly easily. The away games, however, were full of incident and remain much more of a memory to me. In the Scotland game we seemed to be in control until the Scots hit back with two quick tries, one from the front of a lineout and the other from a charged down clearance kick ... The Scottish captain, Peter Brown, who had been kicking goals all day, unaccountably missed the conversion, which meant we were four points behind, not six. I remember thinking at the time that that would prove a costly miss, and I was right.

We came back with only five minutes to go and forced a lineout in the Scottish twenty-five. Delme Thomas leaped high (was there help from Denzil Williams?) and the ball was spun out quickly to the three-quarters. I came into the line and the ball was in Gerald Davies's hands. I could see that the Scottish full-back, Ian Smith, was not far enough across and Gerald had little difficulty in scoring far out to the right. So it all depended on the conversion, and a difficult one it was too. JT [John Taylor], who kicked around the corner with his left foot, strode up to take the kick, looking full of confidence. However, even JT admitted afterwards that he was nervous. There was a deathly hush as the ball sped on its way. Then the touch judge flags were raised and you could almost hear Bill McLaren's gasp of despair in the commentary box. No wonder it was called the 'greatest conversion since St Paul'!

Again, on reflection, I can remember thinking confidently that JT would put it over. Why I don't know, but perhaps that summed up the great spirit and confidence that the players in the team had in each other.

There was just France to go. This is where we had come unstuck in 1969, and what a pressure game it turned out to be. The French had most of the territorial advantage and were pounding away on our line. I pulled off a tackle on their right wing, Roger Bougarel, and then they came again. JT was coming across and I could see he had Bougarel covered. I suddenly decided that he was going to pass. I don't know what made me do it but I went for the interception, something I never do usually. Probably because of the previous tackle, Bougarel had decided not to take me on again. Anyway, suddenly I was in possession, running towards the French line. I had breached the first line of defence but could see the opposite centre and wing coming across. Denzil Williams was up with me somehow, but I was leaving him behind – after all he was a prop. I realized I was running out of time as I was being caught by the two French defenders. At the last minute I caught a glimpse of Gareth Edwards out of the corner of my eye. How he had got there I never will know. So I jinked in-field to check the two defenders and threw a big pass out to Gareth, going at full speed for the corner. He just made it and we had scored three points instead of having at least three scored against us. It was interesting seeing that try on film, and observing just how much Gareth was carrying his leg, for it was at this stage of his career that he was having so much trouble with his hamstring. This was especially so later that year in New Zealand, though he suffered less as the years went by. We all said it was rust from spending so much time in the water, fishing!

The rest of the match saw continual pressure from France, although we managed to get a further six points. They scored one converted try from Dauga and so the score was 9–5 when BJ [Barry John] felled Dauga with an amazing tackle in front of the posts. Barry was not renowned for his tackling, especially against big forwards, and he sustained a broken nose in the collision. Some of the lads teased him that his nose had got in the way and brought Dauga to the ground. There was one more tremendous tackle from John Bevan, again a last ditch affair and then the whistle went – we had won the grand slam!

(From JPR Williams, *JPR, an Autobiography*, William Collins Sons & Co Ltd, 1979)

FERGUS SLATTERY (1970–84)

University College Dublin, Blackrock, Ireland,
British Lions
61 Ireland caps
4 British Lions tests

If ever there was an open-side flanker who, in modern word usage, 'played right up in the faces of the opposition', then surely that was John Fergus Slattery of UCD, Blackrock College, Ireland and the Lions. He was a hard man and, although he could make short, sharp, humorous comments, there was definitely this hard, almost gangsterish side to him, no doubt about it. A 'master of mayhem', he was my choice as open-side flanker for my all-time great *Times* XV.

Throughout a career that spanned sixty-five tests, sixty-one for Ireland, four for the Lions, Slattery was always supremely fit, and was therefore to be found champing all over the pitch in the closing stages as much as he had been when fresh at the kick-off. He was a lot more skilful than some folk gave him credit for, a very good link player, and because of his fitness he was often there when others weren't. But it was that hard edge of his that made him so special.

Certainly Phil Bennett, the great Llanelli, Wales and Lions stand-off, once made the point that he would rather play against any other open-side flanker than 'Slats', as he was called, and Hannes Marais, the South African captain for the Lions tour there in 1974, expressed the view that Slattery was the most effective of the Lions loose forwards and created havoc amongst the South African backs.

Capped first against South Africa in Dublin in January 1970, Slattery was a physically hard six foot one and fourteen stone seven with an edge of pace and a positional sense that rendered him a magnificent support player as well as one who was totally uncompromising, as underlined by the relish with which he thumped into his tackles. At one time the most capped flanker in the world, along with England's Peter Winterbottom, Slattery read the game cleverly and gave wonderful service to the Irish cause, forming, with Willie Duggan and John O'Driscoll, Ireland's loose forward trio in nineteen major internationals.

In 1973 Slattery played a key role in the Irish side which held the All Blacks to a 10–10 draw in Dublin, denying them a Grand Slam. He was then selected for the Barbarians against the All Blacks at Cardiff Arms Park, the match made famous by Gareth Edwards' opening try. Slattery scored a try of his own, and it was his final pass to JPR Williams that enabled the full-back to score near the end. Not surprisingly he was on the two most successful tours by the Lions: Australia/New Zealand in 1971 when he played in thirteen of the twenty games, and then, at the peak of his career, in the unbeaten Lions squad in South Africa in 1974.

On that tour he played in twelve of the twenty-two games, including all four tests, and scored six tries. It was also on the 1974 tour that Slattery was involved in a dramatic situation when the Lions needed to win the last test for an unprecedented clean sweep of the test series. With the score 13–13 Slattery drove over the South African line for a try, only for it to be disallowed by referee Max Baise. But the Lions had no doubt that it *was* a try and that Slattery had been deprived of a much deserved climax to a hugely successful career.

Slattery also captained Ireland seventeen times between 1979 and 1981, and with notable success as Ireland's captain in their tour series win in Australia in 1979, against a side who had dispatched both England and Wales in recent seasons. At the beginning of 1984 he was thirty-four years old when he played in his last international, bowing out against France in Paris, his thirty-third consecutive match since the 21–18 defeat by Scotland at Murrayfield in 1977.

FRAN COTTON (1971–81)

Loughborough College, Coventry, Sale, England,
British Lions
31 England caps
7 British Lions tests

He was nicknamed Noddy because he liked his kip, but there was nothing sleepy about his performance on the field. For Francis Edward Cotton was in every sense a competitor, and one who could claim special gifts not always given to prop forwards. I became aware of those special gifts when I saw the contribution he made to a seven-a-side game for the outstanding Loughborough College squad, and also for the England side which won the world Sevens tournament at Murrayfield in 1973 under his captaincy with victory over Ireland in the final.

On the Sevens field Cotton appeared completely at home in the exposed areas, for Sevens emphasised firstly his adhesive hands, and then his positional sense, and not least that rugged strength and dexterity that enabled him to shine as a ball-provider in the abbreviated version in both scrummage and lineout. As a prop forward in Sevens he showed a lot of the skills you would associate with a flanker.

Cotton was first capped while still a student at Loughborough College. In fifteens he had to do a lot of the donkey work and didn't shine quite as much as on the Sevens field, but there's no doubt that those special gifts that were honed in the Sevens stood him in good stead as a fifteen-a-side forward. In fact he developed as a mighty force, for at six foot two and seventeen stone he was a formidable specimen, physically hard and determinedly competitive. He was probably the finest loose-head of his day, but his technical skill and good rugby brain often made him almost as effective as a tight-head as he was in his normal position of loose-head prop. Moreover, his height gave him an auxiliary ball-winning function at the lineouts, as well as the support role.

Cotton developed into an aggressive and astute scrummager who earned thirty-one caps between 1971 and 1981, and surely would have gained many more but for a suspected heart condition that necessitated his return home from the Lions tour of South Africa in 1980. That had been his third Lions tour following South Africa in 1974, when he played in fourteen of the twenty-two games and in all four tests, and in New Zealand in 1977.

He made a huge impression as a scrummager in the 1974 tour to South Africa, when he took on with relish some very big South African props and hung them up to dry, and gave the Lions a distinct advantage in that area. A quiet, modest giant, Cotton gained his first cap against Scotland in 1971 and his last against Wales in 1981. He linked with Bobby Windsor of Wales and Ian McLauchlan of Scotland to form that formidable Lions front row who made a huge contribution to the Lions unbeaten record over the twenty-two games in South Africa in 1974.

Cotton also shared in England's shock win over New Zealand in Auckland in 1973, in England's Grand Slam of 1980, and in the Barbarians' 13–13 draw with the All Blacks at Twickenham in 1974. I always reckoned he was one of the most skilful prop forwards I've ever seen, as perhaps you would expect from a physical education specialist. He was very special, I must say.

Fran Cotton in his own words

The Lions in South Africa, 1974

British Lions v Springboks: third Test match, 13 July 1974
(The first two of the four Tests had been won by the British Lions.)

The Springboks kicked off with the sun and a gentle breeze behind them. We were forever being told how South African players became superhuman when they put on the green and gold Springbok shirt. For the first twenty-five minutes of this game that theory was justified as they climbed into rucks and mauls as though their lives depended upon it. There is always a period of physical attrition in any Test, but this was fanatical commitment by both teams and for different reasons. One to salvage some pride and self-respect, the other to create history. Both were great motivators.

We were unable to create any rhythm in our game with even Gareth [Edwards] having kicks charged down or unbelievably missing touch. This meant we were under constant pressure inside our own twenty-five. We had never had to cope with sustained pressure like this at any other stage during the tour and I must say that one of the reasons we were able to absorb it was the amount of possession wasted by the Springboks. Sonnekus, the new cap at scrum-half, was giving what is known in the business as a 'dambuster-style' service to his outside-half, Snyman. In other words, he received the ball on the third bounce.

On our first visit into the Springbok half we were awarded a penalty at a scrum and Andy Irvine scored. Snyman immediately replied with a fine drop goal, but within a minute of their equalizing the crucial incident of the match occurred. A ruck formed a few yards from the Lions' goal-line and suddenly Van Heerden, the Springbok lock, raced like a lunatic to stamp on anything with a red shirt on. It was like lighting a powder keg. All hell broke out with both sets of forwards slinging punches from all angles and directions. You could always rely on JPR's support on these occasions and as the fighting subsided he was left there with his feet braced and his fists raised, ready for all-comers. As I turned round there was the instigator of the trouble, Van Heerden, stretched out on the turf.

The whole incident was a disgrace but it was felt necessary to react as a team merely as a means of self-protection. A great deal of rubbish has been said and written about the infamous '99' call and the reason for using it. What happened was, the captain shouted out that number and the team then started a mass brawl. It was only ever intended as a way of bringing the referees' attention to incidents which on frequent occasions in the past they had turned a blind eye to, particularly in South Africa and New Zealand. The attitude was typified in the comment of the referee during the Lions v Canterbury game in 1971, when he informed the Lions' captain that from now on he was only watching the ball and anything else was the captains' responsibility to sort out. The Lions lost three potential Test players in that game and it was their determination to prevent that ever happening again which resulted in the '99'. Quite rightly, the same attitude prevailed in 1974.

From that moment on, the brave early effort of the Springboks evaporated and it soon became apparent that some of the forwards had lost their stomach for battle. Within minutes the Lions swept down the field and Gordon Brown scored from a short lineout, two yards from the Springboks' line. That in effect was game, set and match.

The second-half performance by the Lions was some of the finest rugby I have ever had the privilege to be part of. It was played with total commitment, unwavering concentration, absolute control and support in every phase of play. JJ Williams scorched in for two glorious tries, both from free-flowing three-quarter movements. The game and series was summed up by the last score when Mervyn Davies held the ball at the back of a scrum. Gareth dummied to go one way, then the other, eventually deciding to attack the blind side, only to throw a 25-yard reverse pass to Benny [Phil Bennett] who cool as a cucumber dropped a goal.

The final whistle blew in a 26 points to 9 victory for the Lions, giving us an unassailable 3–0 lead in the Test series. History had indeed been made as we became the only touring team this century to win a four-match series in South Africa.

(From *Fran Cotton, an Autobiography*, Queen Anne Press, Macdonald Futura Publishers Ltd, 1981)

ANDY IRVINE (1972–82)
Heriot's FP, Scotland, British Lions
51 Scotland caps
9 British Lions tests

Andy Irvine was a cavalier of a player who wasn't enamoured of tight defensive rugby football and a lot of touch-kicking. You'll find plenty of people ready to point a finger at Irvine's defensive capabilities, and certainly if you were comparing him with JPR Williams, solely from a defence point of view, then JPR would get the nod. When I recently picked a World side, and chose Irvine at full-back, I got a lot of criticism from some quarters, particularly from my Welsh friends.

JPR Williams was certainly the finest full-back defensively that could be found – he was so physical, and he never held back – whereas Irvine was more the type of fellow who would be thinking, as the ball was coming down from about 200 feet, what he was going to do with it when he got it. And that was why, sometimes, he was subject to error which gave Scots heart failure! But I have seen Irvine with his club, Heriot's FP, and in the district championship, and with Scotland and the Barbarians, and for me he was one of the greatest entertainers in the game because he wanted to run with the ball in an adventurous style.

He had extraordinary pace, off a standing start, and that was another of his great qualities, quite apart from the fact that he was a gifted footballer with safe hands, and a wonderful kicker off either foot. He not only had that flaring pace, but he delighted in using it, and so for me Andrew Robertson Irvine of Heriot's FP and Scotland is certainly one of the top boys, especially from an entertainment point of view. And did he entertain! I can still hear the crowd whenever he got the ball. They started shouting before he'd done anything, because they knew that whatever he did it would be something dramatic, spectacular and entertaining.

Irvine wasn't one to savour close defensive rugby, he liked the ball to be moved by hand. His club, Heriot's FP, had a reputation for open play, and he was their greatest player, symbolising Heriot's approach to rugby, which has always been one of flair and adventurism. Irvine certainly had all those qualities. He was someone who could almost single-handedly light up a game and set it aflame with his sheer daring. Nowadays in defence you have your three-man retreat outfit who will go back and clean up, and counter-attack. Well, Irvine was just made for that. He was one of those class players who take your breath away because they don't do what you expect. That for me is what makes rugby football one of the great games, when a player takes you completely by surprise – and takes the other guys in the field by surprise as well! Irvine was one of the top boys in that department, and he was responsible for some of the finest rugby football in an attacking sense that I have ever seen.

Scotland had some very useful forwards about the place during Irvine's time – McLauchlan, Carmichael, McHarg, hard men all – so the Scottish pack wasn't pushed around much. And then of course you had Gordon Brown who was a world class forward, someone who had a little edge and was prepared to stand his ground, and even to throw a punch or two if it was necessary. So Scotland had a very combative pack, and Irvine made very good use of whatever ball they had. He lent a sparkle to Scotland's back division alongside the great half-back combination of Roy Laidlaw and John Rutherford, who were a wonderful pair. They were Borders players – one played for Jedforest and the other for Selkirk – and they got together and worked things out very well, so Irvine did have that advantage. But even without that, when Heriot's were up against it, it would be Irvine as often as not who would pull them through. He was the player who would light the touchpaper, and you were guaranteed thrill upon thrill when he was playing.

Irvine had a great feel for space. He did things in limited space which other players couldn't achieve, partly because he had that wonderful gift of pace off the mark, and also because he could come off either foot. He was a really tricky runner at pace, and that got him out of a number of difficult situations, and then caused all kinds of problems for opposing defences. His defence, too, was fine when he had to do it. He might prefer it to be somebody else, but when he had to do it he would, no doubt at all. You wouldn't catch him falling on the ball, you'd expect him to run fast and swoop the ball up with three fingers of one hand, and off he'd go. But when he had to do the rough stuff he would do it, jumping to catch the high ball and so on. He gave us some scary moments, but they were worth putting up with just for the sheer delight of seeing him in full cry.

In the 1977 British Lions tour of New Zealand he would pick up a ball near his own line and just run it at the New Zealanders. The audacity of it! They had never seen anything like it before. You'd think someone who did a thing like that needed treatment – give him an injection and he'd be all right again – but Andy Irvine was prepared to take them on, and he did. The New Zealanders still thought in terms of, 'Let's get the bloody forwards right, mate' – eight big solid citizens who would sort you out as soon as look at you, and let the rest of it take care of itself. But even they treated Irvine with considerable awe. He would run from all kinds of crazy places, but he had real faith in his own skill and manoeuvrability.

Irvine had a marvellous capacity to get into top gear in about three strides. If you can do that you can make an awful lot of opponents sit and wonder what's going on: one minute he'd be there, and the next he'd be gone – one blink and he was away. Andy Irvine, the supreme entertainer.

GRAHAM PRICE (1975–83)

Pontypool, Wales, British Lions
41 Wales caps
12 British Lions tests

He was a key member of one of the most feared front-row combines in the history of the game, and a player who most denizens of the front row would rate as the most effective tight-head of all time. Graham Price stood alongside Charlie Faulkner and Bobby Windsor in the Pontypool front row that was nicknamed the Viet Gwent by the entertainer Max Boyce. They were a formidable trio indeed, the first club front row to represent the British Lions when they packed down against the Bay of Plenty in New Zealand, 1977.

Graham Price's contributions were often unseen by the average spectator – but certainly did not pass unnoticed by opposing loose-heads. He was a genuine strong man, but one who played fair, and let his strength and dogged application speak for him. He was very quiet, but what a grinding scrummager he was. Nothing bothered Graham Price, whatever kind of fellow they put against him. He just got on and gradually ground him down, pressurised him to bits. And as far as I can see he did it fair and square. Just shifting a shoulder, a bit more squeeze on, a wee bit pulled down, but nothing that would horrify you! He was just a right, good, solid, strong Welsh prop forward. And his hands weren't at all bad either.

On his debut cap appearance against France in the Parc des Princes in 1975 he scored a spectacular long-range try with a hack-and-chase effort over seventy yards, which piloted Wales to a 25–10 win. It was a startling score by a prop forward, in heavy, sticky conditions. I can still see that hack and chase – it was almost in a swamp, and he hoofed it and hoofed it, and just dived on it in the end. People still talk about that try – it's one of those things that are etched in the mind.

Price went on to gain forty-one caps – a Welsh record for a prop

– and he was an ever-present in the twelve tests of three Lions tours: New Zealand in 1977 and 1983, and South Africa in 1980.

In 1978 Price had his jaw broken in a test against Australia, but the liquid diet which followed was accepted with typical courage and no complaint. A quiet, strong man was Pricey, a favourite son of Gwent, where they revere their prop forwards, and in Graham Price they could claim one of the very best, who more than held his own with strong men from northern and southern hemispheres.

Price retired from the international scene in 1983 when he was thirty-three, but he kept on playing, and he played for Pontypool against New Zealand as a thirty-eight-year-old. They'd say you needed treatment if you did a thing like that!

JEAN-PIERRE RIVES (1975–84)
Toulouse, Racing Club de France, France
59 caps

He seemed an unlikely rugby union type, smallish at five foot ten and twelve stone twelve, with a mass of blond curly hair, and almost always with blood and/or mud to colour his features. He also was an utterly charming personality – off the field. But on it Jean-Pierre Rives, the French flanker, was a hard, totally committed competitor who was prepared to take all the roughing up from opponents intent on curbing his effectiveness in order to further his country's cause.

Rives was a key figure in arguably the best balanced loose-forward trio ever fielded by France: Jean-Claude Skrela, Jean-Pierre Bastiat, and Rives. They featured in eighteen internationals together, with Rives proving not only notably quick but also able to put opponents into reverse with the ferocity of his tackling. He harassed opposing backs into error and was prepared to put his body on the line in order to claim usable ball for his side. It was Skrela who described his as 'a phenomenon, quite unlike any other player in France or indeed the world at that time. He was so fast, so courageous – there will never be another quite like him.'

Such was his allure that a generation of English schoolboys wanted to be French. In his autobiography the English open-side flanker Neil Back has written: 'I had always admired Jean-Pierre Rives and remember watching him in that fabulous French side as a kid. He was so arrogant and so talented. He was also blond, like me. It seemed only natural that I should switch to his position from scrum-half.'

Rives claimed the first of his fifty-nine caps in the 27–20 defeat of England in 1975, having gained national experience at Schools, Junior, Students, Universities, and Under-23 level, as well as playing for France B when just nineteen in 1971. He made a very special impression on my countrymen in his second cap appearance in 1975 with a notable display of pitch coverage that was to become the hallmark of his style.

Having featured in France's Grand Slam of 1977 he captained his country to their 1981 Grand Slam – one of the highlights of his thirty-four tests as captain. Another high point was his leadership of France in their 24–19 victory, by four tries to two, over the All Blacks in New Zealand in 1979 – an event which occurred on 14 July, France's Bastille Day.

Eleven of Rives's first thirteen tests ended in victory, and he demonstrated his courage in Sydney in 1981 when, having dislocated a shoulder in the first test against Australia, he actually played in the second test despite considerable discomfort.

Rives proved an inspirational captain, an astute tactician, and a man of strong will who encouraged his playing colleagues into reaching for their full potential. It was indicative also of how he preferred to play the game that, having thoroughly enjoyed his first Barbarians experience in Wales in 1977, he was instrumental in forming the French Barbarians in 1979. No wonder that the whole of France regarded the 1978–84 period as the Rives era.

Jean-Pierre Rives in his own words

The spirit of the Barbarians

In 1977 Jean-Pierre Rives was chosen for the British Barbarians team to play the 1977 British Lions to mark the Silver Jubilee of Queen Elizabeth II. It was just six months after France's controversial grand slam success, achieved by playing a 10-man game that was criticized at the time for its dull and unadventurous approach. After playing in that Barbarians game against the British Lions, which the Lions won 23–14, Rives said:

> It meant a lot of things to me, to play for the Barbarians. This game was very, very special. A special spirit. For me, it was like having passed the church every day, and this one time I went inside. The church of rugby. It was a great honour; an event of great spirit.

From this match would emerge the germ of an idea to launch an equivalent club in France, to be known in years to come as the French Barbarians. Rives, inevitably, was the guiding hand behind its creation; the romantic who fell deeply and hopelessly in love with the spirit and cause of the Barbarian approach to rugby football. The club was founded in August 1979. He said in later years:

> The idea for the French Barbarians came from friendship. We played in that match for the 1977 Silver Jubilee, but also at that time the players in the French Grand Slam team of that year said they wanted some team to carry on such a great spirit. To show the rest of French rugby this example of that special spirit.
>
> It seemed a wonderful prospect to create the French Barbarians, a club which reflected friendship and spirit, the finest parts of our game. So we spoke with our president, Albert Ferrasse, and vice-president, Guy Basquet, and we had great help from the English Barbarians. They

said we had to be very careful to look after the spirit; to keep that special spirit. I am very pleased that a Barbarian rugby club now exists in France because it is something for the future. Now the spirit is improving...

Rugby must cross all barriers; it must pass above them. Like in Ireland. They play together for only a few hours in a winter rugby season, but they do [play], and that crosses barriers. Even those few, brief hours are important, they are a light for others to follow to a better future. Rugby, in that example and many others, has shown it can build bridges, create harmony in a divided world. I believe so strongly in that role for rugby in the future. To show the world, to show politicians and people who believe killing is the only way forward. If rugby can show that to the world, it will have succeeded in its most severe task.

(From Peter Bills, *Jean-Pierre Rives: A Modern Corinthian*, Allen & Unwin, 1986)

GRAHAM MOURIE (1977–82)
Taranaki, New Zealand
21 caps

Graham Neil Kenneth Mourie, an open-side flanker and Taranaki farmer, has been rated alongside Wilson Whineray as the greatest New Zealand captain of them all. And assuredly he made his mark not only as an astute and inspiring leader, but also one prepared to face criticism for his stand against South African participation during the apartheid times. During 1981 Mourie decided not to play against the touring Springboks, a courageous moral stand.

At six foot and thirteen stone eight he was no giant, but as a farmer he always was superbly strong and fit, so that he and his colleagues usually lasted the pace in impressive fashion. As an open-side flanker he made his presence felt in attack, and he also was a devastating tackler with strong anticipatory powers. In the tests against France his tussles with his opposite number, Jean-Pierre Rives, were of the highest quality. But Mourie's greatest contribution was probably as a highly intelligent tactician with the ability to inspire confidence among his colleagues.

Having played with a New Zealand B team in their undefeated tour of Argentina in 1976, Mourie gained his first full cap for the All Blacks against the British Lions in 1977. He captained New Zealand to Italy and France in 1977, and was captain of New Zealand's first ever Grand Slam tour of the Home Unions in 1978. He returned on tour of England, Scotland and Wales in 1979–80 and led New Zealand to their series win against Australia in 1982. Mourie was an outstanding captain whose colleagues never questioned his decisions because they had such faith in him. His record as a captain speaks for itself.

In the Centenary game between New Zealand and Wales at Cardiff in 1980, Cliff Morgan declared, 'Today I saw the greatest forward display the world could ever wish to see.' He was describing Mourie's performance in that match. I can still see the All Black flanker combining with David Loveridge to launch a counter-attacking scoring move over the length of the pitch for a try by Hika Reid, and also a sizzling try by Mourie after his feint pass to a decoy runner. That was Mourie, a non-stop, superbly fit action man.

However, 1982 was Mourie's last playing season, for he was banned in 1982 when he accepted payment for his autobiography, published in that year, thus declaring himself a professional under the rules of those times. He played sixty-one games for various New Zealand sides, and suffered only six defeats. Mourie captained New Zealand in nineteen of the twenty-one tests in which he played between 1977 and 1982, and he impressed with his organisational gifts and tactical sense, which enabled him to adjust tactics to suit the trend during play. Typical of his tacticianship was his manoeuvre in the second French test in 1977. The New Zealand pack had been having a tough time on that tour against the heavy French forwards, who had knocked them about quite a bit in the first test. So Mourie decided to run the puff out of them – it was his idea, with manager Gleeson, to run those big French forwards all around the paddock with short lines and quick tap kicks until they were clear out of gas. Mourie's plan worked. New Zealand won 15–3.

PART FOUR

1980s

**Grand Slams
Partnerships
1984 Wallabies
1988 Wallabies**

_____ *Portraits* _____

GRAND SLAMS

ENGLAND STRUGGLED through most of the 1980s – their one
success being Bill Beaumont's Grand Slam-winning side of
1980. In 1984, Scotland won their first Grand Slam for fifty-nine
years and Ireland in 1985 were deprived of a slam by a 15-15 draw
with France. But for most of the decade it was France who dominated with the superb athleticism of the likes of Blanco and Sella.
They won the title outright three times, including two Grand Slams
in 1981 and 1987.

Little did I realise in 1980, as I watched Bill Beaumont being
chaired from the Murrayfield pitch by triumphant England supporters, that I would later enjoy Bill's company and his good
common sense as rugby union summariser in the BBC commentary box. England had just clinched the Grand Slam for the first
time since 1957, and for the eighth time in all, with victory over
Scotland by 30–18.

Bill showed the same sound judgment as a commentary pundit as he
had done as captain of England in their mighty 1980 series, when they
claimed a huge haul of eighty points in their four Championship games,
with victory over Ireland 24–9 at Twickenham, France 17–13 in Paris,
Wales 9–8 at Twickenham, and Scotland 30–18 at Murrayfield.

Bill Beaumont equalled the record for England captaincy that day
with his thirteenth appointment, and gave such an inspiring performance as to clinch his selection as Lions captain in the following tour
of South Africa. His forwards in particular responded to his lead by
churning back much quality delivery that marked them out as one of
the most effective England packs of all time: Fran Cotton of Sale,

Peter Wheeler of Leicester, Phil Blakeway of Gloucester up front; Bill Beaumont of Fylde and Nigel Horton of Moseley in the boilerhouse; and Roger Uttley of Wasps, John Scott of Cardiff, and Tony Neary of Broughton Park in the back row. Fuelled by that splendid pack, Steve Smith of Sale and John Horton of Bath ran the show – Smith all power and aggression, Horton of the twinkling feet and safe hands.

Against Ireland, England's forwards won the lineouts by twenty to fifteen, and the rucks and mauls by twenty-nine to nineteen. Enough said! Even Ollie Campbell's pinpoint penalty placements on the fifteenth, nineteenth and twenty-first minutes merely delayed the inevitable. There followed England's first ever win in the Parc des Princes, and their first Paris win for sixteen years, with a 17–13 margin that included two timely drop goals by John Horton, who thus underlined the value of this method of scoring. Those two drops took England to a 17–7 lead, and actually were scored when England were down to fourteen players, Roger Uttley having gone off to have his head stitched.

Undoubtedly the highest drama occurred in the Twickenham game against Wales, which was an abrasive affair marked by the ordering off after only fourteen minutes of Paul Ringer of Llanelli, the Welsh flanker, for a dangerous tackle. The referee was David Burnett of Ireland, and Ringer became only the second player to be sent off in an international at Twickenham, following the New Zealander Cyril Brownlie in 1925.

There was more drama to come, for even with their numerical advantage England couldn't cross for a try. But full-back Dusty Hare spared their blushes for, whereas Wales tried four different kickers and failed to convert any of seven goal-kicks, Hare slotted three penalty goals, the last from wide out on the right touchline, allowing England to gain victory by one point in injury time. That winning Hare penalty goal was a magnificent effort as being slotted from his difficult side. It marked only the second win by England over Wales in seventeen years.

However, England went on to claim the Slam in style, with five cracking tries in their 30–18 defeat of Scotland. It was a superb contest at Murrayfield, marked by the three sizzling tries scored by the Orrell wing John Carleton, who demonstrated a keen sense of where the action was going to be. His first try owed much to the sidestep and clean break achieved by the current head coach of England, Clive Woodward of Leicester, and Woodward went on to create another score for that slippery customer Mike Slemen of Liverpool. Carleton's hat trick of tries was the first by an England player since HP Jacob of Blackheath achieved the feat against France at Twickenham in 1924.

At 19–3 at half-time it seemed all over bar the shouting, but to their credit the Scots staged a revival with tries by Alan Tomes of Hawick and John Rutherford of Selkirk. Andy Irvine of Heriot's FP scored ten points to create a new Scottish Championship record of thirty-five points, while Tony Neary became his country's most capped player with forty-three.

Four years later it was the turn of the Scots, for in 1984 Scotland got the Grand Slam, and they thoroughly deserved it. They played some good stuff, and they played some percentage stuff as well. It was the forwards who gave them the launch-pad. Colin Deans was the hooker, a former pupil of mine in Hawick. He was a good, strong boy, hard as nails, and so quick. He is also a very likeable lad – but perhaps I'm biased! He got fifty-two caps, a record for hooker.

That Scotland team was a very well balanced outfit. John Jeffrey at No 6 was another of those 'wind them up set them running' types who would keep going all day. Finlay Calder on the other flank, and Derek White at No 8, made up a potent back row. White was a class act as well, very good at the tail of the lineout. Those were three guys who would just run all day and, allied to the tight five, they had a pack for all seasons.

The French produced some beautiful rugby in the 1980s, with Sella and Blanco strutting their stuff, and little Berbizier running the show from scrum-half. They won Championships galore and two Grand Slams – 1981 and 1987. The French certainly dominated the Five Nations tournaments and played a fluent game that was a pleasure to watch. But to my mind the wonder of the decade came from the southern hemisphere – the Wallabies Mark Ella, Michael Lynagh and, above all, David Campese.

PARTNERSHIPS

I N RUGBY, combinations of players are often as wondrous to behold as individuals. In my half century of commentating I have seen quite a few who have given me enormous pleasure.

Half-backs

Roy Laidlaw and John Rutherford were a famous Scottish half-back partnership from the Borders, and they were neighbours: Jedburgh and Selkirk are only a dozen miles apart, so they were able to pop over and work with each other. The two of them honed a wonderful partnership for Scotland with a fine blend of contrasts. Roy Laidlaw was a tough, nuggety, physically strong little fellow who had an amazing ability to flick out his hips and throw bigger men out of the tackle. And of course he had a dogged determination to do well. John Rutherford was all silken skills, and exuded class. He had wonderful vision, and could comfortably run the show practically without breaking sweat.

Playing in neighbouring clubs is a great help. But there was another famous half-back partnership, Barry John and Gareth Edwards, which was even closer because they played for the same club, Cardiff. Those two were like blood brothers, they could practically read each other's thoughts. They were also both very confident fellows, not cocky – though there was a cocky touch to Barry John sometimes – but they believed in their own ability, and the fact that they played together so often at club level as well as at international level made them a real ham-and-eggs partnership.

Edwards and John were a contrast as well as a blend, providing an amalgam of the great skills and class touches. Gareth was so physically strong, a former physical education specialist with a barrel chest and immense strength in legs and hips. And of course he had that challenge, he wasn't the sort of scrum-half who got the ball away out of the road as quick as he could. He was quite happy to take on men bigger than himself, and he would survive. As for Barry, of course, he was all lovely little class touches, and he always had a feel for what was on. He had a way of running that suggested to opponents that he would be easily knocked over – but he wasn't! He had a natural gift of change of pace, and he had his special trade mark when sometimes he seemed to dither, almost as if he didn't know what to do – and then he was gone.

Edwards and John were a great pair, individually brilliant and really formidable as a combination because they played together so often that their partnership was just instinctive; each one knew where the other would be and what he was doing. They had a sort of telepathy that was amazing to behold.

Gareth had a good partnership with Phil Bennett too, but that was a bit different. Whereas Barry would glide through opponents, Phil would sidestep, there would be a sort of splodge of movement and he would be gone. Phil was also a more physical player than Barry, who wasn't the greatest tackler in the world. In fact he often left much of his tackling to his flank forwards. Bennett was a more powerful individual, but with wonderful control of pace and direction.

But Barry and Phil had a lot of similarities too. Phil may have been slightly more physical, but they had the same change of pace, the same wonderful boot on them. They could put a ball on a sixpence with the quality of their punting, and tested opponents by putting it in exactly the right places. They were both very capable of running the show with the boot, if it was necessary. For Wales to have two guys like that at the same time – so fortunate!

Michael Lynagh and Nick Farr-Jones were Australia's halves in thirty-two internationals and they proved a superb combine – Lynagh, skilled and creative and Farr-Jones a constant threat. He was a very physical scrum-half, a big guy for that position. When I first saw him I thought, 'You're too big, son,' but with his size he definitely had a physical element to him, which gave him the ability to engage flank forwards and make them think of him first before they went for Lynagh. So Lynagh benefited from the fact that Farr-Jones was a potential breaker.

That was another thing about Gareth Edwards and Barry John. Gareth took so much of the heavy stuff that they had to watch him because he was a breaking scrum-half. He had a wonderful service, but he would always be looking for a break, and because of his physique he was sometimes prepared to have a go when the break really wasn't on. Farr-Jones was much the same, a big strong boy, while Lynagh was so quick off his mark, with those twinkling foot-steps, and he had the ability to come off either foot, in sidestep, and he was a lovely punter of the ball as well.

Craig Chalmers and Gary Armstrong were another very good pair from the Borders who combined really well, and Gary was also a breaker. Opponents always had to watch Armstrong, and that took a bit of pressure off Craig. They had to make sure Gary had got rid of the ball because he would bide his time, but when the time came he would have a go. He was a remarkably strong guy for a little fellow. The kickings he took! Gary certainly put his body on the line for club and country.

Alec Hastie of Melrose did so too. His body could be bruised and beaten and he wouldn't care so long as he did his job. Chisholm and Hastie, both of them from Melrose, played together in some ten internationals between 1955 and 1960 as a half-back pairing. That was another ham-and-eggs combination but they sometimes had to operate behind packs playing second fiddle and so took a bit of stick with immense courage and resolve. They deserved an invite to Buckingham Palace for their bravery!

I remember Cardiff in 1968, I've never seen such a brave performance. The pitch was like a swamp, but the forwards kept putting the ball back to Hastie at scrum-half. There was mud and water dripping off every inch of him, and they still kept putting the ball back. He must have been praying, 'Please catch it and just tidy it up,' but back it came from the lineout as if the Scottish forwards were saying, 'Here you are, Alec, all the best, good luck.' That performance stays in my mind as an example of supreme bravery.

Hastie and Armstrong were very similar. Both were utterly brave, they would put their bodies on the line, take all the kicking that was going, and tackle till the cows came home. Wonderful players, those two. And Laidlaw was another. He was Gary Armstrong's mentor, and Gary succeeded him as Jedforest and Scotland scrum-half. Victoria Cross characters, all of them!

Most scrum-halves try to avoid bumping into people because after all they're usually wee guys, but others, like Farr-Jones or South Africa's Van Der Westhuizen, seem to enjoy the physical side. So scrum-halves seem to divide into two lots: little dainty performers like Berbizier, who steer clear of the physicality of the game but are wonderful link players, with a cheeky touch; and others, like Farr-Jones, who could have played as flankers, big strong guys who like to take people on.

Midfield partnerships

There have been some wonderful midfield pairings, Jeff Butterfield and Phil Davies of England for instance. They were a great pair: Butterfield all class and technical excellence and change of pace – his skill level was very high – while Phil Davies was more of the knocker-down who terrorised his opposite number with cracking tackles, and who could take a ball into physical contact. They were that kind of mix, two class players in their own distinctive styles, and they served England well.

With Bleddyn Williams and Jack Matthews of Wales it was the same kind of mix. Matthews was the physical one, like Phil Davies, and Williams was the one with the feel and the touch, the silky skill that you saw in Jeff Butterfield. I don't remember the Welsh pair kicking much, just the handling seemed to be enough. Those two pairs of centres were very similar – the ideal blend is when one of them knocks people over and the other does the smooth stuff.

Carling and Guscott, that was also a centre pair that gave England sterling service. Guscott was tremendously skilled and polished, but so in a way was Carling, a stocky, burly man who had that physicality about him, but also quite a bit of pace. They weren't quite the blend that Matthews and Williams were, or Butterfield and Davies, but there was certainly a nice mix, and they were very effective. Guscott was perhaps the classier type of player, all rhythm and pace, but Carling was a much better player than he was given credit for, a very effective foil, and of course he was a very successful captain. They played off each other very well.

The Wallabies Tim Horan and Jason Little were another very successful pair. They were nicknamed Helmet and Chook, and their partnership was a feature of the 1990s – they played together thirty-five times. Horan was a flying machine. I don't think I've ever seen anyone as quick off his mark as Tim Horan, he was so quick at accelerating from a standing start. That ability to turn on the power was Horan to a tee, and he was also a very good footballer, changing direction very quickly. Whereas Jason Little was full of lovely little touches, not so much the crash-bang-wallop player but little flicks, changes of pace and so on.

And then there's the present Irish pair of Brian O'Driscoll and Kevin Maggs. Maggs does the rough stuff, while O'Driscoll is the fancy runner. But O'Driscoll now is also bringing determined and technically sound tackling to his running and handling. He's a very good defensive centre now, and puts in a lot of tackles. He's a rounded citizen, is O'Driscoll, and I think he'll come to be regarded as one of their greatest midfield players, one of the best Ireland has produced. And over the years Ireland has produced some pretty classy midfield players. Mike Gibson for a start!

1984 WALLABIES

I THINK that the biggest impression ever made by a touring side in the UK was that made by the Wallabies in 1984. It might be a bit too much to say that they revolutionised international rugby, but certainly they produced a form of back play that was so challenging and so exciting that people were really taken aback by the sheer quality of it. In that 1984 tour they lost four games and drew one out of a total of eighteen. But they won the internationals with a Grand Slam: played four, won four, and scoring 100 points to thirty-three. They did so with good solid forward play, but also with a new concept of back play in which they introduced a whole series of loop moves, dummy moves, changes of pace, switches and so on, that really amounted to virtually a new concept altogether.

They had the ideal people to do it, when you think of Mark Ella and Roger Gould, the great big full-back at six foot two and fifteen stone; and of course the inimitable David Campese, who will always be my number one player for excitement and thrill, and making you sit up and take notice. And they were very strong up forward as well. They had a fellow called Rodriguez, a former Argentinian, a prop forward who was a really hard boy and gave them a tremendous scrummage. And there was a hooker, Tommy Lawton, the biggest hooker I've ever seen, and he could really get about the pitch as well. Lawton was very formidable. And then of course there was the great Simon Poidevin, one of those flank forwards you just wind up and set running, and he would run all day, a phenomenal fellow from the point of view of keeping a high pace going throughout the game – he would appear all over the place.

These were members of a very efficient pack, but it was the back play that really opened our eyes: Mark Ella, Michael Lynagh, Nick Farr-Jones, Gould – and Campese, who was a law unto himself. I once said to Bob Dwyer, who coached the Australians, 'How do you coach Campese, who is so very much an individualist?' And he answered, 'Well, Bill, I make it a point never to interfere with bloody genius.' And that was Campese. He was a thrill to watch, and I enjoyed doing commentary when Campese was playing more than any other time because you never knew what he would be up to next. It was the uncertainty, and the challenge, and the cheek of the fellow that helped to carry the commentary along.

The touring Wallabies of 1984 really did bring a new concept of dazzling interplay in midfield that simply took the breath away. When they made it to Murrayfield with the prospect of a remarkable Grand Slam over the home countries, they took the place by storm. And it seemed in every sense appropriate that the score that clinched their Slam was out of the top drawer and scored by the remarkable David Ian Campese.

We were delighted to produce a South of Scotland side who managed to beat those 1984 Wallabies at Mansfield Park by 9–6. And this was an Australian side who had already beaten Wales by 28–9, England 19–3, and Ireland 16–9 (and went on to defeat Scotland 37–12). Yet here they were, having beaten those three international sides, losing to the South of Scotland. There was a celebration and a half that night! But above all I remember the comment of Alan Jones, the Australian coach, that evening. 'Man, you're a crowing rooster one day,' he said, 'and a bloody feather duster the next!'

Alan Jones was one of the greatest personalities that I've come across in rugby football. Maybe he wasn't the most popular, because he was so forthright – he just said what he thought and people could take it or leave it – but I found him a fascinating fellow, and he was really at the heart of that style of Australian back play which made us sit up and gasp, and which put its mark on rugby in this country. Alan was certainly very blunt, but I had a lot of time for him. And when it came to covering matches he was always so helpful to me.

Mark Ella, the Wallabies' stand-off, was a class act of course. He didn't seem to run on the ground, he seemed to run above it. And he had wonderful gifts of deception and very high skill levels. Ella not only had great pace, there was also his change of pace – he seemed to be going along comfortably in third gear and then, suddenly, woosh, he was gone. And he didn't seem to have done anything different! He kicked well too. Mark Ella and Campese between them contributed hugely to that very successful side.

And as for the forwards, each one did his job well, and so as an accumulated effort they were really splendid – a very good front row, and the flanker Poidevin, who was something else! They were a lovely side, scoring 400 points in eighteen games, and in the internationals it was played four, won four, a clean sweep. They were wonderful, really wonderful.

It was at the Randwick club in Sydney that this way of playing was devised. And Alan Jones was of course connected with Randwick. Those Australian backs were putting into operation the Randwick style, where they'd been playing that kind of stuff for a while. And what a style it was! It certainly left a lot of our midfield players with their mouths open. 'Did you see that?' Or rather, 'Did you *not* see that?' That was the kind of thing going through our players' minds. But it was really riveting to watch. And the whole thing was done at such pace. Flipping a ball over your shoulder is one thing, but to do it when you're flat out, and send a colleague the other way with the ball, that was wonderful to behold. Unless you were on the receiving end! And with people like Ella and Campese they were extremely difficult to beat, especially with Gould coming in from the back, picking his time and place so brilliantly, coming in as a big man with pace, and therefore capable of breaking any but the best tackle.

Mark Ella scored in each game of that Grand Slam: a try against England, a try and two drop goals against Ireland, a try against Wales, and a try against Scotland. That's an amazing record for a stand-off half. It just shows the quality of the fellow, not only in the way he launched other people, but in the way that, having done so, he suddenly appeared somewhere else like a tame genie, and at pace. He seemed to have such lovely light footwork. Ella was very special. And of course with Campese you had a player who could open up any side with his sheer impertinence – and class.

Michael Lynagh was a gifted player too. 1988 was his great year over here, but he made a terrific impression in 1984 as well, when he was brought in as a replacement and suddenly galvanised things. Lynagh was a great goal kicker too. He scored ninety-eight points in that Australian tour of 1984, and that's quite a haul, and gives some impression of his capabilities. To have Ella at stand-off and Lynagh at inside centre! It was a tremendous pairing, especially with Campese floating about as well.

And there were also a lot of other people of great talent in that side, especially Nick Farr-Jones, a world class scrum-half. Farr-Jones was a big boy for a scrum-half, and therefore lethal on the burst. He reminded me a bit of Gareth Edwards on the short burst, and in his ability to break a tackle. Farr-Jones took some holding, and he was a confident fellow as well. He used to go sideways sometimes to introduce a change of direction, and also so that people could run off him and check the defence. And Gould might come in off him from full-back, so there was a whole selection of moves and calls. The knowledge of each other's play and style, built partly on the Randwick experience, was devastating. We found great trouble in coping with it.

It would be interesting to see how they would get on today against the cluttered midfields and the very well organised defences of these days. I just wish the Ellas and Lynaghs and Campeses and Farr-Joneses could play now, just to see how they would fare. They'd certainly find it harder, because the midfield is so cluttered that it's very hard indeed to create an incision, you have to be very hot on your handling and your running off the ball in order to do it. It's becoming progressively harder, and we're getting more punting in the game than there has been for some time. I sometimes get the impression we may be drifting back to the 1950s, when there was so much kicking for touch because of defences blocking the midfield – that was a very grey period.

It was a real shot in the arm to have the likes of the 1984 Wallabies coming over and at that high level, when winning was so important and there was so much at stake, to produce that kind of running rugby football. To score 100 points in four test matches, that was really something, it turned the game of rugby on its head. And I suppose it pointed out to players over here that there really were opportunities out there for opening up tight defences. But your skill levels and in particular your ball transference had to be spot on. These skills didn't just come along but had to be worked on, you had to slog at them. That was the real lesson of that Wallabies tour, you've really got to work on your skill level and your interplay. It comes from practice and from doing it hundreds of times.

They were great, the 1984 Australians, certainly the most exciting touring side that I've ever seen. It was a real feather in the cap of the South of Scotland, our own local lads, to beat them 9–6. I was doing the commentary on that day, I remember well. The match was played in a swamp, and that certainly helped us, because those Wallabies weren't quite as effective when the conditions were heavy and the ball slippery. Of course, they could handle a wet ball as well as or better than anybody, but they were so accustomed in their own country to playing in reasonable conditions, that the 'glaur' was a bit of a shock to them.

In 2002 the achievement of the 1984 team as the only Wallaby line-up to have completed the Grand Slam, defeating England, Ireland, Wales and Scotland during one tour, was honoured by a special award from the Sport Australia Hall of Fame. Mark Ella accepted the award on behalf of the team, while Andrew Slack, who had captained the touring side, confessed to letting 'the odd tear flow' in the after-match speech, in which he singled out for special mention the coaching of Alan Jones.

1988 WALLABIES

IN 1988 the Australians came over again, captained by Nick Farr-Jones, and toured England and Scotland, but not Ireland, Wales or France. That Wallabies side was coached by Bob Dwyer with Bob Templeton, two great characters, but curiously enough they lost three of their first four matches. They were not the world-beaters of 1984, but all the same, they still managed to score 357 points in thirteen games. And in their last six games they scored thirty-four tries and 211 points, so they made up for being turned over three times earlier on, when they lost to London 10–21, the North of England 9–15, and the Southwest 10–26. Those were the defeats they suffered. But then Campese and the rest really got into gear. Campese scored two tries in the international against Scotland at Murrayfield, and Tommy Lawton, that great big heavy hooker, also scored two tries in that win by 32–13, just brilliant following up and instinct about where to be. And Lynagh kicked five goals.

That 1988 tour was the one in which Michael Lynagh dominated, scoring sixty-one points, and really established himself as a class stand-off. But it was Campese who scored the tries, including one in the 28–19 defeat by England at Twickenham as well as those two against Scotland at Murrayfield. But the real high point of that great tour came at the end with the Australians beating the Barbarians 40–22 at Cardiff. That was when Campese scored an absolutely magical try, changing pace and coming off each foot, dummying and dithering and doing everything that was possible and a lot of things that weren't! What a try it was. He beat almost the entire Barbarians side to score it. And he got a standing ovation, the like of which I've never experienced anywhere before. A standing ovation for a visiting player is a rare thing at Cardiff, and it went on and on, very emotional! In the commentary box you felt a great sweep of admiration coming up. The crowd didn't sing, they just cheered and clapped, clapped and cheered, and it went on for ages.

I have already mentioned the Hawick balls I used to take around with me and feed to some players, notably Gareth Edwards and Gerald Davies. One day at a practice session I gave Campese one and told him, 'That'll put a yard on your speed.'

'I don't need a yard on my bloody speed,' he answered, but he took the sweet all the same and held it up to the light. 'Would I pass a bloody drug test with this inside me?' he asked.

Another day he left an Australian training session, and came over to me and said, 'Hey, Bill, you got any of them bloody sweets?' And Dwyer was standing there flaming, 'What the hell's he doing over there?' But Campese fancied those Hawick balls, and he was going to have one, whatever Dwyer thought.

In the Australians' 32–13 win over Scotland the rain came lashing down but the Wallabies just kept handling the ball. Even in those difficult conditions their handling was superb, and they didn't need to change their game. I think it's the old story that if you keep on handling you'll get better at it, and you'll feel the weight of pass that's required, you'll manage to work the ball out of the tackle. You have to accept you'll make a number of mistakes early on, but eventually, just as with the Australians and the Randwick experience, it will click.

Those Australians were prepared to handle in any conditions. I sometimes wonder if we in the UK are discouraged from continuing to handle just because of our ground and weather conditions. We tend to say, when it's raining, let's kick and put the pressure on the other side and get them to mishandle. But those Australians didn't; they wanted the ball, and they wanted to use the ball, although it was much more difficult in conditions when the rain was pouring down and there was a slippery skim on the ball. They didn't seem to let that bother them – they may have kicked a little bit more, but they still mainly handled the ball because that was their bread and butter at home.

The Australians of the 1980s had quite a good scrummage and quite a good lineout, their set-pieces were as good as they needed to be. But they also always tried to keep to the style they knew, irrespective of whether conditions were amenable or not. That was how they wanted to play, and how they wanted people to see them – as a team that not only could play skilful rugby but in doing so could entertain. They wouldn't stop entertaining just because it was wet. So they had a lot to tell us, not only about the machinations in midfield, but also through the players' sixth sense of what to do and when, which came about just through having done it time and time again, in practice and in matches, starting with Randwick. Practice, they say, makes perfect. Those Wallabies underlined that concept.

PORTRAITS

BILL BEAUMONT (1975–82)
Fylde, England, British Lions
34 England caps
7 British Lions tests

Having had the pleasure of sharing BBC television commentary on a number of occasions with William Blackledge Beaumont, who did the summaries, I can testify to the sound common sense and down-to-earth, friendly attitude of one of the true greats of English rugby union football. A man of no frills, he is a very likeable fellow whom I enjoyed working with. When it came to good common sense of the Lancashire type he was out on his own; as a summariser he got his points across well; and he did it all in a way that made people warm to him. Bill Beaumont sounded honest, and he was honest.

A willing workhorse who eschewed the glamour role for one of graft and grind, Beaumont performed his part so successfully that he was to prove not only a doughty forward but also a hugely popular and effective captain of the 1980 Lions in South Africa, the first Englishman to do so for many years.

Beaumont was capped first against Ireland in Dublin in 1975, but he had a disappointing entry to the international fold, as England won only one of the first eight internationals in which he played. However, this quiet achiever, who started out as a Fylde reserve team full-back at the age of sixteen, applied himself with such vigour and enthusiasm to acquiring the skills of the game that he gained thirty-four caps for England, as well as playing seven tests for the British Lions. One of the most popular players in the history of the game, Bill Beaumont captained England to a Grand Slam in 1980, their first in twenty-three years.

At six foot three and fifteen stone, he was a very dependable lineout specialist as front jumper, and a superb scrummager. He achieved significant success as a captain, and not only for England – for instance he was in charge when Lancashire won the county championship, and when Northern Division defeated the All Blacks in 1980. In that year he was also voted Player of the Year. Beaumont would scrummage till the cows came home, as well as win ball at the front of the lineout, and he was also a skilled ball-handler in his quiet way. His personality was stamped all over that 1980 Grand Slam year for England.

After joining the Lions in New Zealand as a replacement in 1977, he forced himself into the test team with his outstanding lineout play and his mobility round the field. On that tour he formed a successful partnership with Scottish lock Gordon Brown, and played an important part in the Lions' victory over the All Blacks at Christchurch. In 1978 he was offered the England captaincy, and his ability to lead by example brought a new energy to the England team.

After leading England in their 1980 Grand Slam it was no surprise that he was appointed captain of the British Lions team to tour South Africa. He was always a very successful captain, not least because he was so well liked.

Bill Beaumont won thirty-four caps for England, thirty-three of them in consecutive tests, captained his country in twenty-one internationals and played seven tests for the Lions. Very sadly, he was forced to retire from playing the game in 1982, at the age of twenty-nine, on medical advice, after sustaining a neck injury during the county championship final.

Bill Beaumont in his own words

The Art of Captaincy

After England won the grand slam [in 1980] a lot of people came up to me and asked me what makes a successful captain. The answer is very easy – 15 very good players. That, without any doubt, is the most important ingredient. The critics said that after three years in the job I personally had made great strides as a captain and that is how I was able to lead England to the grand slam. But in fact, although I had improved a great deal in my tactical appreciation, the simple truth is that I was in charge of a much better team than I was in 1978...

All I ever tried to do as captain of England or the Lions was to be a player's player. I trained and played for my team and I never asked any player to attempt anything that I was not prepared to do myself. I revelled in being in the thick of the action throughout every match, at whatever level, and I hoped to inspire others to give 100 per cent too ... The captain is no superior being in any shape or form and he should always muck in. The coach may choose to distance himself a fraction from the team – but a good captain can never do that.

There are all sorts of arguments about what is the best position to captain a side. There is no conclusive answer, but I have found lock forward ideal. There is no better position from which to have a definitive view of the forward battle and to plan or change tactics accordingly. At every scrum I can feel exactly how the other 15 forwards are faring and I know better than anyone what is happening in the lineout or in the loose. I can tell our half-backs when to nurse our pack or when to stretch the opposition from side to side, and if I miss some of the finer points of the back play, I always have a pretty shrewd idea how the respective back divisions are playing by the direction I have to take to the breakdown after a set-piece. It is certainly easy to lead by example from lock and if I can lift the performance of our pack then I am making a big step in the right direction ...

The captain's role off the field, of course, is to encourage harmony and build up team spirit and confidence, and the most important job is to make newcomers feel at ease. Quite often it takes a new player half a dozen matches before he feels he can play without overwhelming inhibitions; for my first two years in the team I expected to be dropped at any moment. I always made a special point of trying to help new players feel at home and looking after them as much as possible. If they were worried or nervous they were unlikely to produce their best form. [My first captain] Dave Rollitt's approach to me at my first trial – 'Who the hell are you?' – is not necessarily the best way to make a man feel relaxed, welcome, at ease, and determined to follow Rollitt to hell and back.

I tried to arrange match tickets and tea tickets for new players so that their families were catered for and the players had nothing to worry about except the game itself. I would make a special point too of encouraging them during the game and congratulating them on every good piece of play I spotted early on to help them gain confidence. If a new centre put in a crunching tackle or a new full-back found a good touch, I would run past and say well done.

Too often young players are expected to prove themselves first before being fully accepted by the old campaigners. This is an old-fashioned, out-dated attitude that does a lot of harm because it inhibits the newcomers. There is a tendency for someone to be overcautious for the first few caps in the hope that if he does nothing wrong he will be retained in the team. This is a negative but prevalent attitude. I tried to encourage players to play their natural game on the positive basis that if they do something outstanding they will surely remain in the side.

(From Bill Beaumont, *Thanks to Rugby*, Stanley Paul, 1982)

OLLIE CAMPBELL (1976–84)

Old Belvedere, Ireland, British Lions
22 Ireland caps
7 British Lions tests

He had all the appearance of a skinny young fellow in need of a good square meal, a lad who at five foot eleven and twelve stone three might not survive the physical hurly-burly of the international rugby union arena. But Seamus Oliver Campbell proved the doubters wrong by emerging as one of the most strongly equipped stand-off halves ever to wear the green of Ireland, and what is more, as a dead-eye goalkicker whose 217 Irish points in twenty-two tests gave him the highest scoring average in Irish test history with 9.8 per match.

I remember hearing of a fellow who asked, one evening at the Old Belvedere club ground in Dublin, what was that 'boom-boom' noise he could hear from the semi-darkness. 'Ah, that's Ollie,' was the reply. Sure enough, Ollie Campbell was honing his goal-kicking skills in the gloaming, all on his own and with patience and concentration.

It all proved worthwhile because Ollie, a modest and friendly man, proved time and again that he had focus and the big-match temperament. One recalls a particular occasion at Lansdowne Road when Ireland played Scotland in Dublin in the most foul conditions of wind, rain and slush. That was in 1982. Yet Ollie the Boot thumped over six penalty goals and a drop goal – all of Ireland's points – to gain victory by 21–12. It was the most amazing demonstration of the goal-kicking art that I can remember, every strike piloted to take advantage of the boisterous breeze, and each one hit with magical precision, despite the treacherous underfoot conditions. That display was a crucial part of Ireland's 1982 Triple Crown triumph, in which Campbell registered forty-six of Ireland's sixty-six points.

Ollie Campbell tended to be particularly hard on my countrymen, for in Dublin in 1980 he also slotted three penalty goals, a drop goal and a conversion, to give Ireland victory by 22–15. And in 1983 he stroked over four more goals in victory by 15–13 at Murrayfield.

Despite his slim build, Campbell sailed into his tackles like a kamikazi pilot, and he punted from hand with touch and feel. Not only that, but in his rivalry with Tony Ward he overcame criticism of being 'only a kicker' by developing an awareness of what was on as well as the ability to make an incisive break.

That rivalry with Tony Ward split Ireland, because Ward was a flamboyant performer who liked running with the ball and taking people on, while Ollie was more of a thoughtful kind of kicker. Ward had a lot of support in Ireland, twice being awarded the accolade of European Player of the Year. Irish selectors got some stick when they picked Campbell, but they were right as it turned out, because he won the Championship for them. That day in Dublin in 1982 you wouldn't have believed he could possibly have steered the ball as he did because the wind was howling, the rain pouring down – it was like a swamp. I'll never forget that goal-kicking – I couldn't believe my eyes, in those conditions. He was something else!

A double British Lion, he had hamstring trouble in South Africa in 1980, missing eight of the first nine games, yet played in three tests and scored sixty points in his seven games. News of Campbell's goal-kicking skills reached New Zealand, so that by the time the Lions got there in 1983 the All Blacks had been warned not to concede penalties even at halfway. In New Zealand he played in eleven of the eighteen games, including all four tests, scoring all the Lions' points in the first test with three penalty goals and a drop goal. He was the tour's top points-scorer with 124 in eleven games, from a try, eighteen conversions, twenty-two penalty goals, and six drop goals.

COLIN DEANS (1978–87)
Hawick, Scotland, British Lions
52 caps

It was as a teacher of physical education that I first came across a stocky eleven-year-old at Trinity Primary School in my home town of Hawick in the Scottish Border country. I recognised his surname and enquired if he was related to Peter Deans. 'He is my father, sir,' said the lad with obvious pride. 'Right,' I said. 'You're a hooker then.' You see, I had played alongside Colin Deans's dad in the green jersey of Hawick where I knew Peter Deans as a rugged, durable, tough hooker. I was highly amused when Colin decided to title his book of memoirs *You're a Hooker, then.*

How relieved and pleased I was therefore to see Colin make such progress as to achieve a record fifty-two caps for a Scottish forward. Some feat! He was a remarkable exponent of the hooker's art, being blessed also with flaring speed off the mark that got him into places he wasn't expected to be, and he had safe hands too and a keen positional sense that rendered him an exceptionally gifted support runner. In fact, he was probably the best attacking hooker Scotland has yet produced.

He also worked hard to achieve accuracy in throwing, so much so that his lineout practitioners welcomed his presence as he very seldom missed his target. He captained his club Hawick in 1979–80 and 1984–6, and was a key member of the Scottish side that won the Grand Slam in 1984. His fifteen captaincies of Scotland also included a Championship share in 1986.

Colin Deans toured with the Lions in New Zealand in 1983, but was unfortunate to miss out on the tests because, although widely regarded as the better hooker, he had to yield to the tour captain, Ireland's Ciaran Fitzgerald. So Deans had to watch from the bench as the British Lions lost all four tests, but he made a big impact in provincial games as arguably the quickest hooker in the world game.

It was from his mother Isabel that he inherited that turn of speed, for she was a primary school relay stalwart with an edge of pace she passed on to her son, to the benefit of Hawick and Scotland. In 1988 Colin Deans was awarded an MBE.

Colin Deans in his own words

1984 Scotland v France for the Grand Slam

So the vital day, 17 March 1984, dawned ... What a roar went up when we inspected the pitch. It was like the lid being blown off a pan of tatties. Back to the dressing room, strapping put on, muscles loosened up and a talk from Adam Robson, the then President, and out on to the field.

The French looked really mean and menacing. Rives was moving up and down like a lion stalking a deer. The referee's whistle went and the French kicked off. It was soon evident they had come to win. They powered into every scrum, maul and lineout.

One thing we had learned during the campaign was to defend and tackle, and we needed all our determination to halt Rives's men. The French missed an early opportunity to score but eventually Jerome Gallion broke from a scrum and got a try which Jean-Patrick Lescaboura converted.

But all was not lost. It had taken a mighty effort by the French to get that score and they must have wondered what they needed to do to crack our defence wide open. Our full-back Peter Dods got a penalty goal to make it 6–3 in favour of the French at the interval.

It was midway through the second half, after Lescarboura had kicked a penalty goal, that the turning point came for Scotland. From a French throw-in to a two-man lineout the ball was intended for Gallion, the play-maker. Instead David Leslie was there for Scotland and in the collision which followed Gallion was stretchered off.

The Bear [prop Iain Milne] was simply immense that day. He really destroyed the French scrum. Their second row were punching him all through the game and his face was badly marked afterwards, but The Bear just growled, absorbed it all and put on more pressure.

I next felt we had it won when there was a scrum in the middle of the field. When it broke up the French forwards were bickering among themselves and that was a sure sign they were rattled. Sure enough French indiscipline did cost them dear and Dods, in magnificent kicking form, put over two penalty goals. France, though, were by no means finished and Lescarboura had a good drop goal. Again Dods kicked a penalty to level the scores.

Then at 4.23 pm that afternoon came the most exciting try I've seen scored in my career. We had worked our way up to the French line, when I threw in the idea that we would peel from the lineout. However, Jean-Luc Joinel got his fingertips to the ball and deflected it towards the French line. Jim Calder reached up, grabbed it and fell over the line for a try which Dods converted. French frustration then saw Serge Blanco hurling himself at Dods in the closing minutes and the Scottish full-back kicked the resulting penalty just to make sure.

Peter Dods got a black eye during that game which had anxious mums shielding their children from the sight. But he played magnificently and scored 17 points in our 21–12 victory. Dods finished up with a new championship record for Scotland, having notched 50 points in one international season. Scotland finished up with the elusive grand slam. And for once Jim Telfer finished up with a smile.

(From Colin Deans, *You're a Hooker, then*. Pan Books, 1989)

JOHN RUTHERFORD (1979–87)
Selkirk, South of Scotland, Scotland, British Lions
42 Scotland caps
1 British Lions tests

He should have been nicknamed Gentleman John, for John Young Rutherford was not only one of the fairest players ever to grace the Scottish game; he also had a certain elegance of style that proved most frustrating to opponents, who discovered he was a slippery customer and much more difficult to snare than he seemed. Perhaps it was because of a deceptively lazy style of running, allied to subtle change of pace and wonderful body balance on the run, that he presented such a tricky target, not to mention his superb pace and placement of pass; and a booming punt that was part of his wide kick variety.

A product of the Scottish Border club of Selkirk, he proved a huge aid to colleagues around him with his decision-making, and his uncanny judgment of how to put a partner into space. He had superb command of punted ball, placing great pressure on opposing defenders, and his ability to gather points with drop goals was another Rutherford trademark, as underlined by his Scottish record of twelve drop goals in major internationals – to which he added seven test tries.

Capped first against Wales in 1979, after five appearances for Scottish B teams, Rutherford opened his international scoring account in his second test with a try against England in the 7–7 Twickenham draw in 1979. He was first choice for Scotland in the 1980s, and in 1981–82 he achieved the remarkable feat of scoring in six consecutive internationals: drop goals against Australia and England, tries against Ireland and France, and then drop goals against Wales and Australia.

At one time Rutherford was the second most capped stand-off in the history of the game (forty-two) following Jack Kyle of Ireland, who was capped forty-six times for his country. At six foot one and twelve stone three Rutherford had impressive weight of tackle, and we have seen what a splendid half-back partnership he formed with Roy Laidlaw from neighbouring Jedburgh.

Rutherford toured with Scotland in the Far East in 1977, France in 1980, New Zealand in 1981, Australia in 1982, and Romania in 1984. He was with the Lions in New Zealand in 1983 and played in the third test as a centre, where he scored a try. At the initial World Cup tournament in 1987 he had the misfortune to aggravate an old injury in the first game against France in Christchurch, and had to return home. But on his top form Rutherford was a class act, and a key performer in Scotland's 1984 Grand Slam.

SERGE BLANCO (1980–91)
Biarritz, France
93 caps

Without question Serge Blanco deserves to be rated the most famous French rugby player of all time, and of course one of the truly great rugby union full-backs, if not the greatest, for he was the complete athlete. Big at six foot one and thirteen and a half stone, quick, highly skilled, and very sharp in reaction, Blanco had a sense of adventure that endeared him to his Biarritz club supporters, the whole of sporting France, and indeed to opponents all over the world who had reason to marvel at his exquisite gifts.

The Blanco record almost says it all. His ninety-three cap appearances were a world record at one time, his 233 test points included a record thirty-eight tries, with six as a wing, and a record thirty-two tries as a full-back. He captained France in seventeen tests, including the 1991 World Cup, and he played in French sides who won or shared six Championships, and marked up two Grand Slams (1981, 1987).

Blanco had rare positional gifts, a sixth sense of where to be and when. He revelled in surprise attacks from the deep and in subtle intrusion, and at full pace he was an impressive target very hard to torpedo. He epitomised French flair and at times took the breath away with the sheer audacity of his attack play. He performed all the full-back skills with confidence and assurance. Among his scoring feats was a peach of a drop goal in a French victory by 17–15 over England at Twickenham in February 1987, and he scored one of the great counter-attack tries with a thrilling touchline scoring burst against Wales at Cardiff in 1986.

He already had made New Zealand sit up and take notice when in the first test against the All Blacks on the French tour there in 1984 he suddenly appeared like a friendly genie, chipped ahead with precision, regathered and sailed home for a memorable try. And having scored a try, two penalties and a conversion in the 20–20 draw with Scotland at Christchurch in the 1987 World Cup, Blanco then materialised again in the wing position for the crucial try against the Wallabies that took France into that 1987 World Cup final.

With the scores at 24–24 in the last moments of the match, France launched a last attacking move with No 8 Laurent Rodriguez, centre Denis Charvet and scrum-half Pierre Berbizier making ground up the middle. Blanco received the ball from Rodriguez some forty yards from the opposition tryline and set off for the corner, despite his injured hamstring, to scorch past four Wallaby tacklers for a thrilling try.

Blanco indeed was a special type of player who could bring a crowd to its feet in joyous acclaim. And the other side of the great man was demonstrated at his last appearance at the Parc des Princes which was against Wales on March 2 1991. France outplayed the Welsh by 36–3 and Blanco, their captain that day, signed off with a brilliant performance that included the opening try following a seventy-yard thrust and a conversion from the touchline that rang down the curtain on a truly brilliant career.

To mark the occasion of Blanco's impending retirement he was presented on the touchline with a beautiful piece of silverware, whereupon he walked over to a little boy in a wheelchair and gave the trophy to him. The youngster was simply thrilled, and speechless with delight. Blanco – a true great and a gentleman with a heart as well.

MARK ELLA (1980–84)
Randwick, New South Wales, Australia
25 caps

Mark Ella was one of three Aborigine brothers, all of whom played tests for Australia. It was during the Wallabies' tour to the UK in 1984 that Mark stamped his personality on an Australian effort that brought them a unique Grand Slam of the home countries, and, for Mark, a quite remarkable feat. For he not only scored a try in each of the tests against England, Ireland, Wales and Scotland, but, even more remarkably, he also dropped two goals, one with each foot, in the Irish test. On that Wallabies tour he played in ten of the eighteen games and was fourth top try scorer with five tries and two drop goals. An astonishing record for a stand-off.

Mark played first grade rugby in Sydney as a seventeen-year-old, and he and his brothers, his twin Glen and Gary, introduced something of a new concept to the Australian effort in the form of flat alignment of the back division, and a series of loop moves done at pace and with the stand-off positioned close to his scrum-half.

There also was an element of sleight of hand in his game, and fingertip transference, as well as intuitive action. All of this had been part of the Ella boys' style in the Matraville High School XV and the Australian Schools' tour, and when the three brothers got home Australian coach Bob Dwyer was eager to tap their potential, for his

Mark Ella, perhaps the most talented inside back ever to wear the Wallaby jersey, celebrates their Grand Slam-clinching victory over the Scots in 1984 with team-mates David Campese and Andrew Slack.

Michael Lynagh is at the centre of the Australians' victory celebrations after defeating England to win the 1991 World Cup at Twickenham.

David Campese, the greatest entertainer of them all, leaves Rory Underwood in his wake as he surges towards North of England's line, 1988.

Jonathan Davies outstrips the opposition with his blinding acceleration to score a remarkable try in the Wales–Scotland international in Cardiff, 1988.

Ieuan Evans earned my spontaneous accolade of 'Merlin the Magician' with this wondrous try against my fellow countrymen at Cardiff in 1988.

John Kirwan, the All Black wing who wrote his name all over the 1987 World Cup, powers his way past France's Sella to score a try in the final.

Fiji wins the Hong Kong Sevens tournament for the second successive year in 1991. The abbreviated game was just made for Fiji's style of play.

Waisale Serevi, the 'Mr Sevens' of the Fijian squad, on his way to scoring yet another try in the Hong Kong tournament of 1993.

Mesake Rasari, another Fijian Sevens specialist with the physique of a second-row forward and the ball-handling skills of a stand-off, goes for the line in the 1992 tournament.

Will Carling leads out the England team against France at Twickenham, 1991. The match was a cliffhanger, with England winning 21–19 to secure the Grand Slam.

Rory Underwood, the first England player to reach the magical figure of fifty caps, scored fifty test tries – an achievement bettered only by David Campese (sixty-four). His international brother Tony could play a bit as well!

The mighty England side of 1992, Grand Slam winners for the second consecutive year, line up at Twickenham before trouncing Wales 24–0.

Rob Andrew, the highly gifted stand-off who played a key role in England's successes in the early 1990s, gets my vote as the best stand-off of them all – though they won't agree in Cardiff!

Dean Richards, the mighty England No 8, cornerstone of an invincible pack, was one of those players who could change the whole course of a game.

famous Randwick club. 'This is Randwick,' he told Glen, 'and you're the star boy.' Dwyer deserves a lot of the credit for encouraging the adventurous off-the-top-of-the-head play perfected by Mark Ella and his brothers.

Mark was a hugely gifted artist with a wonderful variety of passes with which to put colleagues into gaps, and with short and sharp fingertip transference that frequently manufactured space on the outside. He was like a jaguar in his running, in total balance at full pace – he was a class act without any doubt. I had never seen players criss-crossing like that, passing behind the back, over the shoulder – it was breathtaking, revolutionary.

First capped against New Zealand at Sydney in 1980 Mark, five foot ten and eleven stone seven, played in twenty-five tests between 1980 and 1984, and scored seventy-five points with a full house: six tries, three conversions, eight penalty goals, and seven drop goals. His brother Gary gained six caps, and his twin Glen played in four tests, but the three brothers never played together for Australia, although they were together in that Australian Schools party who took the world by storm in 1977–78.

Mark had the distinction of being captain of Australia in New Zealand in 1982, when he was just twenty-three, and there are many Australians who regard Mark Ella as the most talented inside back ever to wear the Wallaby jersey.

DANIE GERBER (1980–92)
Eastern Province, Western Province, South Africa
24 tests

Daniel Mattheus Gerber set a South African record of nineteen test tries as one of the great midfield practitioners during a turbulent period of South African rugby experience. He demonstrated great sharpness off his mark for such a burly citizen – he was six foot and weighed fourteen stone – and thus was hard to arrest, particularly when he was in full flow. He also had the gift of maintaining full pace over a distance, which made him a formidable attacker. On top of that he could hit hard in copybook tackling, and had a devastating effect when launched in broken play.

Gerber's test debut was against South America in October 1980, while South Africa at that time of isolation had a test programme comprising unofficial sides such as the South Sea Barbarians, South American teams and the New Zealand Cavaliers. After representing South African Schools as captain in 1977 he made his Eastern Province debut a year later, but two more years passed before, as a twenty-two-year-old, he had his first experience of test rugby. That followed his two splendid performances for the Orange Free State and the Junior Springboks against Bill Beaumont's 1980 British Lions.

On the South African tour of South America in 1980 he scored six tries in five matches, including a try in each of two tests. And he achieved other extraordinary try-scoring feats, as when he claimed three against England in 1984, a year after he had represented the Barbarians with two tries against Scotland and four against Cardiff. He was South Africa's Player of the Year in 1984, and in 1986 he celebrated the International Rugby Board's centenary by scoring two tries for the Overseas Unions in their 32–13 win over the Five Nations XV at Twickenham.

When in 2001 *The Times* newspaper asked me to select my World XV, I had no hesitation in naming Danie Gerber as outside centre alongside Mike Gibson of Ireland. What a pairing that would have been! Some people might argue that Gerber had scored a lot of good tries, but against slightly weaker opposition, since he was at his best during South Africa's period of isolation. All the same, the fact is that in those matches he certainly gave every indication of being a class player. Physically he was such a powerful player, and when you allied to that physique his acceleratory pace off a standing start, and his ability to maintain that pace, he was rightly regarded, and not only in South Africa, as the best midfield man of all.

ROY LAIDLAW (1980–88)
Jedforest, South of Scotland, Scotland, British Lions
47 caps
4 British Lions caps

Roy James Laidlaw will always be specially remembered by Scotland's rugby supporters for the two tries he scored against Ireland in Dublin which really sealed Scotland's Triple Crown triumph in 1984, to be followed by victory over France for a Grand Slam.

Those two tries were extraordinary scores as they were from the set-piece, and were achieved with Laidlaw's distinctive close-to-the-ground running style, combining exceptional balance with pace. Laidlaw created a record Scottish half-back partnership with John Rutherford in thirty-five major internationals during the 1980s, when the two of them provided Scotland with a secure hinge: Laidlaw all bustling aggression and courage in the Scottish forward tradition, Rutherford all grace and poise and elegance, with wonderful punt control and placement, and smooth launch into his balanced running.

It spoke volumes for Laidlaw's determination that he gained forty-seven caps despite the fact that at club level he had to keep his head above water in testing circumstances, often at the heels of a pack who struggled for a supply of quality ball. Jedforest scrum-halves like Laidlaw and his successor Gary Armstrong had to live on titbits, like hunting dogs always on short rations, because Jedforest seemed chronically short of muckle brutes up forward.

Both Armstrong and Laidlaw were immensely courageous, they would come at you all day. Laidlaw's willingness to do his full whack in the unglamorous chores was apparent in the zest with which he launched himself into tackles, and the relish with which he used his stocky build of five foot seven and eleven and a half stone to sink opponents.

Capped first in Scotland's 22–15 win against Ireland in Dublin in 1980, Laidlaw was the eighth player from the Jedforest club to be capped, and went on to play in thirty-one consecutive internationals until injured in the French match of 1985, which caused him to miss the games against Wales and England in that season.

A former pupil of Jedburgh Grammar School, Laidlaw set a record of sixty-eight appearances for South of Scotland, for whom he scored eighteen tries. Captaining Scotland against the Fijians in 1982, and in five other cap internationals, he went on five tours of Scotland. He also had the honour of leading the Lions in two provincial games of the 1983 New Zealand tour, in which he played in all four tests. In the third test he was linked at half-back with Ollie Campbell.

PIERRE BERBIZIER (1981–91)
Lourdes, France
56 caps

It was at Murrayfield in 1986, when Scotland were playing France, that their scrum-half Pierre Berbizier nearly won the game for his country with a remarkable piece of quick thinking. Gavin Hastings had just kicked off in his first international, and had put the kick straight into touch. The Scots were heading towards the middle of the pitch, expecting a restart scrummage. But Berbizier had a better idea. He stood on the touchline where Hastings had kicked out, threw the ball in to himself, ran up the touchline a full seventy yards, and touched down in the corner for a try.

I was commentating at the time, and the first words that rose in my mind might not have been entirely suitable for sending out on the air. With a gulp I managed, 'Oh, that was rather cheeky!' The Scottish side thought Berbizier's ploy was sharp practice, but it wasn't at all. His feet were in touch, his throw was straight, it went the five yards, and Hastings had put a kick-off straight into touch. So Berbizier was quite within his rights and deserved to be congratulated for his mental agility, as well as the speed with which he had scuttled down the line to score that try. Luckily for us, Scotland just managed to win the match 18–17. That ploy of throwing in to yourself is used quite a bit today, especially by adventurous players like Jason Robinson.

Pierre Berbizier started his rugby life playing for Lourdes as a full-back before becoming one of France's most gifted scrum-halves. Jacques Fouroux, France's coach at that time, recognised Berbizier's gifts but also saw that at five foot seven and ten stone thirteen he was too small to be a world class full-back. However, his agility, ball-handling skills, toughness and good rugby brain suggested to Fouroux that he could make a good scrum-half, and so it proved. Berbizier went on to become France's most capped scrum-half, playing fifty-six times between 1981 and 1991.

He made his national debut against Scotland in 1981, where his tactical astuteness contributed to a France win by 16–9. That was also the year that France won the Grand Slam, with Berbizier playing a key role, and he helped them to yet another Grand Slam in 1987 and to reaching the World Cup final that same year. He was a very distinctive little fellow, very quick and tidy. In the tradition of French scrum-halves, he was a 'big chief whiteshirt' and ran the show. You saw him talking to the big forwards, people twice his size, and he'd look at them as if to say, 'You do as you're told!' In fact his nickname was *le Patron* – the boss.

The French have a tradition of having their captain in the scrum-half position. He's at the midway point between the forwards and the backs, and he's the link man. And they also seem to have produced a number of little guys who are quite bossy. Gallion was like that, and Fouroux. Fabien Galthié, who was holding the captain's job till he got injured in 2002, is in the same mould, although physically he's bigger. The others focus on him, there's no doubt, and he too seems to be a strong personality. So now there doesn't seem to be very much in-fighting among the French and Galthié, I think, is largely responsible for that. He's got their support all the way, and I believe he would have made a big difference in that game against the Irish that the French just lost in February 2003. But the French will always regard Berbizier as 'Le petit general'.

DAVID CAMPESE (1982–96)
Australian Capital Territory, New South Wales, Australia
101 caps

I love to see rugby football where there's a sense of adventure, and where the players take risks. David Campese was very much one of those, as well as being a player with all the skills, and all the gifts of deception. But he also had a cheeky touch to him, he liked to tilt his lance at people, and to leave big forwards floundering in his wake. He had that kind of cheeky, challenging touch that I thoroughly enjoyed. As a commentator you're always aware of the quality of play on the field. Your commentary really depends for its interest on what's happening out there. Well, whenever Campese was playing you never had any doubt, your commentary would always be lifted by what he was doing on the field, because he was an artist, and a cheeky artist into the bargain.

Look at all the wonderful tries he has scored. Take the try for the Wallabies against the Barbarians at Cardiff in their 1988 tour, in which he ran more than forty metres, and in that spell left three or four Barbarians literally sitting on their backsides. The whole ground rose to their feet to acknowledge brilliance, sheer genius. I was doing the commentary that day, and it almost took my breath away to see how the whole ground rose to that try.

It was the cheeky touch to him that I particularly liked, the yoicks! and tally ho! touch to some of his play. Of course it occasionally broke down. He gave away a crucial try to the British Lions in the third test at Sydney in 1989. But that's Campese, where the good far outweighs the bad, if bad it can be called. For me, as a commentator, it was a delight when Campese was playing because of the sudden adventurousness that would spark a game into life. He had that ability, that 'Come and catch me' mood that I loved. He was always calling for the ball, shouting 'Mine!' and 'I'm here!' And as it turned out this was a wonderful type of decoy, because he often distracted people who thought he was going to get the ball. It tended to upset the opposition. Some people (but not me) thought he was too cocksure. But his colleagues knew they had a gem there. They just reacted with, 'Well, that's Campese.' As Bob Dwyer said, you don't interfere with genius. No doubt he occasionally got a ticking-off from Michael Lynagh or Nick Farr-Jones when he attempted something quite outrageous. Farr-Jones was Australian captain during part of David Campese's reign, and I think he had a calming influence. And Campese also played with Mark Ella, another good influence who could help keep things in perspective. But anybody who tried to drill Campese was a fool.

He was a terribly difficult fellow to get the measure of because nobody knew what he was going to do. *He* didn't know! I think it was Michael Lynagh who once said, 'One of the great joys of Campese's play is that he never knows what he's going to do next, so neither does the opposition!' And he had all those gifts, including a wonderful change of pace: one minute he'd be doddling along, and then he was *gone*! I don't think anyone did that better than Campese. There was a try against Scotland at Murrayfield in 1984 that was unbelievable. He handled away on the right touchline just outside the Australian 22, and he got all the way across the field to take a pass for a score in the left-hand corner. You would have thought at least five guys would have got him, but they never looked like it.

His great art lay in the challenge, the unexpected aspect of his play, the sudden surges of brilliance out of nothing. He had a little hitch kick in his play which often checked defenders. I don't think he knew himself how he did it, but it was very, very effective. He'd just be running along when suddenly there was a kind of one-and-a-half, two-and-a-half step. The local Queanbeyan newspaper in New South Wales, where he came from, called it 'Campese's struggletown shuffle'.

For me Campese was the great entertainer, he could light up a match. There was no way you could tie him down. His record of 101 caps and 315 points speaks for itself. He scored sixty-four tries, sixty-four international tries in 101 games – a world record. Even for a guy who played in so many matches that's extraordinary.

But he was also a cheeky chappie who would speak his mind. And although a number of people resented the remarks he made, I think the majority appreciated Campese because he said what he thought, whether or not it ruffled a few feathers. When he criticised the English style of rugby football, saying that it was very limited, and because it was so dependent on forward play threatened to kill the game of rugby union, he upset quite a few people. But I may say that his remarks went down very well with the Celtic countries, especially Scotland and Ireland! For all the criticism of him, people really thought he was a star. Certainly I did.

Maybe it was the Italian side of him that gave him his sparkle. But it was also the type of game that the Australians played. They were probably the most attractive of international sides, certainly since the war. The Australians have always had that desire to entertain, whereas many other teams just have a desire to win. Campese loved to win as well, of course, but I don't think he'd want to shoot himself if he didn't.

Campese must be the only rugby player in the world who has had a dish named after him. In Queanbeyan a local restaurateur was so thrilled by Campese's play that he devised a special steak dish which he called *filet Campese*. The people of Queanbeyan, they thought he was God! But I found him a very modest fellow, for all his bluster and challenge. Once I ran into him at the Hong Kong Sevens, in the foyer of a hotel. I began telling him how much, as a commentator, I depended on people like him, how thrilled I had been at his performance in the Sevens. And he kept looking at the ground and shuffling his feet, as if it embarrassed him to have all this praise heaped on him. And that surprised me, because until that time I had thought that he might be a bit pleased with himself – but he was the exact opposite! Here was a guy who didn't mind telling people where they could go, and how 'bloody English players can't play bloody rugby', and here he was being embarrassed because I had praised him.

One year Campese's club was invited to the Melrose Sevens, the prestigious tournament where seven-a-side rugby started, way back in 1883. Melrose have always been regarded as the great Sevens exponents, and on the day of the match the Borders folk were rubbing their hands because it was a filthy day, raining stair-rods, solid water. 'Wait till we get Campese in this mud bath,' they said. But he made a complete mug of them. His team of Randwick won, and he scored a try against Melrose in which he slithered, kicked ahead, slithered again, kicked it through, and scored. 'I wouldn't have scored that bloody try,' he said, 'if it hadn't been so sticky!' He was the star of the whole tournament in conditions that were completely against his style of play. But he mastered it. That was Campese.

PHILIPPE SELLA (1982–95)

Agen, France

111 caps

After I had chosen my World XV for *The Times* from players on whom I had provided commentary, I was gently chided by Philippe Sella, of Agen and France, who pointed out that there was not one Frenchman in my side. That came as something of a shock to me. I hadn't realised the omission, and it certainly was a serious one. For Sella himself had to be a strong candidate for one of the centre positions. After all, he still is the world's most capped player with 111 caps, of which 104 were as centre, six as wing and one as full-back. He once played forty-five tests in a row, and had a test haul of thirty tries for 125 points. His haul of twenty-nine tries as a centre is a world record.

At five foot eleven and thirteen stone two, he didn't seem exactly an impressive physical type, and yet he was exceptionally strong, sharp into his running and with impressive body control that enabled him to veer away from tackles. He had this ability to ease himself away from outstretched fingers, running with his body in a kind of fish-hook position, and he had an ability to twist his body away when he felt the tackle coming, the hands reaching out. I haven't seen anyone else do that to such a degree. It made him very elusive. He was like a yacht, almost flat to the sea. And of course he had great change of pace, besides being a willing and punishing tackler himself.

Sella had a shattering experience on his debut test against Romania in Bucharest in 1982, when he was concussed and spent the night in hospital, to be given the shock news on recovering consciousness that Romania had won 13–9. As a twenty-year-old he registered two tries against the Argentine Pumas, who regard a try conceded at home as akin to a family bereavement, and throughout his career he somehow always managed to find space in cluttered midfields, which marked him out as a very special talent.

A teacher of physical education, Sella is one of only six players to have scored a try in each match of an international Championship. This he achieved in 1986, to set himself alongside Carston Catcheside of England, Johnny Wallace of Scotland, Patrick Estève of France, Gregor Townsend of Scotland, and Philippe Bernat-Salles of France.

Sella represented France as they won the international Championship six times, and shared in their 1987 Grand Slam when he scored one of the great individualist tries against England with an interception and a sixty-metre sprint. In fact, a feature of Sella's contribution to French success was the cool, level-headed way in which he married French flair to his own personal ability. Very quick, and with that unusual running style which included weave, sidestep and pace change, he brought leadership and organisation to the French back division as well as quality in linkage which helped colleagues to perform. He captained France in six tests, and played in the first three World Cups – a final in 1987, a quarter-final in 1991, and third place in 1995, when France beat England in his last test as a thirty-three-year-old.

Among his other memorable feats was to celebrate his hundredth test in a 22–8 win over New Zealand at Christchurch in June 1994. He also represented Agen in four national finals, of which two were won. There was general wonderment in French rugby circles when Sella was ordered off for punching in a match against Canada in Ontario in 1994. For Sella throughout his career had proved a fair and sporting player. Certainly his superb fitness as a PE teacher contributed to his amazing record of 111 test appearances, a mark that may never be exceeded.

NICK FARR-JONES (1984–93)
New South Wales, Australia
63 caps

Rugby folk in the United Kingdom were first made aware of the huge potential of a tallish Australian scrum-half called Nick Farr-Jones when he toured with the Wallabies in 1984, aged twenty-two. A law student, Farr-Jones had played club rugby with Sydney University, where he was spotted by the famous Australian coach Alan Jones, and signed up for the 1984 tour. He became an important member of that famous Australian side which adminstered a Grand Slam to France and the UK countries, in the process playing some of the most entertaining rugby I have ever seen.

Big and strong, Farr-Jones showed great confidence from the beginning, scoring a try against Scotland in the final test, and working well between a strong scrum and that sensational Wallabies back line which included Mark Ella, Michael Lynagh and David Campese. Farr-Jones formed a strong partnership on that tour with Ella, who benefited from the threat posed to opposing defences by a powerful scrum-half able to take on the mantle of an extra flank forward. At Murrayfield he scored a try off a lineout that was such a cheeky effort, running up the front of the lineout and crashing over in the corner to catch everybody by surprise. His powerful physicality enabled him to bump off a couple of tacklers on the way.

After Ella's retirement Farr-Jones went on to create a superb half-back pairing with Michael Lynagh, and those two played as a partnership in a world record of forty-seven tests. An engaging personality, he had a lot to do with the Australians becoming such a popular outfit in the tours of 1984 and 1988, and not just because of the type of rugby they played with such panache. He himself was a most impressive player, very strong.

Nor was that the only record to the Farr-Jones name. After the 1987 World Cup, the captaincy of Australia was given to him when he was only twenty-five, and he proved to be an able captain, showing intelligence and tactical grasp. He went on to captain Australia in a record thirty-six tests.

The Wallabies under Farr-Jones had mixed fortunes at first, but he played an important part in restoring their confidence following the Australian defeat by the British Lions in 1989, when some observers considered he had been outplayed by the Lions' scrum-half, the Welshman Robert Jones. However, Farr-Jones led the Wallabies to victory over the All Blacks at Sydney in 1991, and was influential in motivating the Australians to their success in the World Cup final at Twickenham in that year, when they triumphed in a hard battle against England to win 12–6.

At five feet ten and thirteen stone two, Farr-Jones was big for a scrum-half and impressively strong, with a long pass, high organisational skills, vision and flair. A lawyer by profession, he proved a good decision-maker on the field as well as in the courts, and a strong player who scored nine tries in an illustrious international career.

JOHN KIRWAN (1984–94)
Auckland, New Zealand
63 caps

If ever a player used the World Cup to underline his huge potential, that player was John James Kirwan of Auckland and New Zealand. He was first capped as a nineteen-year-old against France at Christchurch in 1984, but it was in 1987 that Kirwan leapt to superstar status, simply writing his name all over that inaugural World Cup in New Zealand. In that tournament Kirwan scored six tries in four games, two of them against Italy (including a sensational seventy-metre effort in the opening game), two against Wales, and one each against Fiji and, in the final, France. He was a key member of the All Black side which dominated world rugby for the next three years.

Kirwan was an impressive physical specimen at six foot three and fourteen stone seven, combining size, strength and speed. Big, strong and direct, he could sidestep off either foot, and had a hand-off like the kick of a mule. He could also stand up in the tackle and off-load in support play. From the time in 1983 when Alex Wyllie, the Auckland and later New Zealand coach, plucked the big lad from the lower echelons to a place in the Auckland squad, the former butcher's apprentice proved one of the most powerful wings of all time, and one who set all kinds of records in try-scoring. He once ran in eight tries during a Ranfurly Shield game for Auckland against North Otago, four tries for New Zealand against Wales in Christchurch in 1988, tries in eight consecutive tests, sixty-seven tries in ninety-six games for New Zealand, and 199 tries in 267 games in first-class rugby in New Zealand.

Kirwan joined David Kirk in deciding against touring South Africa, then under an apartheid regime, with the rebel Cavaliers in 1986. In 1994 he joined the rugby league club, the Auckland Warriors, for two seasons. He also played club rugby in Italy, where he played and coached as well. He now coaches the Italian team, which in 2003 responded to his work by producing its best perfor-mances since entering the Six Nations competition.

There is no doubt that Kirwan would have proved a huge success in any era, and in my opinion he was a better bet as a winger even than Jonah Lomu. Kirwan was more skilful than Lomu, a better defender, very quick, and a better all-round footballer. Many people would plump for Kirwan as the best wing New Zealand has pro-duced. In fact, Kirwan had everything.

MICHAEL LYNAGH (1984–95)
Queensland, Australia
72 caps

Michael Patrick Lynagh will always have a special place in Australian rugby lore, not only as Australia's most capped stand-off with seventy-two, nor as the world's record points-scorer in major internationals with 911, until that mark was passed by Neil Jenkins of Wales (1,049 in eighty-seven tests), nor indeed for his record of having played international rugby against seventeen different countries. What has endeared Lynagh most to countless Australian rugby supporters is the try he scored against Ireland in Dublin in the quarter-final of the 1991 World Cup. Remember the scene? Australia trailed 15–18 in injury time, and all Ireland was preparing to raise the roof when the final whistle went, and then the Wallabies produced one desperate final move for Lynagh, who could always sniff a try, to dash over for last gasp victory by 19–18.

And Australia of course went on to win that 1991 World Cup with victory over England by 12–6 in the final. Lynagh played a huge part, amassing sixty-six points in that tournament from two tries, eleven conversions, and twelve penalty goals.

At five foot ten and twelve stone nine, Lynagh was a compact, tidy practitioner, and although his nickname was Noddy he certainly never dropped off during a long playing career as a gifted all-round athlete with quite an edge of pace. He became Queensland's stand-off when he was just eighteen years old, and was first capped in 1984 as a twenty-one-year-old against Fiji in Suva. In that same year he showed his versatility when Australia toured the UK for, with Mark Ella established as Australia's stand-off, Lynagh took on the role of inside centre as to the manner born. He played in that position in all four tests of the Wallabies' Grand Slam, contributing forty-two points. And he was overall top scorer on that tour with ninety-eight points in eleven games.

When the great Mark Ella retired in 1984, unreasonably early in the opinion of many Australian fans, Lynagh took over the stand-off position and made it his own, forming a fruitful half-back partnership with Nick Farr-Jones in a record forty-seven tests. In fact, he became one of the world's most successful No 10s. A voracious accumulator of points, he once scored thirty-seven in a single match against Canada, twenty-eight against Argentina, twenty-four against France, and twenty-one against Scotland. Lynagh spent eleven years in international play before retiring after the 1995 World Cup.

Lynagh played in three World Cup tournaments for Australia: in 1987 when they reached the final, in 1991 when they were Champions, and in 1995 when they were quarter-finalists. Outside Australia he played club rugby in Italy, where he helped Benetton-Treviso to reach the 1993 cup final, and in England, where he created a fine partnership with Philippe Sella of France and François Pienaar of South Africa for the Saracens, notably when they were cup winners in 1998.

JONATHAN DAVIES (1985–97)
Neath, Llanelli, Cardiff, Wales, British Lions
32 Wales caps

It was against Scotland at Cardiff in 1988 that Jonathan Davies underlined, in one gorgeous move, those remarkable gifts that endeared him first to Welsh rugby union supporters, and then to the adherents of Widnes rugby league club. From a lineout on Scotland's 22 Davies took the ball at pace, slotted a grubber kick with perfect touch and angle to the Scottish goal line, and then accelerated at such blinding speed as to reach the ball first for a remarkable try.

That simple-looking move demonstrated not only the Davies gifts of punting skill at pace, angle of thrust, brilliant placement, and judgment of what was possible, but it also marked him out as a young man with high confidence in his skills and assessments. His brilliant individualist effort brought Wales back into the game after the Scots had taken a 7–0 lead. But more Davies magic was to follow. With Scotland leading 20–19, Davies conjured up two drop goals of magical accuracy for a Welsh victory by 25–20 in what was described as one of the greatest games ever seen at Cardiff.

Those weren't the only drop goals slotted by the Welsh maestro. In all he popped over a Welsh record of thirteen drop goals in cap internationals, which placed him seventh in the world order, behind Hugo Porta (26), Rob Andrew (21), Naas Botha (18), Stefan Bettarello (17), Diego Dominguez (17), and Jean-Pierre Lescarboura (15).

Davies had a remarkable introduction to test rugby when, in his first capped match against England at Cardiff in 1985, he scored a try and a drop goal in victory by 24–15. And my countrymen have every reason to rue that Davies drop-goal magic, for he stroked over drop goals against Scotland in 1986 and 1987, and in 1988 he put over two more, as we have seen. He had the honour of captaining Wales against Canada, New Zealand, Samoa and Romania in 1988, setting a rare example with tries against New Zealand and Samoa. It was in 1988 that he scored drop goals in three consecutive internationals, against England, Scotland and Wales.

Davies was a gifted practitioner, with safe and soft hands, genuine pace and pace change, and kicking accuracy. But as his country's fortunes dwindled in the dark years of the 1980s, he became the target of criticism which finally persuaded him to change codes in 1988, and throw in his lot with rugby league. There he had the good sense to beef himself up for his spell with the Widnes club between 1988 and 1995, making a huge impression, and winning Great Britain honours before, in 1995, he returned to the Cardiff rugby union club with the advent of professionalism in the union game.

Davies climaxed his rugby career with appearances against Scotland, France and England in 1997 as a thirty-three-year-old. Following his last international appearance for Wales against England in 1997 he had eighty-one cap international points to his name from a full house of five tries, thirteen drop goals, six penalty goals and two conversions.

Since then Jonathan Davies has established himself as a TV summariser for the BBC, thus lending his rugby league and rugby union playing experience to his broadcast assessments, which are given in knowledgeable and forthright terms.

IEUAN EVANS (1987–98)
Llanelli, Bath, Wales, British Lions
72 caps
7 British Lions tests

He left four of my countrymen sitting on their backsides wondering exactly where he had gone. That was Ieuan Cenydd Evans in 1988, displaying quite wondrous try-scoring brilliance at Cardiff towards a Welsh win by 25–20. Evans received the ball somewhere in the region of Scotland's 22 and proceeded to demonstrate virtually every form of deception, with swerve, feint, pace change, and running angle, to score one of the finest tries I have ever seen. As I said at the time, 'It was magic, magic all the way, not even Merlin the Magician could have done any better.' And don't forget, Merlin was Ieuan's compatriot!

A year before, the Canadians had cause to experience similar feelings to those Scots. For in 1987 in the World Cup match at Invercargill, New Zealand, Ieuan Evans proceeded to gather in no fewer than four tries in a Welsh victory by 40–9. He even topped that with six tries for Wales B against Spain in 1985. One of the most exciting runners ever spawned by the Welsh game, he also could come off either foot in a blink of the eye, and clearly revelled at tilting his lance at all comers.

A compact five foot eleven and thirteen stone five, and a graduate of Salford University, Evans was capped first in a 9–16 defeat by France in 1987. For the next eleven years he gave his all in the Welsh cause during a bleak spell for Welsh fortunes, when that proud rugby-playing country suffered some appalling defeats. During that period Evans gained a then record of seventy-two caps, and ran in thirty-three test tries – another Welsh record. He also claimed a Lions test try, so that his overall haul of thirty-four placed him fifth in the world rankings at the end of his international career in 1998. His Lions try in the third test against Australia in 1989 caught the inimitable David Campese in error behind his lines for the ever-opportunistic Evans to dash in and dot down. That try turned the series in the Lions' favour.

Evans toured with the Lions in Australia in 1989, New Zealand in 1993, and South Africa in 1997, and played in seven of the nine tests. A favourite son of Stradey Park, he played 230 games for Llanelli, scored 193 tries, played in seven cup finals, and shared in a league and cup double in 1992–93. He scored the winning try for Llanelli against the touring Wallabies in 1992.

Evans played his part when Wales claimed a Triple Crown in 1988 and a Five Nations Championship in 1994. In 1998, having moved to Bath, he shared in their thrilling European Cup success over Brive by 19–18. But before that he had already received Welsh hero status, and this was underlined in 1993, when he scored the try by which Wales beat England 10–9, thus denying them a Grand Slam.

PART FIVE

1990s and the Present

**Grand Slams: England – and Scotland
The World Cup
The Professional Era
The European (Heineken) Cup**

Joost Van Der Westhuizen   (South Africa 1993–)
Jonah Lomu   (New Zealand 1994–)
Keith Wood   (Ireland 1994–)
Christian Cullen   (New Zealand 1996–)
Jonny Wilkinson   (England 1998–)
Brian O'Driscoll   (Ireland 1999–)
Jason Robinson   (England 2001–)

GRAND SLAMS:
ENGLAND – AND
SCOTLAND

D<small>URING THE</small> 1990s England won three Grand Slams, in 1991, 1992 and 1995; and that is some feat – played twelve and won twelve internationals in those three seasons. And with handsome totals of scores: eighty-three points in four games in 1991; 118 points and fifteen tries to four in 1992; and ninety-eight points and nine tries to two in the four games of 1995. So their dominance was there for all to see. At one time or another they put virtually everybody to the sword, beating Wales 25–6 in 1991, Scotland 25–7 and Ireland 38–9 in 1992, and Wales 24–0, in 1992, at Twickenham. In 1995 there were thirty-one points against the French, twenty-three against Wales in Cardiff, twenty-four against Scotland at Twickenham, and twenty against Ireland in Dublin.

Wonderful stuff there! And just think of some of the players who were around then: backs like Webb, Halliday, Carling, Guscott, Rory Underwood; Rob Andrew and Dewi Morris as halves – Rob Andrew I was happy to choose for stand-off half in my all-time World XV, which didn't go down too well in Wales, but I just had to accept the criticism I got for that!

And when you look at that England pack, in 1992 for example, Leonard, Moore and Probyn – what a front row that is; Bayfield and Dooley, big, strong, heavy, gifted; and Skinner, Richards and

Winterbottom in the back row: Winterbottom tearing about all over the place, covering all areas of the park, knocking people over, and Richards, so powerful; when he had the ball no one else got it, he would stand there and protect the ball magnificently. And Skinner, an all-round blind-side flanker of great skill. Those England sides had a total game, from front row to full-back. I recall that Webb, the full-back, scored sixty-seven points in the 1992 championship, and that included three tries.

So England were totally dominant at that time, and they played some great rugby football. At times they tended to place a lot of faith in their forwards, but that was perhaps understandable because the English packs of those days were very powerful indeed, and made for all seasons, as it were. England still played some great running football; with Will Carling and Guscott in midfield, Rory and Tony Underwood on the wings, they had virtually everything. They had Simon Halliday as well, who could play wing or centre. At half-back Rob Andrew and Dewi Morris were very well equipped, so they were a side that could hit you anywhere – they could take you on up front, in amongst the backs, midfield. There were times when you wondered if there was any weakness at all in those England sides. Certainly they created one of the great halcyon eras for English rugby football at international level with their three Grand Slams of 1991, 1992 and 1995.

But there was quite a lot of criticism of England at the time because of a feeling that they placed too much faith in their forwards, and depended an awful lot on the Andrew boot. Rob Andrew had such an educated boot, he could produce any kind of kick that was necessary: garryowen, diagonal, chip kick ahead, he had the lot. So you could understand England wanting to use that to put pressure on the opposition, and also to ensure that they didn't make a guddle anywhere and give the opposition a chance to counter-attack.

Perhaps some of the criticism was justified. But at the same time England did also let the ball go on occasion, and when they did they were formidable indeed! With that in mind, perhaps they could have been more adventurous, they could have had a go. But they were playing Five Nations and then Six Nations rugby football, and they had big, powerful forwards, though maybe not the fastest in the world, so in a way it was sensible to try and keep the ball reasonably close to them. At the end of the 1980s the England backs were playing some champagne rugby, but I think they got a bit of a bloody nose when the Scots beat them in 1990 and took the Grand Slam they thought was theirs. After that they maybe went into their shell a bit more than was strictly necessary.

I've kept many of the big sheets I always used to prepare before each match in my commentating days, with all the details of every player and so on, and one of these sheets is for that crucial Grand Slam decider at Murrayfield on 17 March 1990, when Scotland and England were both going for the Slam. That match wasn't quite unique, but it was certainly very unusual, a tremendous occasion. As we all know, Scotland eventually won 13–7, and I suppose from our point of view it was one of the most enjoyable victories ever over the auld enemy because it was so much against the odds.

England hadn't had a Grand Slam since Bill Beaumont's team in 1980, but they were definitely the favourites for one this time. In their three victories over Ireland, France and Wales they had scored eighty-three points and conceded only thirteen. They thrashed Ireland 23–0 at Twickenham with tries by Guscott and Underwood. At the Parc des Princes their pack had steamrollered the French, with more tries from the backs; and they had beaten the Welsh 34–6 at Twickenham with two tries from Rory Underwood, who was in peak form.

Just look at the England side: backs like Carling, Guscott, Underwood, Andrew and Hill; forwards like Rendall, Moore and

Probyn, Dooley and Ackford, and Skinner, Teague and Winter-bottom. What a magnificent pack of forwards. And I have to say that when I watched England train on the day before the match, I was very impressed indeed. They never dropped a pass and had big men rumbling about and handling like backs. My wife Bette was watching with me and we agreed it would take a miracle for Scotland to beat this lot.

Came the day, and the England team ran out. But then the Scotland team *walked* out, led by David Sole who was an inspirational leader, and the sight of the Scotland team walking out slowly and deliberately made a great impression. The crowd responded with tremendous fervour, and I remember Rob Andrew saying to me that the singing of 'Flower of Scotland' was louder than being in Cardiff. It lifted the Scottish team to heights of endeavour that some people didn't think they could achieve, and it may even have thrown the English off their stride a bit, because they were not the awesome crowd I had watched at practice the day before.

Scotland's tactics were brilliant. They had a plan that suited them. For example, they mucked about at the lineouts so that England were never sure who was going to be where, and that upset them. And of course the whole Scottish team played out of their skins. From the kick-off the Scottish forwards attacked their opposite numbers with terrific intensity, and they used strong rucks to drive the English backwards.

So against all the odds Scotland prevailed, and a special delight for me was that the crucial try was scored by Tony Stanger, who was a former pupil of mine at Wilton School and Hawick High School. It was a particular thrill for me to be doing commentary when Tony scored that important try that really won the match for Scotland, as I recalled that he had learned his rugby with me as a ten-year-old in Hawick. So when I said, 'They'll be dancing in the streets of Hawick tonight' after Tony's Grand Slam-clinching try, I knew what I was talking about!

That was undoubtedly one of the great days in Scottish rugby history, because over the years Scotland, like Ireland, have had few great successes like that. They've been few and far between, so when they do come they give great joy throughout the country. Certainly that victory which gave Scotland a Grand Slam lifted the spirit of the whole of the country. You could feel it everywhere – soccer players, tennis players, hockey players, all of them just rejoiced along with the rugby people. So that one will stay in the memory for a long time.

England were pipped at the post by Australia in the 1991 World Cup, and that may have surprised some people. The Wallabies may not have been the better side in some respects, but they were definitely the more adventurous, and more liable to produce the unexpected. With the likes of Campese a surprise was always on. He was a wise old bird, was Campese. The Australians were a pretty good team, and I always had the feeling that they were capable, at their very best, of the most enterprising and entertaining play. They had a good mix of solid, hardworking forwards – nothing very special but good ball winners and good support runners – and of course the backs with the likes of Farr-Jones, Lynagh and Campese were capable of great things. In one area they were just outstanding, better than anybody else, and that was in that sleight of hand I was talking about earlier, slipping the ball over their shoulder and so on. So I thought they were justified world champions.

England sometimes tend to flatter to deceive, I've often thought. And that may be as true today in 2003 as it ever was. They're capable of a quality of rugby football that the other home nations just can't match at the moment. They must be seen to go into the 2003 World Cup if not as favourites then near the top, and they are capable of winning it. But it worries me that sometimes they don't deliver. I just hope they get to the final, and when they get there they lose to Scotland! You can't expect anything better than that.

Sometimes England think they're better than they are, that they've won before they've actually won as it were. But they should make a big impact in the World Cup, and even carry the banner for the home nations. They've got all they need: a good squad, the back-up, everything.

THE WORLD CUP

WHEN THE idea of a World Cup came up, and the first tournament was organised in 1987, at first I treated it with a bit of scepticism. I wondered how it would be successful, how they would incorporate all the smaller countries who couldn't really hope to compete against the likes of the All Blacks, Wallabies and Springboks, and how it would work with different countries playing in different styles, referees' interpretations, all that kind of thing. But having been at the World Cup in 1987 in Australia and New Zealand, I had to admit it was a huge success, with some wonderful rugby football. So that really changed my mind and I think it's a marvellous tournament. There may be some difficulty with law interpretation between the hemispheres but we seem to have muddled through very well, and it's now thoroughly well established and much looked forward to. I think what it needs now is for one of the Home Unions to break through, to break the dominance of the southern hemisphere countries.

To many people, that match at the Concord Oval, Sydney, on 13 June 1987, when France won the second semi-final and pipped Australia 30–24 through an injury-time Serge Blanco try, was one of the most exciting games of rugby ever played.

The Wallabies had defeated the French on the same ground in Sydney a year earlier, so they were favourites to win again. But the game seesawed back and forth, with the lead changing hands six times. The Wallabies were driven forward by the brilliant tactician-ship of half-backs Michael Lynagh and Nick Farr-Jones, while the French had good mauling forwards and real pace behind the scrum.

The score stood at 24–24 when the game was just about over. But then came the French forwards and backs combined to take the ball deep into Wallaby territory. There were injured and exhausted players scattered all over the field, the move seemed to have broken down, but then the French No 8 Rodriguez fed Blanco, who burst over twenty yards to dive beyond Tommy Lawton's lunge, and touched down in the corner to win the match. New Zealand easily beat France in the final, but it was that semi-final game which caught the attention of the world.

In 1991 the Australians were the champions, and deservedly in my opinion. In the semi-final they broke Irish hearts with Lynagh's match-winning try three minutes into injury time. England had a very hard game against the French at Parc des Princes in the quarter-final. Brian Moore, who was their hooker that day, wrote that 'there was never a match which had its tension and bite ... An English team which was bent, but refused to buckle under intense French pressure.'

Then there was the final at Twickenham and Australia's 12–6 victory. Although there was only one try, both sides played some tremendous rugby. It was strange because England had got to the final by playing to a tight format, keeping the game close with their tremendous pack. But in the final, they changed their style and tried to play a lot wider. It didn't come off and David Campese, who was the great star in that Australian side, of course, said after the final: 'If you want to play fifteen-man rugby you have to learn it. You can't just turn up on the day and play that type of game.'

If England had stuck to the ten-man style they had played to before, I suppose it's possible that they might have won. Rob Andrew passed the ball much more than usual, but still England didn't get a try. So maybe England played the wrong game, or perhaps it was the Australian defence, which was rock solid. England had some great players: Jason Leonard, who is still on the international scene twelve years later, Brian Moore and Jeff Probyn, those two second-row giants Paul Ackford and Wade Dooley, and a formidable back row. But in spite of backs of the calibre of Will Carling, Jeremy Guscott and Rory Underwood, England just couldn't pierce through Australia's defence.

Cliff Morgan wrote afterwards, 'This sporting battle was genuine and worthy of an honoured place on the world stage – above all else in its spirit and gallantry. The 1991 World Cup final had integrity and it was a flourish of triumphant rugby.'

I have kept my worksheet from that match, of course, and this is what comes back to me as I look at it:

You probably couldn't have had a better contest, with England playing Australia, both teams full of class players. England with Webb at full-back; Halliday, Carling, Guscott and Underwood; Rob Andrew and Hill at half-back; and look at that front row: Leonard, Moore and Probyn; then Dooley and Ackford, six foot six and seventeen stone six, and six foot eight and seventeen stone nine; then an abrasive back three: Skinner, Teague at No 8, and Winterbottom – what a threesome that was.

The Australians had one or two fellows who weren't so well known: Roebuck at full-back, Egerton on the right wing. However, they had Jason Little and Tim Horan together at centre, and they were a great pair, having come up together throught the ranks as it were, playing as youngsters in the Australian Schools side, both from the same club, the South club. They were a great pair, blending so well – different types in a way, with Little long-striding, a thoughtful player, and Tim Horan full of get-at-'em.

And then of course on the left wing there was Campese, playing in his sixty-fourth international in that World Cup final in 1991, having first played in 1982 against the All Blacks. He was just a star, and if I had to be asked who was my favourite player, purely from a commentator's point of view, I would pick Campese, simply from the surprise element in his play – you never knew what he would do next, and I don't think *he* did, but it was riveting and enthralling, and a delight to watch.

And then there was Lynagh and Farr-Jones. Could you have a better half-back pairing? Both of them in their fifty-third international match,

Lynagh with 681 points at the time, and Farr-Jones such a strong player, five foot ten and thirteen and a half stone – he actually looked heavier than that.

The forwards – I don't suppose you would rate them much to look at them, but by golly what an eight they were: Daly, Kearns and Ewen Mackenzie; McCall and Eales were the lock forwards, John Eales of course world class, out of the Brothers club and just twenty-one years old, six foot seven and fifteen stone twelve; and then Poidevin, Coker and Ofahengaue – I always worried about Ofahengaue because by the time I'd pronounced his name he'd scored the try and kicked the goal – they were a great threesome, Poidevin roaming about all over the place, Coker a clever No 8, good back-of-the-lineout man, and of course Ofahengaue who was just immense.

It was a great Australian side, but England gave them a run, 12–6 the final score, Mackenzie got the one try, a prop forward out of the Randwick club in Sydney, and the rest of it was Lynagh kicking goals and Jonathan Webb kicking a couple of penalties for England. So that was a great occasion really, the first World Cup final to be played in the UK at Twickenham. Disappointment for England, but Australia definitely a side that could play any type of game that was required, with class men like Little, Horan, Campese, Lynagh and Farr-Jones. World class players, each one.

The 1995 World Cup was also wonderful. Joel Stransky's drop goal won the final for South Africa against New Zealand, so the host country won the Championship. That's a wonderful memory. And Stransky's drop goal happened only a short time after Rob Andrew had done the same thing to win the game for England against Australia, a magnificent effort that took England to the semi-final.

England had high hopes of at least getting to the final. But then they ran into New Zealand and a gentleman called Jonah Lomu. This is what I said about it at the time:

The match exceeded expectations. It was ablaze with movement, with Herculean forward exchanges, with shuddering tackles aimed at knock-

Gavin Hastings, Scotland's Captain Braveheart, scores a spectacular 70 metre try in Paris, February 1995, which clinched Scottish victory over France by 23–21.

Gary Armstrong, Scotland's tenacious, committed, and exceedingly brave scrum-half, combined quick service with hard-hitting tackles and the ability to sniff out a try.

Sean Fitzpatrick, New Zealand's longest-serving hooker and captain, breaks through the Wales line in the All Blacks victory in Auckland, 1988.

Zinzan Brooke, one of New Zealand's most creative forwards of all time with his wonderful ball skills, even had the ability to drop a goal from fifty yards, as in this All Blacks defeat of Wales in 1997.

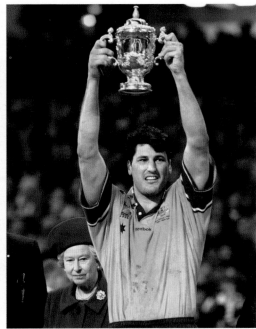

Matt Burke, Australia's most capped full-back, has scored more than 800 points in major internationals, including twenty-five tries.

John Eales, perhaps Australia's most gifted lock ever, hoists the trophy after leading the Wallabies to World Cup victory over France in 1999. Eales, a member of the Australian side that won the World Cup in 1991, could kick goals as well.

Christian Cullen is not only New Zealand's most capped full-back with forty-five tests in that position; he is also the All Blacks' most prolific try scorer, with forty-six. Some talent!

Joost van der Westhuizen, South Africa's long-serving scrum-half, showed his attacking and defensive powers in the 1995 World Cup, where on several occasions he even flattened the mighty Jonah Lomu.

Brian O'Driscoll, Ireland's captain and inspirational centre, is not only fast into his running, with flaring acceleration, but also a dependable and committed defender.

Jonah Lomu of New Zealand shreds the England defence with one of his four tries during the 1995 World Cup semi-final in Cape Town. A lightning-fast wing of six foot five inches and nineteen stone three pounds, Lomu was the sensation of the tournament.

England expects! Jonny Wilkinson drops yet another goal at Twickenham, against Australia in 2001, when he scored all twenty-one points in England's victory. Almost infallible with the boot, he is also a thunderous tackler.

Jason Robinson rips through the Scottish defence as England power towards their 2003 Grand Slam. Robinson has already claimed eleven tries in just twenty internationals.

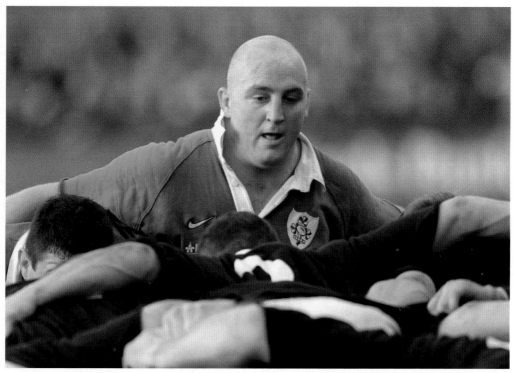

Keith Wood, Ireland's hooker and former captain, is an exciting runner with ball in hand. Dogged by injury, he remains an influential presence.

Jason Leonard, master prop, has scrummaged for England in more than 100 tests – an extraordinary achievement, especially considering the physical pressure placed upon front rows.

My last commentary assignment at Murrayfield: Scotland v. France, 23 February 2002 – a long, long time since my first one there in 1953.

My greatest world XV at *The Times* celebration, Dorchester Hotel, March 2001. *Back row, from left*: Barry John (special guest), Mervyn Davies, Zinzan Brooke, Colin Meads, Fran Cotton, Fergus Slattery, Gerald Davies; *front row, from left*: Rob Andrew, Graham Price, Sean Fitzpatrick, Bill McLaren, Mike Gibson, Gareth Edwards, Andy Irvine.

ing opponents backwards but which, in general, were fair; and with some spectacular handling which gave the capacity crowd a thoroughly entertaining afternoon. It was a personal triumph for Lomu. He scored four of New Zealand's six tries with thunderous runs in which he left opponents grasping thin air. He crashed through tackles like an earth-mover and demonstrated that he is singularly athletic, highly skilled, and possesses an edge of pace that catches opponents by surprise...

That the All Blacks were focused and alert to the main chance was shown by the manner in which they caught England cold at the beginning of each half. New Zealand coach Laurie Mains said at the post-match press conference that they had planned for the All Blacks to take the initiative right from the start. The twenty-two-year-old fly-half, Andrew Mehrtens, took the kick-off for which Sean Fitzpatrick had opted on winning the toss, but instead of the orthodox kick to his for-wards, he put in a delicate little chip shot, like a wedge at golf, to the blind side and just over the ten metres. It was a sucker punch which caught out England. Within seconds of that crafty start New Zealand had created a bridgehead from which Lomu crashed past three tackles for the opening try less than three minutes into the match. Two minutes later the All Blacks made a clear declaration of intent when, from their own 22, Walter Little and Glen Osborne counter-attacked in a blaze of black. Just when the move seemed still-born, Kronfeld appeared like an express train to crash over for Mehrtens to convert. When the fly-half added a penalty goal New Zealand were fifteen points up in eleven minutes and playing a scintillating brand of rugby that England just could not match. It was 25–3 at half-time from Mehrtens' conversion of Lomu's second try and a dropped goal from Zinzan Brooke which underlined my own view that he is the most skilled and tactically aware forward in the world game. He gathered a loose ball some forty metres out and smacked over a cracking goal, that put the icing on an already very rich New Zealand cake...

To their credit, England kept their heads high and, inspired by Dewi Morris, who recovered from a shaky start, they staged an admirable rally and a see-saw spectacular to ring down the curtain with two tries each for Will Carling and Rory Underwood ... Yet each time England threatened serious revival the All Blacks countered to effect. They were rewarded by Lomu's fourth try, from a huge Mehrtens spin pass, converted by Mehrtens, and then a dropped goal for the talented fly-half. It brought his tally to fifteen points in the match, and seventy-five from four games ...

The final score after a contest of rare movement and mighty endeavour was 45–29, and the All Blacks emerged as even firmer favourites to win the World Cup for the second time.

The South Africans shaded New Zealand in the end, of course, thanks to that brilliant Stransky dropped goal in the last minutes of extra time. But there is another thing I'll never forget about the 1995 World Cup final in South Africa, and that was when Nelson Mandela turned up in a South Africa jersey. That really suggested a unity in South African affairs which had been missing for so long. It was lovely to see Mandela use that great occasion – that great World Cup final – to signify, perhaps, a unity of purpose in South African affairs. It was very encouraging and I will remember it as long as I live.

THE PROFESSIONAL ERA

F OR MOST of the last decade, as the game has adjusted to the new professional era, England's dominance in the Six Nations tournament has been quite marked. They won the Grand Slam three times, and took the Triple Crown six times in eight seasons. Only England's bête noir – an indomitable French side with back-to-back Grand Slams – stopped them in 1997 and 1998. But England and France have dominated the early years of the professional era.

I suppose I'm a professional myself in the sense that I'm a broadcaster, and when I first came into journalism I was sometimes ostracised in that I was regarded as a professional and therefore didn't really have a place in the game. But at heart I'm an amateur, I loved the game the way it was, when you played for fun. Everyone wanted to win, but you played for fun, you trained on Tuesdays and Thursdays and you played on the Saturday, and the rest of the week was your own.

It seems to me that rugby football is a job now, and as a result a certain amount of enjoyment has been lost. Where there used to be a desire to win, now there's a *need* to win because of the financial implications of success or failure on the field. On the other hand, there's some real quality rugby being played because there's no doubt players are fitter than they've ever been, physically harder and stronger, and perhaps even more committed to the task.

But that has worrisome bits too – the physical contact of rugby football worries me greatly. I never cease to boggle in amazement at what the human frame will stand in the way of impact and thrust, but today you can be standing there, minding your own business, and suddenly get thumped and barged about twenty yards further away. There are some areas of professionalism I don't approve of greatly. Rugby's a hard enough game as it is, you get knocked about plenty without introducing an additional element that makes it even fiercer than it is.

I loved the game the way it was when you played for your town because you had a pride in your town, but now you can go and play anywhere if the money's good. It worries me a little bit that even at local club level we embrace New Zealanders, Australians or South Africans who want to experience rugby football here. That may break down national barriers a bit, but the trouble is that for every southern hemisphere player who comes and plays in a Scottish club side, or indeed for Scotland, a Scottish youngster doesn't get the chance. I would rather fail with a Scottish side playing with Scottish men born and bred, than be successful with a side that had half a dozen no doubt very good players whose right to play for Scotland was somewhat tenuous.

There's no doubt that rugby can benefit a lot from a really good southern hemisphere player coming and joining a club side. Sean Lineen, for instance, from New Zealand, has made a huge contribution to rugby at international level. But I would rather New Zealanders played for New Zealand and Scots for Scotland. You can't get it as clean cut as that, I know, but it's a bit worrying that in order to try and achieve success we reach out for players whose connection with the home team is very narrow.

In the old days they were perhaps too strict about professionalism. You couldn't be seen even talking to a reporter – they came down on you like a ton of bricks. Once when I was at Hawick I wrote a little thing for the paper, I don't think it was even about rugby, and I was up before the President of the Scottish Rugby Union. He was the manager of the local branch of the Bank of Scotland, and I was marched in past all the tellers and into the inner sanctum, and told, 'Billy, you did something for the paper, don't do that again!' I was petrified he'd tell my dad!

Hawick had quite a number of players who went to rugby league and did well there: Drew Turnbull, Darcy Anderson, David Valentine. I played with David Valentine at Hawick and in a Scottish trial, and he captained the Great Britain rugby league side, and was tremendously successful; but once he was over the other side there was no return. When rugby league players came back you wouldn't see them in the Hawick clubhouse; they were professionals and never the twain shall meet!

THE EUROPEAN
(HEINEKEN) CUP

THE HEINEKEN Cup is another step forward, I regard it as a step beyond club rugby. Playing against other clubs from other countries helps our players to see if there's anything new they might pick up to improve their own game. It's a high standard in Europe and you have to play well there to survive. I think at first it came as a bit of a shock to our players to experience the intensity and physicality of the game as it's played, say, in some of the French clubs. They're tough guys out there, and it can be a new dimension as far as the physical challenge is concerned. At the same time, you broaden your own knowledge of the game and can learn so much from others. It's a handy breeding ground for young players. If they can survive in the European Cup they're well on their way to the kind of pressure they'll have to withstand if they aim to go higher into international play. Europe is a very good stepping stone into the international arena. The European Cup is a tournament that can be compared to the southern hemisphere's Super 12. It gives our players a chance to play the top clubs and players in Europe at the highest level possible. Next to an international, the final is maybe the biggest game you can play.

And also there's some lovely rugby played. You can get a French side that fancies themselves a bit, and it's a delight to see them, even though they might make mistakes and have the odd disaster. It's a thrill to see that kind of adventurism, which I don't think we have enough of in this country. I think we're too careful with our club rugby, we play a lot of percentage games and I'd like to see us taking more risks sometimes.

I remember the first European Cup final in January 1996 at Cardiff Arms Park. Toulouse beat Cardiff 21–18 in extra time with a penalty under the sticks in the last twenty seconds. The Welshmen were devastated. Another game I commentated was the 2001 final in Paris, between Stade Français and Leicester. I've kept the worksheet I prepared before the game, as I do before every game, and the memories come back as I look it through.

Leicester were carrying the torch for British rugby that day. But look at the Stade Français side: at full-back Dominici, one of the most elusive and quickest wings you could imagine, already with twenty-one caps to his name, but played at full-back that day; Thomas Lombard, a great muckle brute of a wing three-quarter, he had already played twelve times for France; Comba the centre, thirteen caps, and Gomez, six caps; and then Diego Dominguez, one of the great creators in rugby football, at stand-off. And they had an all-international pack: Marconnet, Landreau, De Villiers, Auradou, James, Moni, Pool-Jones and Juillet – every one an international player.

But Leicester put against them a side loaded with international players as well: Tim Stimpson was at full-back, Geordan Murphy of Ireland on the wing, Leon Lloyd at centre, a very creative player who had won two caps as a replacement against South Africa, Pat Howard, a cracking player who had got his first cap for the Wallabies against New Zealand in 1993, Winston Stanley who had played forty times for Canada; and Austin Healey was there at scrum-half with thirty-seven caps. And look at the pack: Rowntree, West and Garforth, Martin Johnson, Martin Corry and Neil Back – all internationals. And Will Johnson the No 8 forward, he was Martin Johnson's brother.

So you can see the quality of that final – it had all the ingredients for a tremendous match, and that's exactly what it was. Leicester won by 34–30. Dominguez kicked nine goals. Leon Lloyd scored a couple of tries, and Neil Back got one as well. It was like an international match really, and the quality was great.

I went along to a Leicester training session the day before just to make sure I could identify all the fellows, and I had my big sheet with me with all these details on it. I was asking Dean Richards, who was of course their coach, about one or two things, and he noticed what I was carrying.

'What's that?' he asked.

'Oh, that's just my worksheet. Details about the players and so on.'

'God almighty,' he said. 'Do you mean to tell me you do one of those for every match?'

'Every match. It keeps me out of mischief. Maybe a lot of fellows don't need to, but I like to fill up my double foolscap sheet, and on the night before the game I've got every detail I think I'll need for the game. I just go over the whole lot and try to keep in mind one or two little items.'

'I never realised there was so much homework in it,' he said.

'Well,' I said, 'you had to do a lot of homework too, to get Leicester to the final.'

But he was amazed, he just kept shaking his head. And I was quite pleased Dean was impressed, because of course he was very impressive himself, as a great player as well as a very successful coach. And believe me, that was some game to take on, playing Stade Français in their own patch. But they did it. And they won.

It really was a tremendous effort, Leicester scoring three tries to none, a terrific achievement. And they were a delight to do commentary on that day.

PORTRAITS

RORY UNDERWOOD (1984–96)
Leicester, RAF, England, British Lions
85 England caps
6 British Lions tests

Rory Underwood was one of the most dangerous wings ever to wear the red rose of England, for he possessed quicksilver acceleration, could maintain pace over a distance, and was a solidly built lad of five foot nine and fourteen stone who simply revelled in making for the line at a rate of knots. As a result, he played in ninety-one tests, eighty-five for England and six for the Lions, and scored fifty test tries, forty-nine for England, and one for the British Lions in their 20–7 win against New Zealand at Wellington in 1993. His haul of fifty test tries placed him second in world ranking to David Campese (sixty-four).

Time and again Underwood would exploit limited space for tries that didn't seem on, often squeezing into the corner with inches to spare. He was not the most reliable defender, especially if made to turn, and he wasn't the most dependable punter, but given an inch of space he was quite deadly, and there was a surge of expectancy in the watching audience whenever he took off, ball in hand.

When England played Fiji at Twickenham in 1989, Underwood equalled the England record of five tries in a test, set by Dan Lambert of the Harlequins against France in 1907. He also had the pleasure of playing along with his brother Tony in the England side on nineteen occasions. When the Underwoods played together in a test for the first time against Scotland in 1993, it was the first time brothers had played together for England since the Wheatleys, Harold and Arthur, against Scotland in 1938.

Rory Underwood assuredly would have gained even more caps but for his RAF service as a fighter pilot, which caused him to miss tours to South Africa in 1984, New Zealand in 1985, and Argentina in 1990. First capped against Ireland in 1984 as a twenty-year-old, his international career spanned twelve seasons, and as well as being England's record cap-holder at one time, he also holds the world record as the most capped wing with ninety-one. He played in the World Cup tournaments of 1987, 1991 and 1995, and was in England's side in the World Cup final of 1991. He was the first England player to reach the magical figure of fifty caps. On one occasion, when he returned to the England side, the player he displaced was brother Tony.

Underwood represented the Lions in Australia in 1989 and in New Zealand in 1993, playing in all six tests. They still talk about one Rory Underwood effort for the Lions against New Zealand in 1993, when he took off from fifty yards out and, with sidestep, swerve and pace change, scuttled home for an amazing try. That was just second nature to R Underwood.

ROB ANDREW (1985–97)
Wasps, Toulouse, Newcastle, England, British Lions
71 England caps
5 British Lions tests

He was frequently referred to as a kicking stand-off, but Christopher Robert Andrew in fact was a wonderfully rounded player, possessed of all the skills and a cricketer's hands, who conducted his orchestra with a practised hand and the creative gifts of an all-round sportsman. True, he did punt a lot, but that was a key element in those days of England's tactical plan in support of a mighty pack, whose energies were husbanded by the pinpoint accuracy of the Andrew boot. He could call on the slanted diagonal that gave more than one full-back a testing time, or the garryowen, which he hoisted with searching accuracy, or the delicate little chip kick that turned the opposing defence line and gave England's fast followers a delicious target. And of course Andrew, blessed as he was with those cricketer's hands, reduced handling errors to an absolute minimum, and also was able to adjust the weight and direction of the pass to maximum effect in the sucessful launch of his back line, and equally efficiently off the top of his head in broken play.

Andrew thoroughly deserved his many successes for he had something of a fetish for fitness, and so was mostly in prime condition for the fray. Those who criticised him for punting too much had to admit that it was with Andrew at stand-off that Rory Underwood, a school colleague at Barnard Castle school in the north-east of England, scored most of his English record of forty-nine tries, whilst Andrew's gifts in dictating play proved a key factor in Will Carling and Jeremy Guscott emerging as a rare pair of midfield operators. Whether they would have liked more ball or whether they enjoyed chasing after the punts I don't know, but they clearly revelled in taking on opponents underneath Andrew's high altitude bombs.

The statistics of Andrew's extraordinary points-scoring are hugely impressive. He scored 396 points for England in cap internationals, and a British record of twenty-one drop goals. He scored eighteen points on his debut against Romania, twenty-one points against Wales in 1986, eighteen points against France in Paris in 1994, and twenty-seven against South Africa in 1994, when he became the first England player to achieve a 'full house' in an international – a try, two conversions, five penalties and a drop goal. He scored what was then a record thirty points in a single test in 1994, and will always be remembered for his soaring drop goals which put

Scotland out of the 1991 World Cup semi-final, and Australia out of the 1995 World Cup quarter-final in Cape Town. To many, that last-second score that put out the Wallabies was one of the most exciting moments in the series. And he played seventy tests in the stand-off position, another record.

An undefeated century-maker against Nottinghamshire in 1984, Andrew captained Cambridge at cricket in 1985. As a rugby player he captained England against the 1989 Romanians and was a replacement British Lion in Australia in 1989. There he played in the last two tests, and went on to feature in three World Cup tournaments and three England Grand Slam-winning sides. He moved to Newcastle as a player-coach and made his last test appearance in the 1997 Five Nations. The following year he enjoyed further domestic success as he coached Newcastle to the 1998 English league title and in 2000 his side won the Tetley's Bitter Cup.

Talk of Andrew always will touch on the importance of the power and accuracy of his boot. Certainly, his brilliant kicking for England was part of the battle plan, and he did it beautifully. I told him once I wished he played in bare feet! But he was also a player of considerable versatility, capable of playing to any battle plan, and one of the best tackling stand-off halves in the game. Certainly he would be my choice for the World XV stand-off half position, though they might not agree in Wales!

SEAN FITZPATRICK (1986–97)
Auckland, New Zealand
92 caps

Sean Brian Thomas Fitzpatrick is the world's most capped hooker with ninety-two caps, and he also holds the world record for the most consecutive tests, with sixty-three between 1986 and 1995. He also captained New Zealand in a record fifty-one tests. Of those ninety-two tests, seventy-four were won and two ended as draws. He competed in three World Cup tournaments, 1987, 1991 and 1995.

Fitzpatrick is a chip off the old block in that his father Brian was an All Black second five-eighth in the early 1950s. As an understudy to Andy Dalton in the 1987 World Cup, Sean benefited when Dalton suffered hamstring damage, whereupon Fitzpatrick was promoted and became their first-choice New Zealand hooker for a decade.

At six foot and sixteen stone nine, Fitzpatrick brought a powerful frame to New Zealand forward operations, and had a highly successful World Cup in 1987. He also scored two tries against Australia in the Bledisloe Cup. He was a member of the brilliant Auckland squad of the 1990s, during which he captained New Zealand for six years, including the 1996 series win against the Springboks, the first by an All Black team in South Africa. His last cap was against Wales at Wembley in November 1997.

An enthusiastic trainer and a durable competitor, he presented an aggressive and uncompromising manner on the pitch, and was a determined character who continually sought improvement. Initially lacking in lineout throwing accuracy, he worked hard to achieve better results under the encouraging direction of the great Auckland coach John Hart. His first test was against France in June 1986, and he embarked then on twelve seasons at the top, during which he played 347 first-class matches, second only to the legendary Colin Meads (361). Fitzpatrick also claimed twelve test tries – some return for a denizen of the front row.

Sean is a very fair, pleasant fellow, more approachable than some New Zealanders, and a very friendly, decent kind of chap. And he was a good captain. Working in the front row you have to show leadership because you get knocked about quite a lot, and although he wasn't a particularly commanding figure he had clear ideas about what was to be done and how to do it. The result was that he got a good response from his players and revealed real leadership. I suppose it's easier to be captain of a New Zealand side than some others because the players are always so focused, and in New Zealand rugby is their meat and drink. Most of the players know exactly what their job is, what they have to do, and what their targets are. And the captain simply has to egg them along and remind them now and then. But Fitzpatrick led some tremendous All Black performances. He was a credit to New Zealand – it was in the genes, probably.

GAVIN HASTINGS (1986–95)
Watsonians, London Scottish, Scotland, British Lions
61 Scotland caps
6 British Lions tests

It was in Paris as captain of Scotland, in February 1995, that Andrew Gavin Hastings scored a spectacular runaway try which clinched a Scottish victory by 23–21. He had accepted a pass by sleight of hand from Gregor Townsend, prior to thundering over seventy metres for a super score, chased by half of France. Later, on having listened to the TV commentary on the game, he claimed that 'Bill McLaren's voice had carried an element of doubt as to whether I was capable of running seventy metres!'

That try typified the approach of Hastings, which encompassed 100 per cent effort throughout, and a quiet belief in what might be possible. A laid-back character, he had a quiet way of inspiring colleagues to reach their potential, which explains why he was successful as captain of his club Watsonians, of the first Scotland Schools side to win in England, of Cambridge University in 1985, of Edinburgh, of the first Scotland side to win in France in the Parc des Princes, of Scotland twenty times, and of the 1993 British Lions in New Zealand. He was captain of all those teams.

Hastings had a memorable introduction to test rugby against France at Murrayfield in 1986. We have seen how he sent the starting kick-off directly into touch, whereupon Pierre Berbizier took that quick throw-in to himself – and scored a try! As Hastings remarked with some feeling: 'There I was, bird alone, with four Frenchmen running at me, and thinking to myself, "Hell, is this what international rugby is all about?"' But Hastings showed his true mettle on that debut test by sending over six penalty goals in Scotland's victory by 18–17. Some debut!

He earned sixty-one caps for Scotland and played six tests for the Lions, scoring a record 667 points for Scotland and sixty-six more for the Lions. At six feet two and fourteen stone ten, he was big for a full-back, and strong and dependable under aerial bombardment. He was a thumping tackler, a booming kicker of punt, place and drop, a sure handler, and one who compensated for lack of burning pace with aggression and power on the run. And he had a sway of the hips that frequently dislodged enemy tacklers.

In the second Lions test in Wellington in 1993, the All Blacks planned to bomb Hastings into error, but he stood unflinching and secure in one of the great displays of courage and skill. The Lions won 20–7 and the New Zealanders rated him the best full-back ever to tour there.

Hastings claimed an impressive World Cup record: sixty-one points in four games in 1987, sixty-two points in six games in 1991, and in 1995 a record forty-four points (against the Ivory Coast) and 104 points in all in four games. He was Scotland's most capped player with sixty-one until that mark was passed by his brother Scott (65). Now Gregor Townsend is top with 75 caps. They were the first brothers to make their debuts together for Scotland (against France at Murrayfield in 1986). Gavin toured Australia with the Lions in 1989 when they won the test series 2–1, and as captain in

New Zealand in 1993, when they won the second test 20–7 but lost the series 2–1. Small wonder that he was once described as Scotland's Braveheart.

DEAN RICHARDS (1986–96)
Leicester, England, British Lions
48 England caps
6 British Lions tests

I can still see the mighty Dean Richards, six foot three inches, eighteen stone two, with his feet wide apart, knees bent, posterior pushed backwards, ball cradled against his chest in his powerful hands and arms, defying all opponents to take it from him. It was a sight that inspired colleagues to rare deeds of support, and caused opponents to experience huge frustration as the massive frame of the Leicester giant stood its ground prior to heel or release.

The Leicester and England No 8 proved one of the most influential and renowned forwards of his era, and a key figure in one of the most formidable England packs ever to take the field. A colossus never liable to break the sound barrier, but with a nose for where the action would be, Richards was described by the famous Australian coach Bob Dwyer as 'the single most important factor in the Lions' series victory in Australia in 1989'.

The Whitbread Player of the Year in 1990–91, Richards was a highly influential figure in the England Grand Slams of 1991 and 1992, but suffered the disappointment of England's loss to Wales at Cardiff by 10–9 in 1993, which deprived England of what would have been a unique third Grand Slam in a row.

Richards made a distinctive entry into the England fold when, in his first cap against Ireland in 1986, he was the cornerstone of a mighty England forward effort that spawned two debut Richards tries. He scored a third try against Ireland in 1989 and other international tries against Japan (1987), Australia (1988) and Romania (1989). He played for over a decade for Leicester, had a spell in France with the Roanne club, and in most recent times has proved a successful coach of the Leicester squad.

He toured with the Lions in Australia in 1989 and in New Zealand in 1993, playing in all six tests, and making a huge impression on officials and players alike in the southern hemisphere. He made just as big an impression on my countrymen, notably at Murrayfield in 1992, when England led by only 10–7 at half-time, but gained extra impetus when Richards went on as a replacement, and eventually won by 25–7.

When Richards replaced Rodber at No 8, England's whole forward game changed. I can remember him with the ball, his feet planted wide apart and his backside stuck out, and about three Scots trying to unload him. Richards just stood there, waiting till the whole England pack came round him. It was a monumental performance, an occasion when just one man was able to change the whole course of the game, allowing the rest of the pack to build round about him.

As a player Richards was always conspicuously fair. I don't think I ever saw him pull a dirty trick. Big guys sometimes tend to be bullies on the field, liable to fill you in as soon as look at you, but Richards was different. Dean Richards: a mighty man was he!

ZINZAN BROOKE (1987–97)
Auckland, New Zealand
58 caps

Once described by that renowned broadcaster Keith Quinn as having the physique of a god and the skills of a back, Zinzan Brooke

227

once gave in my presence a truly memorable demonstration of his gifts. It was at the Hong Kong Sevens. New Zealand were behind to their arch rivals Fiji with time almost up, and were first to the touchdown to prevent an opposition try that would have sealed it. Touching down quickly, Zinzan Brooke grabbed the ball, ran to the 22 and, left-footed, placed the restart kick with such pinpoint accuracy in behind the Fijian defender that he was able to gather the bounce, run through, and score the clinching try at the other end.

This feat climaxed the match, and was a typical example of the quick thinking that made the older of the two All Blacks Brooke brothers one of the most astute tactical minds in the game. Some time later when I congratulated Zinzan on his astonishing skill level he just laughed, and then said, 'Yeah, bloody great kick, wasn't it?' It sure was!

There is no doubt in my mind that Zinzan was the most skilful forward it has ever been my good fortune to see in action. Just to emphasise that, there is his unusual statistic for a loose forward of having slotted three drop goals in test matches – against England in 1995 in Cape Town when New Zealand won 45–29, against South Africa in 1996 in Pretoria (33–26) and against Wales in 1997 at Wembley (42–7). In all he scored eighty-nine points in his fifty-eight major internationals from seventeen tries, which was a world record for a forward, and, in all, he scored 161 tries in first-class games.

First capped against Argentina in the 1987 World Cup when, not surprisingly, he scored a debut try, he played most of his international rugby as a No 8 forward, and thereafter demonstrated such a range of skills as to suggest that he could have filled in any position in the All Blacks side and would not have looked out of place. Scrum-half or full-back – either would have been meat and drink to him.

He had an acute positional sense, was bulky enough at six foot three and fifteen stone eight to make his mark as an intelligent ball-carrier, and he had a special skill that had Zinzan written all over it

– a huge spin pass that switched the area of attack and frequently caught opponents on the hop.

He made his mark as a Colt in 1985, for Auckland and the Maoris in 1986 and the All Blacks in 1987. Zinzan and his brother Robin, the lock forward, played together in a record thirty-nine All Black internationals. He seldom failed to make an impression, as when he appeared as a twenty-one-year-old replacement for New Zealand against the Barbarians in 1989 and promptly scored a crucial try towards a New Zealand win by 21–10. Zinzan Valentine Brooke undoubtedly was one of the most gifted and creative forwards ever to wear the silver fern.

GARY ARMSTRONG (1988–98)
Jedforest, Scotland, British Lions
51 caps

In boxing parlance Gary Armstrong might be described as more than punching his weight, for here was a slimly built scrum-half who tackled with the explosive effect of players much heavier. He might also be described as Scottish rugby's Braveheart, for if ever a wee man merited praise for sheer courage and tenacity, he was the one.

The tiny Scottish Border town of Jedburgh has one particular claim to fame in that it has produced two of the finest scrum-halves in the history of the game: Roy Laidlaw, who won forty-seven caps between 1980 and 1988, and his disciple and successor Gary Armstrong with fifty-one caps (1988–98). These two were out of the same mould: tough, durable, tenacious, committed, and exceedingly brave. And each ran a protection society for their stand-off partners, John Rutherford of Selkirk and Craig Chalmers of Melrose respectively!

First capped in the 13–31 defeat by Australia at Murrayfield in

1988, Armstrong formed Scotland's half-back partnership with Chalmers on a record thirty-two occasions. But he was also a powerful player and a dangerously breaking scrum-half in his own right. Among a number of highlights to the Armstrong career was his vital contribution to the try by Tony Stanger of Hawick that proved the winner when Scotland beat England 13–7 in their 1990 Grand Slam Murrayfield decider.

Armstrong captained Scotland in fourteen tests, notably when they won the 1999 Championship on points differential. He would have claimed many more than his fifty-one caps but for serious knee damage that caused him to miss nineteen internationals between the Ireland match in 1994 and the New Zealand game in 1996. He scored four international tries: against Wales in 1989 and 1991, Argentina in 1990, and Ireland in 1991, having demonstrated early on his ability to sniff a scoring opportunity at both set-piece and later phase with three tries for Scotland B in 1987. He toured Australia with the Lions in 1989, playing in five games and finishing second top try-scorer with five.

Armstrong joined the newly constituted Newcastle side under Rob Andrew in 1996 and promptly won a premiership medal with them. In that year he regained the Scotland place he had been denied by his serious knee injury. In addition to his scrum-half skills he had a spell as club stand-off and centre in 1993–94, and scored fourteen tries for Newcastle in 1997.

Gary Armstrong could hit with a lot of power, and was a remarkably strong guy for a little fellow. But he had what we call a 'shilpit' appearance, a sort of sucked-in look that made you think he was in need of a good meal. I said so in commentary once, and that was quite a mistake, as I soon found out, because Gary's grandmother gave me a tremendous rocket about it. It was at Mansfield Park, in the stand in front of my own home ground, and she handed me a right ticking off. 'He gets the best food in the Borders,' she told me, and I wasn't going to disagree.

One of the most popular and self-effacing players, Gary Armstrong will always have a warm spot in the hearts of all Scottish rugby folk as one out of the top drawer.

Gary Armstrong in his own words

Scotland v England, 1990

It had already been decided that we would walk out to meet the enemy. It had even been suggested that we would be played on to the pitch by a piper but that was vetoed by the higher-ups. The walk itself, even without a piper, was just incredible. It had been the captain's idea and we all agreed. It would be like a march, with the Scots going out to do battle with the Auld Enemy. Quite simply, I've never experienced anything like it. When we emerged from the tunnel the crowd started cheering and then, when they saw we weren't galloping out as we normally did, they stopped cheering for just a second or two. Then, when they realized what we were doing, the cheering got louder and louder. It made the hairs stand up on the back of your neck. That set the tone for the afternoon and the crowd were like an extra man to us from then on.

The English players had already been out for a couple of minutes and we made them wait on purpose. Then we lined up for the anthems and, again, I've never heard anything like it before and probably never will again. Both verses of *Flower of Scotland* were sung for the first time. It's the best I've ever heard it sung. Usually, when you're standing in the middle of the pitch you hear an 'echo' as sections of the crowd get out of synch. But on Grand Slam Saturday everybody was with everybody else. It summed up the day and it was just brilliant. Whenever I watch that on video it brings tears to my eyes and I think it will continue to do that until the day that I die.

The first ten minutes of the game were a dream for us. We wanted quick penalties, quick lineouts, quick everything. That was the plan and it worked a treat. We were buzzing and the crowd were going crazy. The tone was set with a tap penalty that Fin [Finlay Calder] drove on. He was stopped by, I think, Micky Skinner, but the boys got in behind Calder and drove the English 10 metres up the park. Now the Englishmen knew that it wasn't going to be the pushover they thought it was going to be!

... For the first half hour England were on the back foot. Scotland led 9–4 at half-time thanks to three penalty goals from Chic [Craig Chalmers] but we got a glimpse of what the English could do when Jerry Guscott strode away for a try. Guscott's try gave the English their cockiness back and they began to run stupid penalties, thinking, again, that the game was theirs for the taking. But it wasn't. They got us stuck on our line with a series of scrummages late in the first half.

The English claim to this day that they should have had a penalty try because David Sole was repeatedly collapsing the scrum. I don't think he was. He may have done once – when, very unsportingly, the English forwards rushed to take a scrum when we were a man down with Derek White off hurt and Derek Turnbull still to come on – but other than that I don't think the scrums were being brought down deliberately. In any case, the arrogance of the Englishmen proved their undoing. They were convinced that they were going to get a pushover try and so were scrummaging penalties instead of going for goal ... Psychologically that was a huge turning-point in the game. England thought they had the most powerful scrum in the Five Nations tournament but they came away from five or six minutes' pressure on our line with nothing to show for it.

I was quite relaxed at the interval. Geech [coach Ian McGeechan] had told me before the kick-off that I was to play my normal game. I was to harass the England scrum-half Richard Hill and their No 8 Mike Teague. I think I did that OK and at half-time I was happy enough.

In the second half our try came from a planned move which was codenamed Fiji. I had tried it already in the first half but it hadn't worked. In fact I got a bollocking from Gav because I hadn't drawn Rob Andrew on to me before releasing the ball. Basically, Fiji was a No 8 scrummage pick-up and I was then to draw the stand-off before passing to Gavin who would come into the line at speed, hopefully leaving our winger free and unmarked.

At the back of my mind was the telling-off that Gavin had given me in the first half and so as a result I made a wee half break and delayed the pass a bit. That drew Andrew and Teague on to me and so that was two English defenders taken out of the equation. I lobbed the ball out to Gavin – it wasn't much of a pass and he did well to hold on to it – and he put in a mighty chip for Tony Stanger to run on to, and the rest is history.

The chip ahead wasn't originally part of the move but Geech always taught us that a planned move was just there to open the gap. After that you just have to play what was in front of you. Gav had good vision and improvised the kick ahead for Tony. If Stanger hadn't got the touchdown then Finlay was right there as well and so either way a try was very definitely on the cards.

It was an uphill struggle for England from then. They battled well but we defended better and they just had a penalty goal to show for their second-half efforts. The final ten minutes were unbelievable. England threw everything at us but we weren't going to be beaten and we defended like our lives depended on it. People still speak of that tackle that Scott Hastings put in on Guscott, but even if Scotty hadn't got him then, I believe that Guscott would never have scored. The defence was three deep. After Scott came Gavin and me. There was no way he was getting to the line.

We could still have been playing yet and I don't think England would have scored. That Scottish team was unbeatable on the day. When the final whistle went, the feeling wasn't elation, it was more relief. When we had all made it back to the dressing room, through crowds of Scottish fans who were going wild with delight, it was, to be honest, quiet. We were all drained. I know I was. I was absolutely knackered, both physically and mentally. The medics were going around handing out the drinks but even at that stage we weren't saying much to each other. That was the biggest game I've ever played in, and until the elation of the victory had really sunk in, I have never felt so drained of energy. I was so tired I could hardly lift an arm or a leg. They speak about 'dying for your country', well, I reckon there were 16 guys who almost did that on Grand Slam Saturday. We had no more to give.

(From Gary Armstrong, *Jethart's Here*, Mainstream Publishing Co (Edinburgh) Ltd, 1995)

WILL CARLING (1988–97)
Harlequins, England, British Lions
72 England caps
1 British Lions test

William David Carling of Harlequins, England and the British Lions proved arguably the most successful captain of England, for not only did he perform that function in a world record of fifty-nine tests, but he also can claim forty-four wins as a test captain, another world record.

Awarded seventy-two caps in all for his country, Carling received his first in January 1988 in the 9–10 defeat of England by France in Paris, and he went on to become an influential figure in the midfield as England revived their fortunes in the 1990s. An astute tactician, a determined tackler, and a skilled link man, at five feet eleven and fourteen stone three Carling's stocky frame was not easily torpedoed. He formed an influential England centre partnership with Jeremy Guscott on forty-five occasions.

Carling was England's captain for the first time against Australia in 1988 as a twenty-two-year-old, the youngest for over fifty years, having been captain of England Schools in 1984. He had the distinction of leading England to Grand Slams in 1991, 1992 and 1995; to four Championships; to the World Cup final in 1991 when England lost 6–12 to Australia; and to the World Cup semi-final in 1995 when England lost to New Zealand 29–45. In the quarter-final of the 1991 World Cup, when England beat France 19–10 in one of the most abrasive matches ever played between the two nations, he played a key role to score a fine try in the final minutes, thus putting the game beyond France's reach.

In May 1995 Carling was temporarily removed from the captaincy for some colourful comments about the RFU committee, but reinstated soon afterwards. He led England in the 1995 World Cup in South Africa, scoring two of England's tries in the match against New Zealand. But unfortunately for England, Jonah Lomu, the sensation of the tournament, weighed in with four for the All Blacks. The forty-five points notched up by the All Blacks on that occasion represented the highest score ever conceded by England in a test, of which Andrew Mehrtens contributed twelve points, making him the fastest player in history to top 100 points in test matches.

In 1991 Will Carling led England to their first Grand Slam since 1980, and he also enjoyed leadership of England sides that beat Australia in 1988 and 1995, South Africa in 1992 and 1994, and New Zealand in 1993. Some achievement! In all, he scored twelve international tries for his country.

It was a disappointment for Carling that he was not invited to captain the 1993 British Lions in New Zealand when he was dogged by injury and loss of form. But that did not prevent his selection for the first test, in which he resumed his centre partnership with Jeremy Guscott in the 18–20 defeat by New Zealand in Christchurch.

JASON LEONARD (1990–)
Saracens, Harlequins, England, British Lions
103 England caps
5 British Lions tests

Jason Leonard of Harlequins and England has achieved a quite singular feat of endurance and strength by becoming the most capped forward in the history of the game, having reached his century of caps when taking the Twickenham pitch for England's 25–17 win over France on 5 February 2003. Thus he becomes the third player to gain a century of caps, joining the French centre, Philippe Sella (111), and David Campese of Australia (101).

Even more impressive, without detracting from Campese's or Sella's achievement, is the fact that those 100 caps have been gained as a prop forward, with all the grinding work on shoulders and neck which that entails. In fact, it is one of the most phenomenal statistics I can think of. Jason Leonard is indeed a phenomenon when you think of his going through those 100 tests, with about forty scrummages in each – that's 4,000 in all. It's amazing what the human frame will stand in the way of impact, and Leonard's frame is perhaps the most amazing of all. How could a guy gain over a hundred test caps in that position?

Jason Leonard has slogged away at the international coalface for thirteen years, with all the bumps, bruises and muscular strains that are part and parcel of the prop forward's experience. Indeed, on his hundredth appearance, which was unhappily cut short by a hamstring injury, Leonard had just recovered from a neck injury.

It is also testimony to his commitment to the task of front-row forward that he has functioned equally successfully in test rugby on the loose-head and the tight-head sides. For, most unusually, Leonard could play either side, tight or loose – and he could probably have hooked as well!

Born in the humble London district of Barking, Leonard moved to Saracens and then Harlequins, and has proved the cornerstone to the Harlequins, England and British Lions scrummage since his first cap against Argentina on tour in 1990. He celebrated his captaincy of England against Argentina in 1996 with his only international try, which he scored in a forthright manner, without quite putting together a swerve, sidestep, dummy or change of pace. But there has been no more popular try-scorer.

Very good company, approachable, friendly, and with a delightful cockney sense of humour, Leonard is proud of his birthplace of Barking. Improbably enough, one of his boyhood chums, Glyn Llewellyn, received his first cap for Wales in 1991 on the same day that Leonard got his first cap against Wales. So two Barking boys were meeting for their debut internationals on the same pitch. People from Barking kept coming up to me to inform me of this fact until it got somewhat over-familiar. So when Jason ambled over to tell me yet again, I could only say, 'You're the tenth person from Barking to tell me that!'

Awarded an MBE for services to the rugby union game, Leonard toured three times with the British Lions, visiting New Zealand in 1993, South Africa in 1997, and Australia in 2001. It is unlikely that his achievement of over a hundred caps as a prop forward will ever be bettered.

Jason Leonard in his own words

With the Lions in New Zealand, 1993

The deciding Test was to be played in Auckland – the home of New Zealand rugby. We played well in the first half, building up a 10-point lead, but lost our way in the second half and frittered away every advantage so that New Zealand finally beat us 30–13 to take the series.

It was a bitter blow and a horrible way to end my first tour. But when I came off the pitch, something that really concerned me was the fact that Craig Dowd, in the New Zealand front row, had been doing his best to put me out of action all the way through the match. Everywhere I went, he was trying to kick and punch me at every opportunity. I don't claim to be whiter than white myself, but Craig was being outrageous, targeting me from everywhere, seeking me out and punching me – it was as if he had a personal vendetta against me.

At the dinner after the game, I walked down the steps into the main dining area and saw Craig sitting there at a table full of players and wives. The attractive blonde girl next to him was staring at me, and he was nudging her and pointing at me. She was shaking her head. He suddenly stood up and came over to me.

'Look, I've really got to apologize to you,' he said.

'Don't worry, it's all part and parcel of the game,' I replied magnanimously.

'No, I was out of order, and there's a reason for it,' he explained. He went on to tell me that his fiancée had been staying in a hotel in Auckland a couple of nights earlier with some friends when a group of guys swaggered in and introduced themselves as Lions. One of them said he was Jason Leonard and they set about chatting up the girls. Craig's fiancée wasn't interested, so she decided to head back to her room, but the 'Jason' guy followed her into the lift and tried to force himself on her. She managed to get away from him and run up to her room, where she phoned Craig straight away. He had a fit, and decided to take his revenge on my face in the Test!

It was when he was sitting with his fiancée afterwards and I walked down the stairs that he pointed me out, and it was then that she told him I was not the one who had grabbed her in the lift!

(From *Jason Leonard, the Autobiography*, CollinsWillow, 2001)

JOHN EALES (1991–2001)
Queensland, Australia
86 caps

It's a pity you can't get a quart into a pint pot! That saying was brought home to me in 2002 when *The Times* newspaper asked me to select my best World XV from players on whom I had provided commentary. I chose as the locks Colin Meads of New Zealand and Frik Du Preez of South Africa, for they provided an amalgam of all that is required in a modern test lock forward. But I had one big regret about that selection, which was that there was not room to include the Australian John Eales, who has been one of the most gifted lock forwards to have emerged from the southern hemisphere. A giant of six foot seven and eighteen stone nine, Eales set the ability to kick goals alongside impressive lineout ball-winning, scrummage power and technique, handling skills, and impressive pace for such a big man; and not least a gift for captaincy that brought the best out of his colleagues.

Coming from the famous Brothers club in Brisbane, Queensland, Eales was capped by Australia eighty-six times, the first being against Wales just prior to the World Cup of 1991 in which he played all six games, two at No 8, the others at lock forward. His fiftieth cap was gained in the 15–15 draw with England at Twickenham on 15 November 1997. He could easily have had even more caps but for a shoulder injury that kept him out of the 1993 season. Once chosen as the best and fairest player in Brisbane club rugby in 1990, he was awarded the Order of Australia for services to the community, and his value to Australian rugby is underlined by his feat of scoring 173 points in cap internationals, comprising two tries, thirty-one conversions, and thirty-four penalty goals.

He captained Australia in a record fifty-five tests, of which forty-three were won and two drawn. And he had a merited pinnacle of achievement by leading Australia to the World Cup win in Wales in

1999. He retired from rugby after captaining Australia in their series victory over the Lions in 2001. John Eales was a great captain and a magnificent lock forward with all the qualities, one of the most respected players in the world. I chose him as my replacement lock, but such were his talents that it may be right, as some have insisted, that no team can be complete without him.

One of his most famous feats that endeared him to the Australian support was when in Wellington, and as captain, he took on the testing task of landing a penalty goal that would retain the Bledisloe Cup for the Australians in August 2000, although Stirling Mortlock already had slotted four goals. But Eales took the pressure on himself by demonstrating focus and character in piloting home a far from easy goal for victory by 24–23. Small wonder that his nickname is 'Nobody' – because nobody is perfect!

He also was known as 'Slippery' and 'Spring' Eales, and the second of those nicknames was particularly apt, for few big men have been able to launch themselves skywards in pursuit of lineout ball with the dexterity and body control of John Anthony Eales.

MATT BURKE (1993–)
New South Wales, Australia
68 caps

If ever you were looking for a fellow to pilot over a difficult goal-kick to save your life, Australia's Matt Burke would assuredly be the man to make any short list for the job; and certainly he would be the first choice of virtually all Australian supporters. For not only has he rewritten the Australian record books as Australia's most capped fullback; he has also demonstrated remarkable concentration and composure in the most pressurised conditions to slot crucial goals, as when not so long ago he piloted over a crucial goal that gave Australia victory over the All Blacks – and there are few things the Wallabies enjoy more than putting one over their southern hemisphere rivals.

Time and again Burke has virtually broken the hearts of opponents with the pinpoint accuracy of his goal-kicking. The British Lions of 2001 felt the pain of Burke's brilliant striking when he steered over seven goals and a try for Australia's 35–14 test win in Melbourne, then slotted seven more goals for nineteen points in victory by 29–23 in Sydney.

Capped sixty-eight times for 833 major international points, Burke gained his first cap against South Africa in 1993, and soon made his mark. He had a remarkable series in 1999 when he struck twenty-three points and twenty-four points respectively in two matches against the All Blacks, twenty-five against France in the World Cup final in 1999, and twenty-four against South Africa in the World Cup semi-final. He already had sunk Scotland with twenty-five points and against the Canadians in 1996 he set an Australian record of thirty-nine points.

Yet Burke's amazing goal-kicking was just one important section of his repertoire. He was impressively quick for a big man of six foot and fourteen and a half stone and was a formidable target for opposing tacklers who found it hard to sink him. Burke was an aggressive runner with ball in hand and clearly saw it as part of his function to set a standard of strong physical tackle engagement for his colleagues to emulate. He had a sound instinct of when and where to enter the attack line and when he did, it was with all guns blazing in a manner that appealed greatly to the Australian supporters and specially to those members of his Sydney and New South Wales club, Eastwood.

It is testimony to that Burke judgement of where and when to intrude that his over 800 points included twenty-five tries in major internationals. Burke's nickname at one time was Back-off, but nothing could have been less appropriate for Burke's style, for he had bravery and total commitment written all over him and never once when I have seen him play has he ever looked like backing off.

It was tribute also to his versatility that whilst the vast majority of his caps were gained in the full-back position he also played five tests for Australia at wing and four at centre. He had adhesive hands, a booming punt, sound positional sense and power running, and he was as dependable in attack mode as in the defensive duties in which he revelled, while having the gift of shepherding his quarry into the lane that facilitated his arrest. He was formidable coming into the line because his timing was so good, and of course he always hit the pass flat out, and that made him a great breaker of any but the best tackles.

From the time that he toured the UK with the unbeaten Australian Schools squad in 1990, Burke was marked out as a cap prospect, and he certainly would be rated by rugby folk all over the world as out of the top drawer and a full-back who not only had a firm grasp of all the basics but also a very big heart.

JOOST VAN DER WESTHUIZEN
(1993–)
Northern Transvaal, South Africa
81 caps

You could have been forgiven for assuming that Joost Heystek Van Der Westhuizen of Northern Transvaal and South Africa was a flank forward, for at six foot one and a half and thirteen stone ten he was big for a scrum-half and displayed all the aggression and thrust on the run of a loosie. But it was as a scrum-half that Van Der Westhuizen became South Africa's most capped back with seventy-nine and their top try-scorer with thirty-five. In 1998 he had become the second Springbok to top fifty caps after the lock Mark

Andrews, and to mark that achievement he had the honour of leading the South Africans out at Twickenham.

Van Der Westhuizen not only had impressive physique but he was surprisingly quick off his mark, and those features combined to make him an impressive breaker of the game line and a lad who had to be nailed to the floor, otherwise he would break the tackle and be gone. He could detect a try-scoring opportunity with wonderful anticipatory gifts and he was a splendid defender with an explosiveness into the tackle that not only floored his quarry but at times exploded the ball as well.

It spoke volumes for his versatility that he adapted to three different stand-off halves in his first three cap appearances, although he will long be remembered as partner to Joel Stransky when that gifted stand-off popped over the crucial drop goal that won the 1995 World Cup in South Africa in the 15–12 defeat of New Zealand. One recalls how Van Der Westhuizen wrote his name all over the game against Scotland at Murrayfield in 1998 with a superb try and constant threat in that victory by 35–10. And all Wales looked on in some amazement as he claimed three tries in South Africa's 37–20 Cardiff win in 1996.

Two years later on the tour of the UK he scored tries in three of four internationals. A Northern Transvaal stalwart when they won the Currie Cup in 1998, Van Der Westhuizen will long hold a revered place in South African rugby annals as one of their strongest scrum-halves ever, and one who revelled in the unglamorous defence chores, as when he even sank Jonah Lomu more than once in the famous 1995 World Cup final. He was a flanker-type scrum-half who loved flattening people, really revelling in it. Some scrumhalves steer clear of physical contact but Joost took it in his stride and welcomed it as in the case of Lomu in that epic 1995 final.

JONAH LOMU (1994–)
Wellington, New Zealand
63 caps

It was at a Hong Kong Sevens in 1994 that I watched the New Zealand squad at a training session, and asked the friendly New Zealand manager Gary Merrill who that big Maori forward was as he thundered about like an enraged bison.

'He ain't a bloody forward, he's a bloody wing,' said Merrell. 'Big, isn't he?'

I had to agree. But I was also astonished. I had never seen a wing half that size. This lad was a monster, and no slouch as he later demonstrated in the tournament. There was nothing wrong with his handling either. But at six foot five and eighteen stone nine, Jonah Lomu was bigger than most of the forwards in the tournament. Imagine having to mark Jonah Lomu in Sevens! A nightmare undertaking.

Having spent his early years in a tough area of Auckland, Lomu, son of a Tongan lay preacher, came across rugby at Wesley College and began to appreciate the give and take of the rugby union game and its team spirit and discipline. In his early experience of rugby union he was just a big strong runner with limited knowledge of link play, angles of running, gifts of deception, defence obligation, and tactical appreciation, but he went on to develop not only his skill but his pace, eventually clocking 10.8 for the 100 metres.

He represented his college first XV as a loose forward, New Zealand Under-17 as a lock, and played his first first-class game in May 1994 as a Counties wing. He took the Sevens game by storm, and then became the youngest ever New Zealand All Black international against France in 1994 when just over nineteen. Both tests were lost, the French backs asking questions of the young wing's defensive skills. So Lomu had an unusually early test baptism, only to be left out of the following five tests.

But the following year, 1995, belonged to Jonah Lomu. At the 1995 World Cup he made a huge impression when he demolished England in the semi-final at Cape Town, amassing four tries, as well as scoring two against Ireland, two against Italy, and one each against France, Scotland and Australia. Not surprisingly, he was named Player of the Tournament.

Lomu took everybody by surprise, and I don't suppose many of us had seen anything like him before. In his first fourteen tests he registered thirteen tries. In 1999 he scored eight tries in five consecutive tests in the World Cup, and he weighed in with another three tries in the 69–20 Dunedin defeat of Scotland in June 2000. In his sixty-three caps he has laid claim to thirty-seven tries. And that achievement has been attained in the face of injury and serious illness. At the end of 1995 he was diagnosed as suffering from a kidney ailment that kept him out of action for almost a year. But he was back in the All Black side in their 1997 tour of the UK. He has rightly been called the first superstar of rugby's professional era.

Whilst Lomu is a huge handful for any opposing defenders to sink, he also has a pulverising hand-off in his repertoire, and the threat he poses requires more than one opponent to deal with him. This has the effect of opening gaps for colleagues to strut their stuff. Lomu has the power of a forward with the pace of a back. In try-scoring terms he has been particularly severe on Scotland and England with seven tries each, Australia with six, Italy and France four each, Samoa three, and Tonga two; but he hasn't yet scored tries against Wales or South Africa.

Although Lomu would appear to have plenty more rugby in him, and may well terrorise quite a few more people yet, very sadly there has recently been a return of the kidney complaint that kept him off the field for most of 1996. Lovers of rugby, as well as all those who have come to know and admire the phenomenon that is Jonah Lomu, can only hope and pray that he will shake off this new threat to his career.

KEITH WOOD (1994–)

Garryowen, Harlequins, Ireland, British Lions
51 Ireland caps
5 British Lions tests

In June 2002, when Keith Gerard Mallinson Wood played for Ireland against the All Blacks in Auckland, he joined that distinguished group of rugby union international players who have reached the magic figure of fifty caps. He is now Ireland's most capped hooker with fifty-one despite long injury, and lies twelfth in the list of most capped Irish players.

First capped against Australia in 1994, Keith Wood followed in the footsteps of his father Gordon, who as a prop forward gained twenty-nine caps and played in two of the Lions tests against New Zealand in 1959. Keith overtook his father's achievement by playing test rugby for the Lions in two tours: two tests in South Africa in 1997, and all three tests in Australia in 2001. Against the Springboks in 1997 Wood's brilliant performances contributed not a little to the Lions' series victory.

There is more than a touch of the yoicks! and tallyho! about the Wood style, for he is an explosive runner ball in hand, and relishes the challenge of Six Nations and Lions rugby, in which he has scored an impressive fourteen tries. Originally a star of the famous Garryowen club in Munster, Wood joined Harlequins in 1996, becoming captain in 1997. But he returned to the Irish club for the 1999/2000 season, leading Munster to the narrowest of defeats in the European Cup final. He first captained Ireland against Australia in November 1996, and has proved an inspirational leader, having captained his country in twenty-eight tests including their New Zealand tour of 2002.

At six foot and sixteen stone ten Wood brings a rugged physicality to the Irish forward effort. In 2002 he suffered a shoulder injury which has kept him out of rugby for far too long, but his positive, combative approach to the game has had much to do with Ireland's renaissance as one of the most attractive sides in world rugby.

Keith Wood played a crucial part in depriving England of a Grand Slam in 2001, when the Ireland v England game was held over, due to foot and mouth disease. Wood's try was the result of a peel move at the lineout, a ploy that had originally been dreamt up by the French under Lucien Mias (see p. 56). The French hit on this idea of launching forwards off the lineout and peeling round the front or the back. When Wood scored a try with that peel move it all came back to me, because that was such a devastating ploy, and so hard to stop – as Wood proved, to England's chagrin!

Wood was nominated IRB Player of the Year in 2001, but shortly afterwards he picked up the injury that sadly has kept him out of the game up to the present time.

CHRISTIAN CULLEN (1996–)
Manawatu, Wellington, New Zealand
58 caps

No player ever announced his arrival on the international stage with a louder blare of trumpets than Christian Mathias Cullen, whom I recall seeing in action for the first time at the Hong Kong Sevens in 1996, and boggling at his searing pace, lines of running, and challenging sense of adventure. In his very first test, in that 1996 Hong Kong Sevens, he scored a try and six conversions in the 42–5 defeat of Taipei.

As a teenager, Cullen took the Hong Kong tournament by storm. And to think he was just recently out of school! In the wide open spaces of the Sevens field he revelled in the use of his pace, skill-level and confidence. Opponents found it a little bit easier to put handcuffs on him in the fuller version of the game, but they had to keep their peepers on him throughout every match as he was capable of suddenly erupting in startling fashion to cause alarm bells to ring all over the place.

Cullen could be devastating with that pace of his coming into the line, once he'd picked his place and time. He could also operate well in cluttered confines because he was so sharp coming off either foot, with a blistering take-off. At five foot eleven and twelve stone eight, he was of compact build, and he had a great ability to sniff out the gaps and to change direction when at full speed.

Cullen's entry into the realm of capped players was as devastating as his entry into the line. In his first cap appearance against Western Samoa in 1996 he scored three tries, and in the next game, against Scotland in Dunedin, he scored four more. In a career of fifty-eight tests (so far), between 1996 and 2002, he went on to become New Zealand's most capped full-back with forty-five appearances in that position, and their leading try-scorer, amassing a rich haul of forty-six tries. His 236 points in fifty-eight tests includes three conversions as well as those forty-six tries, but it is his electrifying pace and pace change that make him one of the most exciting players ever to wear the silver fern.

Between 1996 and 2000 he played fifty-one tests in a row, showing dedication to superb fitness and a strong preference for the full-back position, although he did play occasionally as a test centre. It seemed to me that the selectors weren't quite sure what his optimum position was, but I would have played him as a full-back. He was one of those fellows, like Andy Irvine or Gerald Davies, who could add another dimension. One minute you had him and the next he was gone; and he was a good footballer with it.

Of the many spectacular tries he has scored at the top level, they still talk of one he registered against Australia in 1997. Launched by a typically inch-perfect feed from Zinzan Brooke, he scorched sixty yards for a try that just hadn't looked on. In the Tri-Nations game against South Africa in 2000 Cullen scored his forty-third try in forty-eight tests, and his sixteen tries in Tri-Nations is a record. Some talent is Christian Mathias Cullen.

JONNY WILKINSON (1998–)
Newcastle, England, British Lions
45 England caps
3 British Lions tests

He was still short of his nineteenth birthday when Jonathan Peter (Jonny) Wilkinson became the youngest England international player, capped first in victory against Ireland by 35–17 at Twickenham in April 1998. Since then he has developed into a superbly gifted all-purpose stand-off half who has set new points-scoring records for England with, currently, 686 points from forty-five cap internationals, including five tries.

Not only that, but he has also created a reputation as a thunderous tackler, who pile-drives his five foot ten inch and thirteen stone ten frame into shuddering impact, as well as an astute distributor with thumping punt power. A mainstay of the Newcastle Falcons from the beginning, he has benefited from the influence of Newcastle manager Rob Andrew who has guided his fortunes. Having taken on the captaincy of Newcastle, he also headed England in their 40–5 win over Italy in 2003 in the absence through injury of Martin Johnson.

Among Wilkinson's remarkable scoring feats is a consecutive run of thirty points against Wales, twenty-one against New Zealand, and twenty-two against Australia in 2002. In that year he was chosen as International Player of the Year. In the 2003 Six Nations Championship he registered twenty points against France, sixteen against Wales, eight against Italy, eighteen against Scotland, and fifteen against Ireland, and he received the Man of the Match award in a victory which gave England the Grand Slam.

In November 2001 he scored all twenty-one points in England's 21–15 win over Australia at Twickenham with five penalty goals and two drop goals. Incidentally, those drop goals indicate that he is in the process of repopularising the value of that particular way of scoring: so far he has stroked over thirteen in cap internationals, showing an ability to do it with either foot.

At just twenty-three Wilkinson is a dead-eye marksman who scored thirty-five points in three games for the British Lions in Australia in 2001, and has topped the twenty points mark in over a dozen games, including all twenty-seven against the Springboks in Bloemfontein in June 2000. He is only the third player to reach 1,000 points in Zurich Premiership games, and he has equalled the Lions record of eighteen points in a test match. That was against Australia in Sydney in July 2001.

Since gaining his first cap as an eighteen-year-old replacement he has developed into a tremendously rounded stand-off with barely a weakness. He tackles like the crack of doom; he has all the basics, including a mighty punt, safe hands, and a splendid adjustment of pass. And he is a hot handful on the burst, with an ability to shake off all but the most technically perfect tackles. He also exhibits wonderful temperament in the pressurised environment of goal-kicking.

Altogether, Wilkinson is a cracking all-round young player, whose ability to adjust the weight and direction of pass sets up his centres. His clever decision-making – when to kick, when to pass, when to have a go himself – makes it so comfortable for them. And his mighty tackling takes the tackling chore off the shoulders of his flankers. If you've got a stand-off who does his own tackling, the loose forwards are freed up to make a nuisance of themselves all around the park.

BRIAN O'DRISCOLL (1999–)

Blackrock College, Leinster, Ireland, British Lions

38 Ireland caps
3 British Lions tests

One of the most exciting talents in the Six Nations championship, Brian O'Driscoll has experienced both the highs and the lows of rugby union fortune. As a new Irish cap against Australia at Brisbane in June 1999 he had a shattering baptism in a defeat by 46–10, a record Australian score against Ireland. Yet on 9 November 2002, at Lansdowne Road, he experienced a contrasting baptism when he captained Ireland for the very first time, and what is more, to an 18–9 victory over the reigning World Champions, Australia. That was Ireland's first victory over the Wallabies for twenty-three years.

Originally replacing the injured Keith Wood, O'Driscoll has now been Irish captain in nine cap internationals and seems destined for a long reign in leadership, for he has the respect and support of his colleagues as a player with special gifts. He is lightning into his running, with sound handling skills, and he is something of a drop goal specialist, having slotted three of those: one against Romania in 1999, and one in each of the two tests against New Zealand in Dunedin and Auckland in June 2002.

He gave evidence of his huge potential in the Irish Schools side of 1997 out of Blackrock College, and a year later in the World Champion Irish Under-19 side. His meteoric rise to cap status was taken in his stride, and he has developed into a world class centre with that sizzle off a standing start that leaves opponents flat-footed, and fits him out for breaking all but the most technically sound tackles with his strong compact frame of five foot eleven and fourteen stone three.

He has set a new Irish try-scoring record with eighteen, and on two occasions he has scored three tries in a test: against France in a 27–25 victory on 18 March 2002, and in a 43–22 victory over

Scotland at Dublin on 2 March 2002. In both games he was named Man of the Match. He toured Australia with the British Lions in 2001, played in all three tests, and scored a super try in the Brisbane test.

JASON ROBINSON (2001–)
Bath, Sale Sharks, England, British Lions
20 England caps
3 British Lions tests

Of those players one would have liked to mark least of all, Jason Robinson the England wing tops the list. For he is as elusive as a demented ferret, with the ability to come off either foot in a blink, and with pace change to match, and with pattering footsteps that make it hard to judge just exactly what he is going to do – sometimes he doesn't know himself. Already he has claimed eleven tries in just eighteen cap internationals, and no doubt there are more to come. For he is a player who has adapted speedily to the contrasting demands of the rugby union game, having already made his mark in the rugby league version with Wigan Warriors, prior to switching codes in November 2000.

During his spell in rugby league with Wigan he played twelve times for Great Britain, and for England on seven occasions; and he has demonstrated his versatility by playing rugby union for England as both full-back and wing. In 302 rugby league games he sizzled in for 184 tries, and then, after playing rugby union for Bath and Sale, he toured with the British Lions in Australia in 2001 and was top try-scorer with ten. A year ago he was voted the Zurich England Player of the Season.

I was surprised when England first played him as a full-back; I suppose it was because they wanted his burst out of defence, his ability to turn defence into attack. But the fact is that when he was under pressure with kicks he could be exploited because he wasn't used to kicking – they don't kick much in rugby league. As a former rugby league man, he had to learn to differentiate between the ball you run and the ball you hoof back out of the road to get forward momentum going again. If you get tackled when you're behind your forwards they are not amused, because they are rucking at a disadvantage if they are coming in from behind, whereas the other team are rushing towards the ball and have all the momentum.

So kicking is a key factor distinguishing league from union. You rarely kick in rugby league, whereas in rugby union a full-back has got to be able to punt accurately. Another difference is that a fellow who has played rugby league is more inclined to tilt his lance from out of the deep, coming out from behind. That's okay if his judgment's good, but in rugby union there are a couple more players floating about, cluttering up the place, so your judgment of when to run out of defence and when to hoof it and chase it has got to be spot on.

Although I would prefer him in the line rather than at full-back, Robinson is an immense talent wherever he plays. He contributed four tries to England's 134–0 win over Romania in November 2001, and on two occasions he has scored two tries against Scotland: in the 24–3 win in February 2002, and in the 40–9 margin in March 2003. He now has played in seventeen of the last eighteen England internationals, having been capped first as a fifty-minute replacement against Italy in the 80–23 Twickenham win in February 2001. For me, he is one of the most exciting talents in the Six Nations Championship, with his pattering footsteps and a nose for wee gaps.

PART SIX

My World XV

Full-back	Andy Irvine (Scotland 1972–82)
Left wing	David Campese (Australia 1982–96)
Right wing	Gerald Davies (Wales 1966–78)
Outside centre	Danie Gerber (South Africa 1980–92)
Inside centre	Mike Gibson (Ireland 1964–79) (Captain)
Fly-half	Rob Andrew (England 1985–97)
Scrum-half	Gareth Edwards (Wales 1967–78)
No 8	Mervyn Davies (Wales 1969–76)
No 7 (Openside flanker)	Fergus Slattery (Ireland 1970–84)
No 6 (Blind-side flanker)	Zinzan Brooke (New Zealand 1987–97)
No 5 (lock)	Frik Du Preez (South Africa 1961–71)
No 4 (lock)	Colin Meads (New Zealand 1957–71)
No 1 (Loose-head prop)	Graham Price (Wales 1975–83)
No 2 (Hooker)	Sean Fitzpatrick (New Zealand 1986–99) (Vice-captain)
No 3 (Tight-head prop)	Fran Cotton (England 1971–81)

MY WORLD XV

IN 2001 I was asked by *The Times* to select my all-time World XV. It went on over four months, and in the end I had made fifteen firm friends and at least 500 enemies, a lot of them in Wales! I know I have created some controversy. I got the most stick for picking Rob Andrew ahead of Barry John, Phil Bennett or Cliff Morgan. A lovely man from Wales rang and said: 'Hey, Bill, have you taken leave of your bloody senses?' But I will always defend my selection of Andrew. I knew I would get a lot of abuse and I sure did.

But that is the nature of the beast in undertaking a project such as this. You could actually pick maybe three XVs of equal strength because of the quality of players around the world. But you can't get a quart into a pint pot. I have thoroughly enjoyed picking the players and looking back over the years. I love researching things and it has been a delight to look back and revive wonderful memories of the past from a lot of the games I have been fortunate enough to cover. There were some guys whose selection was never in any doubt. In most cases you would try to balance one person's merits against another's, but on the right wing it could only have been Gerald Davies, at centre, Mike Gibson, on the left wing, David Campese, and at scrum-half, Gareth Edwards. They are truly great individuals.

The task of selecting the captain for my team, the replacements, and a referee, I left till last. The captain has to be worth his place, although there have been some successful captains who might not otherwise have been first choice for their position. He has to be a born leader, someone who revels in responsibility and is popular with his colleagues – although one or two captains have been sharp of tongue but got things done regardless of what people thought of them. And the captain has to be a tactician with a clear idea of how his team will play. He must be able to coax and cajole; and he has to feel what is going right and wrong on the field. Most importantly, he has to assess when a change of emphasis is required.

My captain would be *Mike Gibson*, with *Sean Fitzpatrick* as vice-captain, and it would be up to him to assess how the forwards were going and to advise Mike as to what might be required. Gibson had vast experience and was so tactically astute; he was always very aware of what was on and what was possible. Mentally he was very sharp and a lovely personality, a captain who would help his players to play. In some people's eyes Mike might be considered too technical, but people always had respect for Gibson. Sean was a tremendous captain of New Zealand, people looked up to him.

With the game nowadays very much about the twenty-two-man squad rather than just the XV, the choice of replacements is crucial. At prop I would have *Jason Leonard* because he is equally effective on either side of the front row as he showed for the British Isles in New Zealand in 1993. I have huge respect for him. *Keith Wood* would be the reserve hooker because of his inspirational qualities. The lock would be *John Eales*, and when you look at my team I wonder whether he should not have been in my XV. He was a great captain and a magnificent lock forward with all the qualities. The loose forward would be *Ian Kirkpatrick* because he could play in any of the back-row positions.

Nick Farr-Jones is my reserve scrum-half. He was the complete No 9 and a born leader. For strength, power and service you couldn't go wrong with the former Australia captain. *Michael Lynagh* would be cover at both fly-half and centre where he distinguished himself for Australia, and finally *Matt Burke* would look after any of the back three positions at wing or full-back. He is another of those rounded fellows whom Australia produce so often.

As for a referee, well I know I am perhaps biased but I admired Jim Fleming, of Scotland, immensely. He had a light touch, he encouraged people to play with a light hand on the tiller and he had a lovely sense of humour but also had that aura of command. You couldn't be a clever dick with him. Jim was tall, and for me it is important that a referee can see over the top of a ruck or maul. He would be my No 1. But I also had great regard for the two Welsh fellas, Derek Bevan and Clive Norling. Bevan had a voice like a foghorn. Norling was very much the boss and let the players know it. Ed Morrison and Johnny Johnson, both of England, were also top class. David Bishop, of New Zealand, was the best from the southern hemisphere.

Here is my team:

FULL-BACK

I always look for courage in a full-back. He has got to be brave because, although the garryowen is not used so much these days, it is still a potent weapon. It takes a brave guy to stand underneath it, waiting, hearing the enemy hooves bearing down, or leaping high into the air, the fashion nowadays. He also needs courage in the tackle, because there are still situations, even in today's organised defences, when he has to knock his man down, one on one.

Pace is also vital, now that players in this position invariably have played several times on the wing as well. It is the last line of defence and the first line of attack. Pace is important for counter-attacking, allied of course to basic skills and judgment. The full-back must have a feel for when it is right to counter. Counter-attacking is a key function. If he gets it wrong, then he could be knocked down behind his forwards, and then his team is in trouble.

The full-back has an awful lot to think about, so courage, ability to take the high ball, punt, weight of tackle, and pace are required if he is to be well equipped. If he can kick goals, so much the better. In the old days he was the lone sentinel; he did not have his two wings covering. Now, knowing he has support behind him when going for the high ball is important.

Andy Irvine (1972–82)

My choice as full-back is Andy Irvine. Some people might have thought he was a bit vulnerable defensively, but he could catch and tackle. What made him stand out was his attacking genius. When he lit the touchpaper he was devastating. He might not have been as steady as Gavin Hastings or JPR Williams, but his willingness to tilt his lance and have a go made him a joy to watch. He could come off either foot and was very quick. He had a wonderful way of turning defence into attack with a blast of genius. Whenever he touched the ball you knew something special would happen. You had to accept that there would be times and games when you might think, 'What the hell is he doing?' He did so many memorable things, though, and was so deceptive in his running. He gave me the most pleasure. Sometimes he would be thinking what he would do with the ball before he got it, but the pluses far outweighed the odd minus. His greatest game was against France in 1980. Scotland were down 14–4, and Andy had been booed because he had missed a couple of kicks. Then in a trice he had scored two tries, a conversion, and had kicked two penalty goals. He took that game by the scruff of the neck and Scotland won 22–14. Astonishing.

2. Serge Blanco (1980–91)

No doubt the vast majority of people would opt for Serge Blanco as their number one choice, and for me there is very little between the two. He was quite big and well-built, which made him a solid proposition under the high ball. The famous try in the 1987 World Cup semi-final against Australia epitomised his class. He timed his entry perfectly and dipped for the try in little space. He was a player who could bring a crowd to its feet in excitement and delight.

3. Gavin Hastings (1986–95)

Gavin was a player and leader whose record speaks for itself. He was a great defensive full-back, so solid under the high bombardment. He timed his intrusion into the line so well. Seventeen tries says it all. He probably could have done with an extra yard of pace, but he was a genuine stalwart you could depend upon to lay his body on the line. He was also a very popular captain, both of Scotland and the British Lions, whom he led in 1993. A genuine star.

4. JPR Williams (1969–81)

He was the complete player, and what made him stand out was his unbelievable strength. My enduring image of JPR was his shoulder charge at full tilt against Jean-François Gourdon, the French wing, in the 1976 Grand Slam game. It was one of the most frightening shoulder charges I can recall, but it saved the match for Wales. That was JPR, fearless and very confident, an inspiration to those around him.

5. Matt Burke (1993–)

Similar in a way to Hastings with his physical presence, he is very dependable with what I call the unsavoury chores – the high ball, tackle and fall. As with all top class full-backs, he is also a wonderful judge of when to intrude. It is surprising how many tries he has scored, having broken tackles, for he is very difficult to put down. He also has that edge of pace, which is important. He is a fine place-kicker and has a hoof like a siege gun. I would love to see him play on the high veldt. The ball would go a country mile!

Other contenders: *Pierre Villepreux* (1967–72), so crafty, he epitomised French rugby in the 1970s; *Jean-Luc Sadourny* (1991–2001), a brilliant runner from defence; New Zealand's *Don*

Clarke (1956–64), a great goal-kicker; *Christian Cullen* (1996–), a number one finisher; *André Joubert* (1989–97), a South African with the same elegance as Villepreux, and with a deceptive change of pace and astute change of angle.

LEFT WING

A left wing has to have change of pace as well as outright speed; he must be able to kick off his left foot to bring the ball back to the middle of the pitch. I like a wing to have a strong hand-off, whatever his size, and to be able to punt or to chip-kick through. In the cluttered confines in which wings have to work, the ability to punt ahead accurately is very important and is one aspect which wings sometimes neglect. Ideally they should also be strong defensively, be comfortable as part of the back three unit, and be keen to look for work, not merely wait for the game to come to them.

David Campese (1982–96)

My first choice has to be David Campese, who is probably my favourite player of all time. He is the greatest entertainer the world game has seen. He is the Bradman of rugby union. His trademark was his amazing hitch kick. I loved what he did. For a commentator he was always a delight because he would invariably lift a game, and you always knew he would produce the unexpected. He was a law unto himself. No doubt he drove some coaches crazy. But he had that touch of genius, a sense of adventure allied to high skill levels. I remember one game when he was haring down the right wing, seemed to be trapped, but instinctively passed the ball over his head, sensing Tim Horan was inside. The pass was perfect and a try scored.

2. Jonah Lomu (1994–)

Jonah Lomu has made an incredible impression on the world game. His unique combination of power, pace and skill make him stand out as one of the best. He is six foot five and eighteen stone nine, and can run 100 metres in 10.8 seconds. I first saw him at a New Zealand training session for the Hong Kong Sevens in 1994, and mistook him for a forward. Because of his size, people have called him a freak, but he is a great footballer, far better than people give him credit for. His try against Ireland in 2001 demonstrated how much he has matured as a player. He made it look very easy but it was not. It was perfect in its execution: the timing of his entry into the line, the angle of his run at pace, made it look so simple. He is a devastating attacker, and has great balance for a big man. He is a cracker who always takes two or three defenders to stop him.

3. David Duckham (1969–76)

Duckham was one of the great England centres in partnership with John Spencer before he was moved to the wing with such success. He was so effective wide out. He would have scored many more tries if players inside him had used him more. He had a brilliant sidestep; he almost telegraphed it, but still it was devastating. He was the archetypal Englishman, blond hair flowing, who would glide away from opponents. He also possessed an aggressive hand-off. He came into his own with the British Lions in 1971 when he scored eleven tries. He showed how brilliant he was with the Barbarians against New Zealand in 1973. In a team of great players he stood out.

4. Rory Underwood (1984–96)

As the most capped England back, Rory Underwood was a lethal finisher, as forty-nine tries in eighty-five England internationals demonstrate. Underwood not only possessed explosive pace, but he was blessed with a very good physique. He could flick off tackles and had a deceptive sway at full tilt. He scored some terrific tries –

the one for the Lions in the second international against New Zealand in 1993 stands out – and he shares with Cyril Lowe the record for the number of tries (18) in the Championship. Some people may point a finger at his defence, but with the ball in hand he was deadly.

5. Joe Roff (1995–)

Joe Roff of Australia is another class act who has played in fifty-one internationals in a row. He is an unusual fellow with his languid style of running, a lazy style but very deceptive. He is a big chap who has impressed me greatly. He has shown great versatility, is a good footballer and a tremendous attacker. Give him half a chance, as he showed against the Lions during the summer of 2001, and he is in. On the Australian tour to South Africa in 1994 he scored 104 points in five games.

Other contenders: *JJ Williams* (1973–79) of Wales was the master of the chip-and-chase, and one of the fastest wings in Welsh history. *Philippe Saint-André* (1990–97) is the most capped France wing and has lovely control and balance. His compatriot *Patrice Lagisquet* (1983–91), the Bayonne Express, looked ungainly but was hugely effective. *Tony O'Reilly* (1955–70) and *Keith Robertson* (1978–89) were others who stood out.

RIGHT WING

What makes a great wing? The fundamental asset is change of pace. I don't mind if they're big and strong or small and elusive, but speed is vital – the ability to scorch the ground.

An outstanding wing needs great powers of deception, otherwise he can't get away. Control of body movement is also very important because so often wings have very little room in which to function.

The best wings are clever and quick-thinking. They should have good hands, and the ability to assess where best to turn up. I would want my wing to cross-kick to the middle and have the ability to chip the ball at speed.

Wings should also be able to control the ball on the floor. And they need to have a full-back's skills so that they can operate in what is now termed the back three defence.

Gerald Davies (1966–78)

The wing who had everything, the finest I have ever seen, is Gerald Davies. He had all the gifts – but his change of pace was startling and so deceptive. In judging wings you think of who you would least like to mark, and TGR Davies was the one I would have hated to have come up against. He could make you look a patsy. One game I particularly remember was for Cardiff against Pontypool in the Welsh Cup in the 1977–78 season. Cardiff only won about six balls, yet Gerald scored four tries. He wasn't shy defensively either. He was not a big fellow but he tackled, as I often say, like the crack o' doom.

The score that sticks in my mind was for Wales against Scotland in 1971. Delme Thomas took the lineout and the move ended with Gerald scooting around Iain Smith, the Scotland full-back. It was a classic try, simple in the making, but Gerald was in the right place at the right time. Wales won with the conversion kicked by John Taylor. Certainly my number one is TGR.

2. Peter Jackson (1956–63)
His nickname was Houdini because he escaped from so many tight situations. Hugh McLeod, the great Scotland and Lions prop, always reckoned that Jackson scored tries that no one else could. He scored sixteen on the 1959 Lions tour, including one in which he left half the New Zealand side for dead. Jackson had the gift of seemingly floating across the ground rather than running. It wasn't

so much a sidestep with him as a tiny swerve, or a sideways drift, which would send people the wrong way. Slim, quick, and a star.

3. John Kirwan (1984–94)

Kirwan was an unusual type. He had a very physical presence, a big guy allied to speed, which made him a formidable proposition. He had a hand-off like a steam engine and also a very good chip kick. In 1988 he scored four tries in one game against Wales in Christchurch and two tries in the opening game of the 1987 World Cup against Italy. Time and again he would break his way through tackles. His try in the 1987 World Cup final helped to write his name across the tournament.

4. Ieuan Evans (1987–98)

One of the most elusive fellows in the game and the scorer of a record thirty-three tries for Wales. The one I recall was scored against Scotland in 1988. He got the ball near the halfway line, about ten yards in from the touchline. He came off his right foot at least three times in a bewildering run which ended up near the posts. He was also very clever defensively. If you put the ball over the head of a lot of wings they find themselves in trouble but he could almost prophesy what was going to happen.

5. Stu Wilson (1977–83)

Stu Wilson was a special type of player who captained New Zealand from the wing. He had a lovely feel for space and of what was on in tight situations. He was outstanding at keeping the ball alive. He was a member of the great All Blacks Grand Slam side of 1978 and in 1980 played for New Zealand against Wales to celebrate the WRU Centenary. He set up a try for Hika Reid that allowed me to say: 'Hika the hooker from Gnongataha.' I'd been waiting to say that for ages.

Other contenders: There have been other great wings, such as *Arthur Smith* (1955–62) of Scotland, who perfected the chip kick.

Christian Darrouy (1957–67) of France was another great exponent, slinky with superb body control at top speed. *Bryan Williams* (1970–78) of New Zealand was very difficult to put on the floor because of the power of his hips and thighs; and *Simon Geoghegan* (1991–96) of Ireland, who seemed to play the game off the top of his head, was so explosive and never held back. He could light up a game.

OUTSIDE CENTRE

The key attribute for a centre is acceleration and physique. Now the centre has to be so powerful; he is bigger and stronger than ever. A few years ago, a centre would weigh between twelve and thirteen stone. Nowadays he is fifteen to sixteen stone, the size of a forward, demonstrating the extent to which the game has changed.

Because he operates in such cluttered confines and has to work much harder, we don't see such clean-cut breaks anymore. A centre has to have physical presence and aggression and expect to take a real buffeting. He has to be able to take a gap, which shows so fleetingly these days. Colleagues have to have confidence in him and he must convey confidence that he will not miss a tackle. If he half-misses his man, alarm bells start to ring. He must have that dogged determination to keep the door shut.

Danie Gerber (1980–92)

My best outside centre has to be Danie Gerber. He was special, not only because he had the physique and power that made him so difficult to put on the floor, but also because he was a great tackler and so aggressive. He was a fitness fanatic. But for South Africa's exclusion from the world game Gerber, who played for Eastern and Western Province, would have won many more caps. He was at his peak when South Africa were banned.

He was a prolific try scorer. In 1984 I remember he scored three tries in eighteen minutes during the first half of the second test against England. He scored two against Scotland for the Barbarians at Murrayfield, a game to celebrate the opening of the East Stand, and four against Cardiff, again for the Baa-Baas. Another quartet came in the unofficial game against South America when South Africa were trying to fill up the gaps in their calendar. It was a shame more people did not see him at his peak.

2. Philippe Sella (1982–95)

The most capped international player of all time, Sella would, I suppose, be many people's idea of the best of all time. He played 111 times for France between 1982 and 1995 and scored thirty tries. He also made fifty appearances in the Five Nations Championship. He made his debut for Agen while still a schoolboy and was first capped against Romania. He had a wonderful eye for space where none seemed to exist. He looked like a tenpenny rabbit – a stripling. But he was, in fact, very strong, an athlete who was a great breaker of tackles. He was also one of only five players to have scored a try in every round of the Five Nations Championship, a feat he achieved in 1986.

3. Bleddyn Williams (1947–55)

Bleddyn Williams was a product of Rydal School, where he once scored a superb individual try only to be given a ticking off by the headmaster, who said he should have passed. He must have taken notice because, during his career, he was a wonderful creator of chances and a wonderful timer of a pass. As a member of the brilliant postwar Cardiff side, his partnership with Dr Jack Matthews will always be remembered. Together they were a dominant feature of the Wales side for years: Matthews the skilful bludgeon, Bleddyn the rapier. He also scored his fair share of tries, forty-one alone in the 1947–48 season. He led Cardiff and Wales to victory over New Zealand, which gives you an idea of his quality as an outstanding midfield player who proved it with the Lions in New Zealand in 1950.

4. Jeremy Guscott (1989–99)

You cannot ignore the claims of Guscott, who scored thirty tries and dropped two goals, including the kick that won the series for the Lions in South Africa in 1997. One of the most elusive centres, with smooth gliding acceleration, he launched himself on the inter-national stage with three tries on his debut against Romania and scored seven tries in his first six games. He was very deceptive and seemed to accelerate without trying. He was serene, a classic player who had such style. He enjoyed a remarkable midfield partnership with Will Carling. They were the backbone of England in the glory years of the early 1990s. Guscott had it all, yet never seemed to be trying very hard.

5. Jo Maso (1966–73)

Jo Maso, the last of my top five, was an unorthodox citizen who enjoyed taking risks. His trick of passing the ball behind his back at speed became known as the Maso flip. His approach did not always endear itself to the selectors, who thought him too much of a liabil-ity. He was a kind of phantom who glided across the ground, and he had adhesive hands. He calculated when the percentages were in his favour. He was an entertainer – his sense of adventure endeared him to the French public.

Other contenders: *Bruce Robertson* (1972–81), the stylish New Zealander; *Brian O'Driscoll* (1999–), Ireland's wunderkind, who has such huge potential and who invariably makes some-thing happen, doing it all with such a cheeky schoolboyish demeanour; *Japie Mulder* (1994–2001), the powerful South African who could force gaps and who enjoyed a partnership with *Hennie Le Roux* (1993–96), who was another to be admired; *Frank Bunce* (1992–97), a typically hard All Black centre who blotted out the midfield. Bunce could cause mayhem with or without the ball.

INSIDE CENTRE

The inside centre has to be a second fly-half these days, a decision-maker, a clever individual who has the ability to size up the situation very quickly, someone who can act as a very good link and someone who must be able to play his full part in defence.

The role of the inside centre has changed over the years. The 1967 All Blacks under Brian Lochore redefined the position. Ian MacRae, the second five-eighth, was a big straight-running centre from Hawkes Bay, who was able to give his forwards a target to ruck at. All the classy back play that followed, the handling, stemmed from the work of MacRae. It was not something we had seen in the northern hemisphere before.

Now the inside centre is, as I say, a second fly-half, someone able to operate flat and in confined space, someone who has to be creative and who is a great guy for the loop.

Mike Gibson (1964–79)

Mike Gibson has to be the complete footballer and is my first choice. He played in virtually every position behind the scrum. There was nothing he could not do. He did not look very powerful but he was a stern tackler with amazing speed of reaction in the busy lanes. He also could sniff the try line. He was still playing international rugby in 1979 at the age of thirty-six. His international career spanned sixteen seasons, and only Tony O'Reilly could equal that. He was a key figure in Irish rugby for years. Gibson was a brilliant Lion, a player who could fit in anywhere. I would never pick a World XV without him.

2. Jeff Butterfield (1953–59)

Jeff Butterfield was one of the great England centres of all time. He spent eleven seasons with Northampton and made a great contribution to several England Triple Crowns. He enjoyed a memorable partnership with Phil Davies in the England midfield. They were a fine blend – Davies the bump-bump merchant, and Butterfield all class. People still talk about a try he scored for the Lions against South Africa in Johannesburg in 1955; he took a ball on his hip at full pace and left everybody high and dry. He was quicksilver, fast off the mark. Guys loved to play with him because he had this wonderful ability of putting them into space.

3. John Gainsford (1960–67)

John Gainsford, of Western Province, played thirty-three times for his country, making him South Africa's most capped centre. He was big enough and strong enough to break tackles, and he was very fast. Opponents could be put off their stride by the ferocity of his crash tackles. The 1962 Lions found him very difficult to deal with, and he scored a great try in the fourth international.

4. Tim Horan (1989–2000)

Tim Horan is also up there with the best. He played eighty times for Australia, seventy at centre and ten at fly-half, and scored thirty tries – second only to David Campese for Australia. He is Australia's most capped centre, who made his debut against New Zealand in 1989 as a teenager. He was a short, chunky individual with flaring acceleration, which caught people unawares. He recovered from a serious knee injury to play some of his best rugby. A double World Cup-winner and player of the tournament in 1999. Very special.

5. Jim Renwick (1972–84)

A former pupil of mine, whom I remember as a ten-year-old at Drumlanrig St Cuthbert's Primary School. Jim Renwick made his debut as a nineteen-year-old in 1972 and is the only Scot to have scored tries in three consecutive internationals at Cardiff Arms Park. I had the pleasure of seeing him in his formative years, and you had to be careful not to coach his natural talent out of him. He possessed a flashing sidestep, a wonderful feint either way, and was full of cheeky touches. He scored eight tries for Scotland, five penalty goals, four conversions and dropped four goals. An all-round hot-shot.

Other contenders: *Will Carling* (1988–97), England's most capped centre, had an impressive turn of speed and was very phys-ical. He was under-estimated, a far better player than people gave him credit for. *Scott Hastings* (1986–97) was a great defensive centre for Scotland, remembered for his try-saving tackle on Rory Underwood at Murrayfield in 1990. France produced *André Boniface* (1954–66), who often played with his brother, Guy. André was slimmer, a dancing type of player, quick into the gap. Then there was the light-footed *Jason Little* (1989–2000), a great contrast to *Scott Gibbs* (1991–2001), a key figure for Wales and the Lions, who was nicknamed Car Crash. He did not tackle people, he oblit-erated them. From the back he looked like a prop forward. He had a low centre of gravity and there was a feeling of indestructibility about him.

FLY-HALF

A fly-half must be the tactician, the fulcrum of the side, with the confidence to call the shots and to select the percentage options. He must have the ability to change strategy as the game goes along; he must punt accurately with either foot; and he requires soft hands so that in an instant he can provide weight and direction of pass that would prove beneficial to those on either side of him. He needs to have sharp acceleration because his opportunities to break will be few and far between, so they must not be wasted. It is a bonus if he revels in explosive tackling, and an additional bonus if he can slot a drop goal off either foot. The garryowen, the grubber kick, the diagonal punt, and the neat chip ahead also have to be part of his repertoire.

He has to have the confidence and judgment to direct operations and to select the most fruitful ploys, and he must also take a full part in the forward and cover defence systems in operations. I have seen so many wonderful fly-halves down the years, a succession of great individuals who are worthy of the accolade and who deserve mention. There is no doubt that this has been my hardest decision and one that will prove the most controversial; I probably will not be allowed in Wales again.

Rob Andrew (1985–97)

It is extremely difficult weighing up one individual against another, but the most complete all-round fly-half that there has been is, in my opinion, Rob Andrew. England's most capped No 10 had a glittering career. He had the adhesive hands of the professional cricketer, as befits a cricket and rugby blue at Cambridge. It is said that some saw him as 'just a kicker'. Certainly when England opted for a somewhat limited format he proved the ideal pivot. But he was not 'just a kicker'. Perhaps he could have done with another half a yard of pace, but he was no slouch and was far more rounded a player than people give him credit for. When he was at Cambridge he was a runner and a linker; he could play different types of game.

He was never flustered and had an ideal temperament. His orchestration suited the other personnel in the England side. He was a punishing and brave tackler. It was with Andrew at fly-half that Rory Underwood registered so many of his forty-nine tries. On England's 1994 tour to South Africa, Andrew scored eighty-seven points, including twenty-seven against the Springboks at Pretoria.

He was also a drop goal specialist, twice piloting over crucial goals in a World Cup: against Scotland in 1991 and against Australia four years later. He never dodged the unsavoury chores.

2. Cliff Morgan (1951–58)

It was a close-run thing between Andrew and Cliff Morgan, a totally different player. He was always regarded as one of the greatest to have emerged from the Wales fly-half factory, one who turned down a handsome offer to switch to rugby league with Wigan. He was a shrewd tactician and a deadly dangerous attacker. He had an amazing ability of being able to lean sideways on the run like a yacht in full sail, which helped him to ease away from grasping enemy hands with the ball held out enticingly. At five foot seven and twelve stone he was the darling of the Cardiff crowds during the halcyon times of the 1950s. He proved an inspirational figure when Wales won the Grand Slam in 1952 and the Championship in 1956. He was an elusive target who reached a peak with the British Lions in South Africa in 1955, notably in the first international when he scored one mesmerising try and made three others in a 23–22 victory.

3. Jack Kyle (1947–58)

From Queens University and Norfolk Island FC, Kyle is one of Ireland's favourite sons. He proved to be one of the most gifted fly-halves in the world game, one who could be absent-minded at times as when he turned up at an Ireland training session with only one boot. He was a beautifully balanced runner who seemed to float rather than run and who had the ability, suddenly, to find another gear that enabled him to escape opponents. Although he wasn't a big man he was brave and resolute in defence. He was an astute tactician and a dangerous attacker who was remarkably successful considering he had to function on comparatively limited rations under heavy pressure. He was the orchestra leader in Ireland's only Grand Slam-winning side of 1948 and the Triple Crown team the next year. He remains Ireland's most capped fly-half and one of Ireland's most admired sportsmen. He made a huge impact with the Lions in Australia and New Zealand in 1950, when he played in all four of the internationals, scoring six tries.

4. Michael Lynagh (1984–95)

His country's most capped fly-half, Lynagh was a player of such versatility that he proved equally effective at international level at No 10, where he played sixty-four times, at centre (seven caps), and full-back (one appearance). At one time he was the world's top points-scorer with 911. Lynagh was a neat and tidy player, tactically very sound, with superb punt control and with a surge of pace that frequently caught opponents by surprise. He was a dependable defender and played a significant part in Australia's Grand Slam tour of the British Isles in 1984, finishing as top scorer with ninety-eight points.

5. Barry John (1966–72)

Part of that truly great half-back partnership with Gareth Edwards, with whom John played twenty-eight times for Wales and the Lions. After a magical contribution to the 1971 Lions in New Zealand he was referred to as the King. He was an amazing fellow with no great physical presence, and by no means was he a heavy tackler. He had a shrewd brain and, at the end of Edwards's fast and lengthy pass, he always seemed able to make time for himself. He had command of all types of punted ball. He slotted eight drop goals for Wales and had a deceptive running style, which made him a supremely difficult target. John also had a crucial role in the Welsh halcyon period, when they won the Grand Slam in 1971 and Triple Crown in 1969.

Other contenders: *Phil Bennett* (1969–78) was up among the best. He had all-round class and a magical sidestep. *Jonathan Davies* (1985–97), his compatriot, who scored a record thirteen drop goals for Wales, was another complete footballer. *Hugo Porta* (1971–90) was Argentina's inspiration, tactician, points-scorer, and star in sixty-six international matches spread over eighteen years. The New Zealanders *Grant Fox* (1985–93) and *Andrew Mehrtens* (1995–) also deserve mention, while *Mark Ella* (1980–84), one of three brothers who represented Australia, was a master of the short pass. *John Rutherford* (1979–87) of Scotland had all the silken skills and a wonderfully accurate boot, as did *Ollie Campbell* (1976–84) of Ireland.

SCRUM-HALF

The ideal scrum-half has to be very brave because he is in the front line and often has to deal with a big opponent coming around the corner. He must have a pass that suits his partner, and be a master of service off either hand. He has to put the ball where his partner wants it – in the right place at the right pace. He must have a sharp break, as very often he will only have a split second in which to react. He must cover well. He has to have control over the punted kick, especially the one back over the forwards' heads into the box.

Gareth Edwards (1967–78)

Gareth Edwards was the complete scrum-half with the build of a bison, a rifled pass, control of the punted ball, impressive power on the run that rendered him lethal from close range, a highly competitive temperament, a strong helping of self-belief, and a punishing tackle.

He had the physical strength of the gymnast that he had been, which gave him resilience and power. He revelled in taking on bigger opposing forwards and, even when their key target, he yet led them a merry dance. He had a remarkable international career of fifty-three caps in a row, the first against France, in 1967, as a nineteen-year-old. He played ten times for the British Isles, twice in South Africa in 1968 and then with Barry John as his partner in New Zealand in 1971 and Phil Bennett, again in South Africa, in 1974.

He was never dropped by Wales, was the most capped scrum-half in the world at one time, and shared the Wales record of twenty tries with Gerald Davies. He was the first Welsh player to reach the milestone of fifty caps. He was a star in the Welsh golden era of the 1970s, when they won three Grand Slams, five Triple Crowns and seven Championships. He was the youngest Wales test captain, at twenty years and seven months, and led his country on thirteen occasions.

He will be remembered in particular for two breathtaking tries: from his own kick ahead for Wales against Scotland at Cardiff in 1972 when he trotted back downfield covered in mud from head to foot, and for the Barbarians against New Zealand in 1973, also in Cardiff. He was special, the best ever.

2. Nick Farr-Jones (1984–93)

Australia's most capped scrum-half, and another of those half-backs with the impressive physique of an old-style flank forward – five foot ten and thirteen stone two – that enabled him to hold his own in the growing physicality of the modern game. Captain of Australia thirty-six times, Farr-Jones at times played like a ninth forward. He was a punishing tackler, a long passer and a strong breaker, and an astute reader of the game. He created a world record half-back partnership with Michael Lynagh (forty-seven), and their uncanny linkage and astute calling of shots proved a crucial ingredient in Australia's success in winning the World Cup in 1991, with Farr-Jones as captain.

3. Joost Van Der Westhuizen (1993–)

South Africa's most-capped back and record try-scorer (thirty-five). Big for a scrum-half at six foot one and a half and thirteen stone ten, he allied this impressive physical dimension to explosive pace off the mark with which he attacked the gain line. A highly competitive individual who honed his game in the Northern Transvaal, Van Der Westhuizen was lethal on the burst, and a dedicated, hard-tackling defender. He gave one of his finest performances in recording three tries versus Wales in Cardiff in 1996. His linkage with Joel Stransky was a major factor in South Africa's success in the 1995 World Cup, not least when it worked like a charm for Stransky's winning drop goal in the final against New Zealand.

4. Ken Catchpole (1961–68)

Catchpole captained Australia on his debut against Fiji. He stood only five foot five and ten stone, yet he held his own in the hurly-burly of the test game, proving a dependable tackler. His partnership with Phil Hawthorne encompassed seventeen tests, a record at the time, and its success owed much to the speed of Catchpole's pass delivery. Catchpole's foot positioning was a vital element; he had rare balance. He will be remembered as master of the wrist-flicked shortish pass off the floor and off either hand. It was sad his career ended prematurely after injury against the All Blacks in Sydney in 1968.

5. Dickie Jeeps (1956–62)

Jeeps was a forthright, amazingly strong and unafraid character. He was an English version of the stocky powerful breed of scrum-halves spawned in the 1950s and 1960s. Jeeps was England's scrum-half when they won a Grand Slam in 1957, the Championship in 1958, and a Triple Crown and Championship share in 1960. During the Lions tour of South Africa in 1955, his sharp pass gave Cliff Morgan all the help he needed to weave his magic.

Other contenders: *Syd Going* (1967–77) was another of the strong scrum-halves who made a huge impact on the New Zealand game. His compatriot *Dave Loveridge* (1978–85), a farmer from Taranaki, was one of the most complete scrum-halves. *Robert Jones* (1986–95) was one of the most skilful to play for Wales, while *Gary Armstrong*

(1988–98), a Scot, was one of the most courageous wee men, full of grit and a fearless tackler. Finally, *George Gregan* (1994–) of Australia is a durable campaigner, and nowadays an astute skipper.

NO 8

The No 8 has to be the cement of the scrummage by using his arm-strength to pull the locks together, ensuring that the scrummage binding is really tight. Beef is important – ideally sixteen to seventeen stone. Much depends on the physical make-up of the other forwards, but if the No 8 has the size, the leap and technique to prove an auxiliary lineout provider, so much the better because ball creamed off the top of the lineout tail can be of high quality.

The No 8 also has to perfect the timing and technique of his scrummage pick-up routine, and have rapport with his scrum-half and his fellow loose forwards. Also he must ensure that, when he does launch himself off the scrummage, he does not become too upright, but is comfortable in a strong driving position, with ball protection a top priority.

Defensively, he will usually be the second forward off the scrummage. He has to be aware of where the tackle or action points are, so that he can arrive there quickly to augment the effort of his openside flanker to win ball at the breakdown.

Safe hands and the ability to adjust the weight and direction of pass are essential as a skilled No 8. Clearly, too, he has to take his part in harassing the opposing backs into having only minimal, if any, time on the ball.

Mervyn Davies (1969–76)

No rugby player the world over has been more recognised as a class act than Davies, who, emerging at twenty-two from the London

Welsh side of 1969 to cap status as a gangling No 8, had the look of a stray coat-hanger, but developed into one of the greats. A vital member of five Championship-winning Wales sides, he captained them to the title in 1975 and a Grand Slam a year later.

Known affectionately as Merv the Swerve, he was uncompromising, a powerful scrummager, a safe handler and one of the finest lineout exponents who provided much quality ball from the tail, not least the possession that he pinched from the opposition through his craft, application and technical expertise.

He also enjoyed a profitable understanding with Gareth Edwards, especially in scrummage pick-up ploys. Davies proved a key figure in the two most successful Lions tours, 1971 and 1974, in which he played in twenty-five of the forty-eight games, including all the internationals. He was earmarked for captaincy of the 1977 Lions to New Zealand, but a brain haemorrhage sustained in a cup semi-final of 1976 brought about his premature retirement.

2. Brian Lochore (1964–71)

Lochore was six foot three, fifteen and a half stone, craggy, with no spare meat on his bones, and safe hands and a high state of fitness. He was a sure source of lineout possession and made clever use of his role in standing off ruck or maul to create a surprise element. Lochore toured with New Zealand in 1964, playing in thirteen of the thirty games, including a first cap against England. His own tenure of leadership covered eighteen internationals between 1966 and 1970. He captained the most formidable pack I have seen, one that included Ken Gray, Colin Meads, Kel Tremain, Waka Nathan, Ian Kirkpatrick and Sam Strahan.

3. Dean Richards (1986–96)

England's most capped No 8 forward, Richards has to be rated one of the strongest forwards to represent them, a mighty cornerstone in their pack strategy for a decade. Something of a man mountain at six foot three and eighteen stone two, he became an immovable object when he turned his back on the opposition. He would plant his feet wide apart and defy anybody to shift him. He also was phenomenally strong in arms and upper body so that he excelled in ripping ball away from shocked opponents. He helped England to three Grand Slams in 1991, 1992 and 1995, and provided a veritable tour de force when in 1996 England deprived Scotland of a Grand Slam. He played in the 1987, 1991 and 1995 World Cups as well as touring twice with the Lions, playing in all six internationals in Australia and New Zealand in 1989 and 1993.

4. Hennie Muller (1949–53)

The first time I saw Muller was in October 1951 when he scored a try, three conversions and a penalty goal in the Springboks' 43–11 win over a Combined Glasgow/Edinburgh XV. I hadn't seen a 'middle of the back row' forward as quick as him, nor one who slotted goals from all over the paddock. A month later I saw him again at Murrayfield as a try-scorer and captain in South Africa's 44–0 defeat of Scotland. Muller was known as the *Windhond* (the Greyhound) of the Veld and, at five foot eleven and thirteen stone ten, he created a style of No 8 defence that subjected opposing backs to huge pressure and little time on the ball.

When Basil Kenyon, captain of South Africa in the UK in 1951–52, was injured, Muller took over and led the side to a Grand Slam against Scotland, Ireland, Wales and England. In 1949 he was voted the best No 8 in the world.

5. Peter Brown (1964–73)

There might have been a kind of Heath Robinson element to his running style, but Brown was an unusual back-five forward, tactically astute and observant, and not averse to playing it off the top of his head to sometimes dramatic and entertaining effect. He brought to his role an acute sense of position, and an ability to manufacture passes to suit the situation, as when he created a crucial try for Chris Rea in the 16–15 defeat of England at Twickenham in 1971. He had educated hands, was a crafty lineout operator, and had an unusual goal-kicking method, whereby he turned his back on the ball before the run-up.

Other contenders: *Murray Mexted* (1979–85) was one of the most athletic forwards to come out of New Zealand. Mexted, six foot five and fifteen stone nine, was his country's most capped No 8 until overtaken by Zinzan Brooke. He was rated by his countrymen as one of their best players of the century.

NO 7 (OPEN-SIDE FLANKER)

A No 7 has to be quick and prepared to put his body on the line because he is usually the tail-gunner from the lineout and, off the open-side position at the scrummage, he has to be first to the break-down and mine for ball on the floor. His problem is to work within the laws, or at least so that the referee doesn't see anything illegal when he does operate outside them. He has to time his withdrawal from the set-pieces so as to put pressure on the opposing backs, and has to be ready to do a lot of his work on the floor and be ready to take what the New Zealanders call a shoeing. He has to be a secure tackler and have good safe hands as a support runner to his back division.

Fergus Slattery (1970–84)

There were sundry midfield backs and, indeed those further out, who found it no pleasure to play against UCD, Blackrock, Ireland or the British Isles during the 1970s, because a certain John Fergus Slattery made it his business to create some anxiety in their ranks by harassing and hounding them to distraction. His brand of aggressive flank forward play marked him out as one of the greatest of open-side practitioners. At six foot one and fourteen stone seven, he was ideally equipped for this task, a hard physical specimen, brave, totally committed, very quick, and with an impressive work rate based on super fitness. He captained Ireland on seventeen occasions between 1979 and 1981, and led them to a series win in Australia in 1979. In 1971, Slattery toured as a young player with the Lions and reached a peak of performance with the unbeaten squad in South Africa in 1974, when he played in twelve of the twenty-two games, all four internationals, and scored six tries. Hannes Marais, the South Africa captain, said: 'Slattery created havoc among our back division.' Sure enough, that was 'Slatts'.

2. Michael Jones (1987–98)

Michael Jones was first capped for Western Samoa in 1986 against Wales before choosing New Zealand, for whom he made his debut in the inaugural World Cup in 1987. Hugely popular, the Iceman, as he was known, had pace, an explosive quality to his running and, at six foot one and fifteen stone six, carried his weight well and had great ball-handling skills. He allied his creative gifts to ferocious but fair tackling to such effect as to draw from Graham Mourie, the great New Zealand captain, the compliment that in 1987 Jones 'had played as well as any flanker could ever hope to play'. It sometimes surprised folk to discover that Jones, who revelled in the physical exchanges, could be so cool, composed, quiet and modest off the field, and one whose Christian beliefs precluded him from playing on Sundays. A cruciate ligament injury in 1989 restricted his appearances.

3. Jan Ellis (1965–76)

Ellis toured Argentina with the South African Gazelles in 1966 and was given the nickname of El Try Hombre. One can still picture him, at Twickenham in 1970, making a wonderful fifty-five-yard scoring run in which he seemed to be cornered four times, yet by use of pace, change of pace, swerve and feint, he scored one of the great individual tries. At six foot one and a half and sixteen stone, he was ideally built for the loose forward role, and he had a loping stride that masked genuine pace that frequently caught opponents unawares. He also had a way of carrying the ball in a hand the size of a frying-pan. He had a fetish for fitness so that he was still at full throttle in the closing stages of even the most physically demanding contests.

4. Michel Crauste (1957–66)

Crauste was given the nicknames Mongol and Attila because of his sallow complexion and his dark fearsome moustache, and certainly he was a ferocious competitor. He once punched a South Canterbury player during a France tour to New Zealand, only to be punched himself by a local lady supporter who marched on to the pitch. But Crauste undoubtedly was one of the most effective loose forwards to be spawned by the French game. Although no giant at six foot and thirteen stone five, he had safe hands, rare pace and positional instinct. He tackled also with shuddering effect. A son of the soil, he captained France in twenty-two internationals and, in 1960, was voted France's top player.

5. Graham Mourie (1977–82)

At Cardiff in 1980, in the Centenary game New Zealand v Wales, I saw a sizzling try by Mourie after his feint pass to a decoy runner. No giant at six foot and thirteen stone eight, nor a flying machine with his unusual scuttling action, Mourie was a superbly fit action man. He had wonderful gifts of anticipation, tactical nous and he was an intelligent, inspirational All Blacks captain in nineteen internationals.

Other contenders: *Waka Nathan* (1962–67) of New Zealand was nicknamed the Black Panther, for he stalked opposing backs with feline ferocity. *Neil Back* (1994–)of England is one of those flankers that you wind up and set running. At five foot nine and fourteen stone seven, he holds his own with bigger opponents.

NO 6 (BLIND-SIDE FLANKER)

In the scrummage, the No 6 has to be the block down the blind side, the man to shore up the narrow channel and let nothing get by. He has to get in people's faces by helping to harness and hound the opposition backs. Elsewhere his functions are to tackle, support and drive. He has to angle his scrummage drive to keep a tight edifice, while being prepared to cover the fringes and the midfield. At the scrum he has to be able to provide assistance in pick-up moves. At the lineout, if he is big enough to be an extra jumper, well and good, otherwise he is responsible for supporting his jumper, especially near the tail. From the line he must be sharp enough either to support attack or augment defence.

Zinzan Brooke (1987–97)

Although recognised primarily as a No 8, I regard Zinzan Brooke as capable of playing anywhere in the back row (I have another option at No 8). The older of two brothers, Zinzan, at six foot three and fifteen stone eight, was arguably the most skilful and most tactically aware forward to come out of New Zealand. So skilful was he that, all else apart, he scored three dropped goals in internationals. Brooke was blessed with acute positional sense and could bring supporters to their feet by firing huge passes across the pitch, often to devastating attacking effect. There was also his total commitment to keeping the door shut with shuddering tackles. Once in the Hong Kong Sevens, Fiji led New Zealand by two points with time almost up. Zinzan made to place a restart drop kick to the left; instead he pivoted and, left-footed, kicked to the right with such precision as to create a winning try.

2. Ian Kirkpatrick (1967–77)

New Zealand has spawned a rich galaxy of big forwards who can run and handle, but none was more explosive than Kirkpatrick – big enough to have started out as a lock but whose power and pace made him one of the great loose forwards. He scored what has been rated one of the greatest individual tries by a New Zealander, against the 1971 British Isles in Christchurch, when a win for the Lions would have put them two up in the series. Kirkpatrick torpedoed them by thundering around the edge of a maul and powering past four Lions in a fifty-yard run for an incredible score. Kirkpatrick had already made his imprint as a member of the unbeaten 1967 All Blacks in the UK and France when he played in seven of the fifteen games. He made a huge impression, notably in France, with a try in each of the four games, including the international.

3. Derek Quinnell (1971–80)

Quinnell had the unusual distinction of having played for the Lions in an international before being capped by Wales. His Wales debut had an element of drama. Mervyn Davies had to leave the field injured with time almost up in the game against France at Cardiff in 1972. Desperate to get on, Quinnell muscled his way past half of the Welsh constabulary, as well as the touch judge, to make the promised land just in time. Father of Scott and Craig, Quinnell will be remembered for his contribution to Llanelli's victory over the 1972–73 All Blacks, and for his part in that memorable Gareth Edwards try in the Barbarians victory in 1973. He took a pass at ankle height and, with a brilliant take and give, provided crucial linkage in one of the great try-scoring moves. He allied tight forward play with mobility and ball-handling expertise in the open. He toured with the Lions in New Zealand in 1971 and 1977 and was a key figure in curbing Sid Going, the All Blacks' most dangerous back, in 1971.

4. Alan Whetton (1984–91)

Whetton played in twenty-six leading internationals with his twin brother, Gary. His physique – six foot three and nearly sixteen stone – made him a formidable foe with ball in hand, because he could shift as well. The Whettons became integral to some outstanding Auckland and New Zealand pack performances in the 1980s, each being an explosive forward with astute positional sense and safe handling. Up to the 1987 World Cup final, Alan had scored seventeen tries in an All Black jersey in twenty-four games. He was a key member of the New Zealand squad that won the World Cup, playing in all six games, and also excelled in the 1991 World Cup.

5. Laurent Rodriguez (1981–90)

Rodriguez was a huge bull of a French forward who, at six foot three and seventeen stone two, was likened to the great Kirkpatrick in his thundering charges, notably from the No 8 position, from which he would explode with impressive force in pick-up ploys. He had the distinction of playing for France in all three loose-forward berths, also proving a resolute and intuitive defender, as well as a splendid support runner. Rodriguez was a fireman in charge of fitness training and figured as a mighty force on the international circuit for nine years.

Other contenders: *Richard Hill* (1997–) has proved his versatility for England by operating in each of the three loose-forward positions, but mostly as blind-side flanker in arguably the most formidable English trio of all time, alongside Dallaglio and Back. He possesses pace, aggression, experience, power and handling dexterity – and a nose for tries. *Jeff Squire* (1977–1984) of Wales is another of the versatile Welsh loose forwards who could function at No 8 or blind-side. He would never rate as being jet-propelled but moved at a steady lick with total focus, power and stamina.

NO 5 (LOCK)

The No 5 is usually the tallest player in the team, with good reach. He has to be an athlete with the ability to time his jump correctly in mid-line, while also being aware of opposition attempts to disrupt his work, although that is not so easy nowadays because of the spacing rule.

In the scrummage, he has to be accustomed to packing at awkward heights; it is difficult for him to pack low enough to get the drive he needs, as well as the tightness. As the left lock in the scrummage, he has to be aware of the positioning of his feet, so he does not interfere with, say, a channel-one strike. The locks have to achieve a tight bind – they are the solid rampart of the scrummage. If they are loose, so is the rest of the scrummage.

The lock has to have an instinctive feel for the angle of run to get to the next action point and nowadays he has to be able to give and take a pass under pressure. Another problem is to judge when to commit to a ruck or maul. A No 5 may find himself bolstering the attack line or helping to shore up the midfield defence. He has to have strong arms and be prepared to have his ears squashed between the ample posteriors of the prop and hooker.

Frik Du Preez (1961–71)

Representing South Africa and Northern Transvaal from 1961–71, Du Preez played at international level thirty-one times as a lock and seven as a flanker in the days when lineout specialists had to become airborne without lifting from colleagues. He was one of the greatest lineout technicians, with a standing jump measurement that was mind-boggling considering that he was only six foot two and fifteen stone six.

Du Preez developed from a fly-half at school to one of the most gifted locks of all time, a dependable lineout purveyor, with educated hands, a powerful boot, and a grinding scrummager who was astonishingly quick for his size. In his first ten internationals he never lost. He once sent over a seventy-five-yard dropped goal in Pretoria and he had the honour of leading the Springboks on to the field for his final test, against Australia in 1971.

2. Willie John McBride (1962–75)

Claiming a record five British Isles tours on which he played seventeen internationals, McBride reached the peak of an illustrious career when he captained the British Isles to an unbeaten record over twenty-two games in South Africa in 1974. This rugby giant from County Antrim proved an inspirational figure at every level of the game, notably captaining Ireland in 1974 to their first Championship for twenty-three years. As Lions captain in South Africa, his famous saying was: 'We take no prisoners!' One will never forget the delighted reaction of the Irish support when McBride scored his first try with a typical bullocking charge against France in 1975. They raised the roof to underline their massive regard for the giant Ulsterman.

3. Lucien Mias (1951–59)

Mias was one of the most tactically astute players to adorn the French game. He was an influential figure in raising French prestige. During Mias's reign, France not only shared the Championship twice but became outright Champions for the first time in 1959. Yet it is hard to believe that Mias, somewhat disillusioned, gave up the game when only twenty-seven. But France needed him and his return heralded the first series win by a France side in South Africa for sixty years. He was described by colleagues as the Bulldozer with a Brain. That brain spawned one of the most effective tactics of the time, for Mias will always be linked to the lineout peel move by which he sought to breach the strong defensive lines of the 1950s.

4. Robin Brooke (1992–99)

The younger of the two Brooke brothers, he played together with Zinzan for the All Blacks on thirty-nine occasions. Robin was a first-choice lock in seven seasons of internationals, in which he set a world record for a second-row partnership with Ian Jones in forty-seven internationals. A typically strong All Black lock with high skill levels, who revelled in the close-quarter combat of ruck and maul, he scrummaged like an animated bison and seldom failed to win his own lineout ball. But he was also eminently comfortable with the ball in his hands.

5. Martin Johnson (1993–)

'Mean, moody and magnificent' might be an appropriate assessment of Johnson, who has captained England on twenty-six occasions. He is also England's most capped lock, having passed Wade Dooley's mark of fifty-five. In his past ten internationals he has lost once, against South Africa in 2000. He has proved an inspirational captain, not only with Leicester and England, but with the Lions, whom he captained on their tours to South Africa in 1997 and Australia in 2001. He has also captained England to victories over every leading team in recent times.

Other contenders: *Bill Beaumont* (1975–82) was England's captain on twenty-one occasions, most memorably when he led them in 1980 to their first Grand Slam for twenty-three years. *Elie Cester* (1966–74) is remembered in France for being a typical engine-room workhorse; while *Mick Molloy* (1966–76) of Ireland was another one of those quiet achievers.

NO 4 (LOCK)

The No 4 is the workhorse of the pack. Bulk is helpful, not only for scrummaging in which he and his partner provide the core of the edifice, but also to counter the bump and push aspect of the No 2 berth at the lineout. The timing and angling of his jump have to be spot on, so that he must have a strong rapport with his thrower. For the No 2 jumper it is all a question of arms and upper body application.

In the scrummage, he has to be aware of his foot positioning so as to obtain maximum drive, while at the same time ensuring that there is a clear passage for the ball. He also must be aware of the need to counter any opposition attempt to swivel the scrummage.

Colin Meads (1957–71)

Known as Pinetree, revered by all, feared by many, Meads was voted by the New Zealand public as the All Black of the century in 1999. In fifteen seasons Meads played a record 133 games for New Zealand. He first represented King Country as an eighteen-year-old in 1955, and New Zealand against Australia in 1957.

Initially a loose forward, but soon renowned as arguably the greatest lock forward of all time, he was of farming stock. Standing at six foot four and weighing more than sixteen stone, Meads was naturally and immensely strong, brave, physically hard, and totally uncompromising on the field. He was a powerful scrummager and played in fourteen New Zealand internationals in the engine-room in partnership with his brother, Stan. He was a fearsome figure on the charge, often with the ball in a hand the size of a bucket lid. He was always superbly fit, so that he was still running hard in the closing stages of matches.

2. John Eales (1991–2001)

At six foot seven and eighteen stone nine, Eales was destined, over a decade of international rugby, to gain a reputation as one of the world's greatest locks. He was Australia's most prolific source of lineout possession during the 1990s and one of the most sporting.

Unusually for a lock, he took on goal-kicking duties for Queensland and Australia, scoring more international points (173 in eighty-six appearances) than any other forward. He captained Australia a record fifty-five times and, under his leadership, Australia played a dynamic, expansive style. Immensely popular with colleagues, Eales played in fifteen World Cup games, winning the trophy in 1991 and 1999.

3. Ian Jones (1990–99)

Known as the Kamo Kid after that part of North Auckland from which he emerged, Jones became one of the most kenspeckle figures in New Zealand rugby during the 1990s. He is his country's most capped lock, and the second most capped New Zealander ever. His seventy-ninth and last international appearance was in the 1999 World Cup against Scotland at Murrayfield, when he played a big part in a 30–18 victory. Despite his gangling appearance and raking strides, Jones is a well-equipped engine-room operator with exceptional lineout skills, power in scrummaging and dependable handling.

4. Benoit Dauga (1964–72)

Referred to often as the Eiffel Tower of the French lineout during his sixty-three caps from 1964–72, Dauga proved an inspiration to his colleagues during a most successful spell for French rugby, when they won the Championship in 1967 and then the Grand Slam of 1968, while sharing the Championship with Wales in 1970. A former basketball player, he brought that sport's special handling and jumping skills to his rugby, not least to his high quality lineout service and his support running.

Dauga was an unsmiling giant with a special aura of hardness and grim resolve, but he was highly respected by friend and foe, and there was a huge well of sympathy directed towards him when he suffered serious neck damage. He captained his country nine times, scored eleven international tries, and his contribution to the French game was marked by the award of the National Order of Merit and the *Légion d'honneur.*

5. Gordon Brown (1969–76)

Arguably Scotland's finest tight forward, Brown won thirty caps for his country from 1969–76 but made his reputation as No 5 for the British Isles. He was the big workhorse who revelled in close-quarter warfare yet had the instinct and pace to score an impressive eight tries in twelve matches during the Lions tour to South Africa in 1974. He was the youngest lock in the Lions squad touring New Zealand in 1971, but applied himself with such vigour as to become first choice alongside Willie John McBride. He was a very popular tourist on Lions tours in 1974 and 1977. Brown died in 2000 from cancer, aged fifty-three.

Other contenders: *Gary Whetton* (1981–91) of New Zealand was one of twin brothers who played for the All Blacks and won fifty-eight caps. *Mark Andrews* (1994–2001) of South Africa, once a junior water polo international, was especially adept at claiming opposition restart kicks.

NO 1 (LOOSE-HEAD PROP)

A loose-head prop has got to be able to scrummage effectively at a height that is comfortable for his hooker. Size isn't all that important, but physical strength and hardness is, and if a loose-head can weigh in at sixteen or seventeen stone, and still be able to shift that bulk about at a consistent rate of knots, so much the better. Technical expertise is a priority, the ability to impart strain on opposing tight-heads, while also taking any strain they place on you.

Nowadays props have to be skilled in ball-handling and play a vital role in protecting their lineout jumpers. Props must be expert at timing the hoist of their lock skywards at restart kicks. Stamina is a vital ingredient.

Fran Cotton (1971–81)

You had to see Fran Cotton playing in high-class Sevens to appreciate the wealth of skill and mobility that he possessed alongside his natural strength, and the craft and awareness that he developed. He worked hard on his scrummaging, having appreciated that size had to be allied to technical efficiency. He was big enough to take on an auxiliary ball-winning function at the lineouts, as well as the support role. He proved an important member of Bill Beaumont's Grand Slam-winning side of 1980. Cotton's leadership gifts were underlined when he captained England to victory in the World Sevens at Murrayfield in 1973. A treble British Lion in 1974, 1977 and 1980, he played in all four internationals when the Lions won the series in South Africa in 1974.

2. Ian McLauchlan (1969–79)
One of the finest loose-head scrummagers the game has produced, McLauchlan was a tough fellow from Tarbolton in Ayrshire, who spent much of his rugby career causing discomfort to opposing tight-heads at club, district, international and Lions level. He had remarkable success at the highest level, even though just five foot nine and thirteen stone ten, which ensured the nickname Mighty Mouse. McLauchlan also toured with the Lions in 1971 and 1974. He had a ruthless touch to his field actions, and his exhortations when Scotland captain twenty-one times had his troops in a high state of willing derring-do.

3. Jason Leonard (1990–)
The world's most capped forward, he has been virtually a permanent fixture in the England side since 1990. Such has been his strength, versatility and technical expertise that he has functioned

equally successfully as loose-head or tight-head. When he captained England against Argentina in 1996 he scored his one international try. Never liable to break the sound barrier, Leonard nonetheless covered the paddock to the action points in impressive style for one who turned the scales at eighteen and a half stone, thus riding low in the water. His recovery from a serious neck injury, at an early stage in his career, was remarkable.

4. Hugh McLeod (1954–62)

McLeod's fetish for fitness, and a dogged determination still to be running when others gave up, as well as a resolve to match back-division colleagues in skill on the ball, made him a special type of prop forward. At five foot nine and fourteen stone, he was no giant but was an impressively strong man who stood sure against the world's best. Strictly teetotal, he earned the nickname the Abbot from colleagues, who held him in the highest regard.

5. Craig Dowd (1993–2000)

Steve McDowell was never going to be an easy act to follow, but Craig Dowd made quite a fist of it, so much so that he played in fifty-nine tests. He formed the New Zealand front row with Sean Fitzpatrick and Olo Brown on thirty-seven occasions between 1993 and 1997. He played in the same New Zealand Colts side in 1988–89 as Martin Johnson, the England captain. Dowd was immensely strong and big enough, at six foot two and a half and eighteen stone, to do his whack at the lineout, and he was also versatile enough to have propped on both the right and left side of his hooker.

Other contenders: Sir *Wilson Whineray* (1957–65), the first All Black to be knighted, was one of the most successful captains of all time and had the distinction of having a tactical ploy named after him – the lineout peel move known as the Willie-away. *Topo Rodriguez* was the first Argentinian to play for another country. Rodriguez gained fifteen caps as a Puma, then emigrated to Australia and played for that country on eleven occasions (1984–87). *Steve McDowell* (1985–92) was New Zealand's loose-head prop in a rich period for the All Blacks when they were unbeaten in twenty-three tests. He formed a powerful front row with Sean Fitzpatrick and Richard Loe.

NO 2 (HOOKER)

The hooker's first obligation is to win his own ball in the scrum, down whatever channel is nominated. His second obligation is to persuade his props to put enough pressure on the opposition front row, so that he might be able to pinch an occasional opposition put-in, albeit that is far more difficult than it used to be because referees permit squint feeds.

There were times when you could get six or seven strikes against the head, so there was an element of surprise about scrummage play. Now we are in no doubt who will win the ball. The third, and perhaps most important attribute, is accurate throwing-in to the lineout. It is easier now for lineout specialists to win their own throw, because they can be hoisted to indecent heights, but it is rendered valueless if the throw does not hit the target.

The hooker must also be capable of providing upward lift to the big men in dealing with opposition restart kicks. He has got to be physically strong and have a touch of ruthlessness about him. As the middle man of the front row he has to contend with heavy physical pressure from all sides. He must be technically well equipped and have the skill, dexterity and knowledge to deal with the squeeze put upon him. Elsewhere he must be able to make adjustments when things are not going as expected. Genuine pace is a big bonus, not only in exploiting the front of the lineout to put pressure on opposition ball, but also to make the kind of impact in attack that is nowadays expected of all forwards.

Sean Fitzpatrick (1986–97)

Sean Fitzpatrick is the most capped All Black of them all. He rates as one of the great international captains, having led his country a record fifty-one times. His father, Brian, had played in New Zealand's midfield in the 1950s, and Sean, a participant in the World Cups in 1987, 1991 and 1995, showed the same dedication, working hard on his throwing so that he became one of the most accurate. At six foot and sixteen stone nine, he also proved a strong scrummager. His mobility was impressive too, and he was renowned for suddenly appearing in broken play outside his wing, sometimes scoring tries that stem from that kind of intuitive positioning. He was also something of a talker on the pitch, occasionally giving the referee advice about how to go about his task. He was undoubtedly one of New Zealand's most famous sportsmen over a decade of international duty.

2. Colin Deans (1978–87)

Colin Deans was arguably the fastest hooker ever to play for Scotland and the British Isles, with explosive acceleration that frequently got him to places on the field that others, and sometimes some of his back-division colleagues, simply couldn't match. At one time Deans was Scotland's most capped player, and it was testimony to his strength, fitness and durability that he never had to leave the field because of injury.

Scotland's lineout play prospered during Deans's near decade of international duty because he practised his throwing-in assiduously and became deadly accurate in hitting his targets. He made a huge contribution to Scotland's 1984 Grand Slam. When he toured New Zealand with the Lions in 1983, he played in seven of eighteen games but was deemed unlucky not to have featured in an international as his hooking rival was the captain, Ciaran Fitzgerald.

3. Bobby Windsor (1973–79)

Known as the Duke, he was the first of the famous Viet Gwent Pontypool front row to be capped and, at one time, was generally regarded as the number one hooker in Europe. He was also quick for a front-row denizen and he had some great moments as a link man in the kind of dazzling handling moves that were part and parcel of the Welsh repertoire during one of their golden eras. A former captain of Cross Keys, Windsor showed his true potential when he joined Pontypool and became a member of one of the most feared packs in the United Kingdom.

He formed a mighty front-row liaison with Charlie Faulkner and Graham Price, and those three were so successful as a coalface unit that they played together for Wales on nineteen occasions. Windsor proved one of the most colourful characters on his tours with the Lions in 1974 and 1977 in which he played in five internationals overall.

4. Phil Kearns (1989–99)

He was just twenty-two when Bob Dwyer, the Australia coach, pinned his faith in the inexperienced hooker against the All Blacks in 1989. Kearns never looked back, except when suffering Achilles tendon problems. He not only became Australia's most capped hooker – which would have been more but for injury – he was a vital cog in the Australia machine that captured the World Cup in 1991. He had impressive physical statistics at six foot and sixteen stone twelve, set alongside surprising pace and safe hands – hence his eight international tries. He was also tactically astute.

He played in forty-six consecutive internationals between 1989 and 1995. He was partnered by Ewen McKenzie and Tony Daly in the Australia front row on thirty-seven occasions. One of the features of southern hemisphere rugby over the past decade was the keen rivalry between Kearns and Fitzpatrick, with honours fairly even. Kearns has been a much admired member of Australia squads, not only for the quality of his play, but also for his sportsmanship.

5. Keith Wood (1994–)

Wood is Ireland's most-capped hooker, having surpassed Ken Kennedy. He has also passed another great Irishman's record, the twenty-four times that Tom Kiernan captained his country. Wood now has had that honour on twenty-five occasions. First capped against Australia in 1994, he has developed into an inspirational citizen who frequently brings the Lansdowne Road crowd to its feet. There is always excitement when Wood has the ball in his hands. For although six foot and sixteen stone ten, he has a sharp turn of pace and revels in running at opponents or into space, which he has done in rollicking fashion for twelve international tries. Wood toured with the Lions in South Africa in 1997 and Australia in 2001, and played in five of the six internationals.

Other contenders: *Peter Wheeler* (1975–84) was England's No 2 for twenty-two consecutive times during his forty-one-cap career. The Leicester stalwart was a lightning striker when hookers had to fight for their own ball, a double Lion and key member of England's Grand Slam side of 1980. *Bryn Meredith* (1954–62) can claim to have stolen five strikes against the head against the Springboks, a feat he achieved in 1960. He played for Wales thirty-four times and was in the Newport side that beat the Wallabies. A hooker's hooker, Meredith was exceptionally quick about the pitch and a Lion who played in all four internationals against South Africa in 1955. *Eric Evans* (1948–58), a successful captain who never minced his words, was England's hooker and inspiration when they had their successful reign in the 1950s. Made captain at thirty, his career highlight was a Grand Slam in 1957.

NO 3 (TIGHT-HEAD PROP)

The principal asset of the tight-head prop must be his natural strength and his technical know-how, and the ability to exert pressure on the opposing front row to help his own hooker. Support at the lineout for his jumpers is also essential. He is not usually the first out of the scrummage and so he has to have the positional instinct to get to the action point as quickly as possibly.

The tight-head is the anchor and has to be strong enough to put pressure on the opposing loose-head so, when it is their put-in, there is a chance to destroy the channelling they would want to have. A good tight-head can also take the scrummage down low to make it hard for the opposing hooker to see the ball coming in. In the modern way of things, the tight-head has also to be part of the defensive line.

Graham Price (1975–83)

A favourite son of the Pontypool supporters and a superb product of the club's front-row manufacturing company, Graham Price proved a cornerstone of Pontypool, Wales and British Isles packs for more than a decade. He was a key member of the famous front row that also included Bobby Windsor and Charlie Faulkner, all of whom toured with the Lions, Price playing in twelve international matches. He might be best described as a 'quiet achiever', for he went about his business of giving 100 per cent at every outing in an undemonstrative fashion, and without recourse to violence.

He had a memorable international debut against France, in Paris in 1975, when he hacked and chased over seventy-five yards of cloying mud for an individual try that brought strong men to their feet in adulation. It won the game for Wales, and Pricey was the hero of the hour. He was a master of what he did.

300

2. Ken Gray (1959–69)

A former Wellington lock forward who switched to prop in 1961, at six foot two and seventeen stone, Gray was initially regarded as too tall for a prop, but as a typical rawboned New Zealand type, he proved one of the greatest. A fine scrummager, a considerable force as number two in the lineout, and exceptionally mobile, he set something of a new style for big props in lineout play, where he was not only a strong support for his jumpers, but excelled as a ball-winner in his own right, thus providing New Zealand with an auxiliary lineout source.

He captained Wellington to victories over the 1965 Springboks and 1966 Lions; on the New Zealand tour of these islands in 1966–67 he played a key role in the powerful front row scrummaging that was such an important factor in their unbeaten tour record that comprised fourteen wins and one draw.

3. Chris Koch (1949–60)

A South African sheep-farmer, he was a player I first saw in October 1951 when the Springboks beat a combined Glasgow/Edinburgh XV 43–11. He scored two tries in that match to underline not only his handling skills, but his impressive pace for a front-row denizen. He and his forward colleagues gave a telling demonstration of how big forwards need not only to be ball providers, but ball-carriers and distributors as well. A month later Koch played at Murrayfield in a record-breaking 44–0 win over Scotland. Two of their nine tries were scored by Koch. A son of the soil, Koch was a phenomenally strong scrummager and set a new pattern of skilled handling participation by front-row players.

4. Robert Paparemborde (1975–83)

Paparemborde was France's most capped forward until his mark of fifty-five was passed by Christian Califano in the 1990s. A black belt in judo, Patou was one of several genuine strongmen who made a huge impact on the French game as scrummagers and

301

ball-handlers. He was an awkward fellow to pack against in the scrummage because he had unusual sloping shoulders, which made it difficult for opponents to gain any purchase against him, and he was well-equipped, skill-wise, as a former handball representative player, as well as a promising junior athlete. France based their Grand Slam packs of 1977 and 1981 on the strength and experience of Paparemborde in the tight-head role.

5. Ray McLoughlin (1962–75)

At five foot eleven and fifteen stone eight, he proved one of the most feared scrummagers in the world game during his thirteen years of international rugby for Ireland, when he merited a reputation as a strongman who frequently buried or lifted opposing props with a combination of physical hardness and technical know-how. He might be described as the thinking man's prop, for here was a bright, intelligent fellow with a science degree from University College Dublin, who made a study of the mechanics of scrummaging, then applied them to his work at the Irish coalface.

Other contenders: *Iain Milne* (1979–90) was perhaps the most durable scrummager produced by Scotland with the ability to exert pressure on loose-heads. *Christian Califano* (1994–), France's most capped prop, once scored three tries against Romania to demonstrate his mobility. *Phil Blakeway* (1980–85) was a product of the tough Gloucester school, and *Sandy Carmichael* (1967–78) was the first Scot to reach fifty caps.